P9-BZK-727

WAKE
ME WHEN IT'S
OVER

WAKE
ME WHEN IT'S
OVER

*A JOURNEY TO THE
EDGE AND BACK*

MARY KAY BLAKELY

𝕿imes BOOKS

Library of Congress Cataloging-in-Publication Data

Blakely, Mary Kay
Wake me when it's over / Mary Kay Blakely.
p.   cm.
ISBN 0-8129-1699-9
1. Blakely, Mary Kay.   2. Journalists—United States—
Biography.   3. Working mothers—United States—Biography.   4. Coma—
Patients—United States—Biography.   5. Stress (Psychology)
6. Working mothers—United States—Family relationships.   I. Title.
CT275.B57847A3   1989
973.92′092′4—dc19   88-40499
[B]

Manufactured in the United States of America

9   8   7   6   5   4   3   2

First Edition

For
FRANCIS JUDE
and the family who loved him

The old woman I shall become will be quite different from the woman I am now. Another I is beginning, and so far I have not had to complain of her.

—George Sand

ACKNOWLEDGMENTS

Obviously, I was in no position to keep a written record of the nine days in March 1984 reported here. I am indebted to Larry and Gina, who not only kept faith but also kept notes. Their helpfulness through every stage, from collecting hard facts to recalling their most poignant moments, made this work both possible and passionate. I am grateful to Dennis Greenbaum, M.D., and his indefatigable staff at St. Vincent's Hospital and Medical Center for healing my body, then filling in the blanks of my mind. Phyllis Wender, my friend and literary agent, and Ellen Sweet, Julia Kagan, and Elizabeth Scharlatt, my diligent and affectionate editors, read each draft and provided invaluable direction.

I thank Joan Uebelhoer, Cathryn Adamsky, and my remarkable friends in Fort Wayne, Indiana, for their energy and inspiration; George Mack for insightful comments on the manuscript; Jane Myers for her steady friendship through a rocky period; Gabrielle Burton for her thoughtful conversations between chapters; Susan Harney and Carrie Tuhy, my soul mates and friends through twenty-five years and nine unforgettable days, for their most sublime loyalty; my brothers Paul and Kevin for being dependable family seers and advisers; my sons Ryan and Darren for their spirited independence and affection while their often preoccupied, not to say outright absent, mother kept getting stalled in 1984; and Howard, my dear friend and comrade in parenting, for his willingness to review our history with courage and humor. I thank my parents, Kay and Jerry, for the unstoppable love and abundant support they've showered on their five children.

I suppose every human being would behave more thoughtfully if we all knew in advance that our story would appear in print someday. Few of us have that luxury, and certainly the private people who appear on these pages with me did not. The difficult lessons described here reveal my family and friends during their most vulnerable times. I therefore thank the reader in advance for understanding that embarrassment and foolishness are honorable passages in the human condition.

CONTENTS

WAKE
ME WHEN IT'S
OVER

Prologue:

THE GRIEFS

i

For the entire drive to the Detroit airport on March 21, 1984, I stifled the urge to ask Howe to "please step on it." My foot pressed to the floor on the passenger's side, I kept scanning the highway for mile markers, as if by sighting the tiny green signs far in advance I could propel us toward them through sheer force of will. While my heart pounded—audibly, I thought—Howe stared placidly through the windshield.

It made no sense to prod him, though, since he wasn't receiving many messages from me that disconnected year. I knew he wouldn't feel my distress, even if I'd announced it. "If you moved any slower, you'd grow leaves," his old college roommate once kidded him. During the last five years of our marriage he had moved with the speed of a tortoise, unaffected by my frequent bouts of anxiety, regarding them as the tragic but inevitable consequences of being born a hare. Even in emergencies—and catching my flight for New York qualified as one, in my mind—the maximum speed he reached was a slow, steady cruise.

We left for the airport each month at the last possible minute, I suppose, because the adrenaline-pumping drives took our minds off where I was going, who was waiting on the other end, why I'd be moving on soon—facts of 1984 that depressed Howe down to his soul. It had been three years since our separation, but he was still buried in the emotional white winter following divorce. Angry and hurt, he'd sat through the long negotiations with his arms folded sullenly across his chest, facing me across the mediation table like a one-man army of underground resistance.

His current defense was a kind of cool detachment, especially present when he was performing some kindness for me lest I regard it as approval for my desertion as "wife." That we still loved each other only made things more provocative.

I'd tried to achieve a cool detachment of my own but succeeded only intermittently. A familiar line or expression would trigger memories of a happier past, and I'd mourn the losses all over again. I would hear the kids laughing at his jokes in the living room and remember how I loved his wit—a whimsical, self-deprecating humor he couldn't afford to share with me these days. Howe had his own peculiar take on things: While other family members were shocked, for example, when my sister Gina quit college that year, one semester short of her degree, he wrote her a note of complete empathy: "It's nice to know there's someone else willing to keep the rest of the world off-balance by driving on the wrong side of life's road."

I wanted to be the kind of woman who could handle the tension and traffic jams that Howe's irregular employment and unusual driving style guaranteed, but I wasn't. By 1984, with two sons to raise under mounting debts, I craved order over adventure. The same qualities that had attracted me to him in the first place—his unflappable calm wit during crises, his wholly nonconforming approach to life—became the very reasons I finally had to leave the marriage.

While we were in agreement intellectually that the marriage was over, we were at odds emotionally about where the relationship was going next. I proposed being friends, an offer that sounded like an empty proposition after ten years of being husband and wife. We conducted ourselves stiffly, self-consciously, unsure how to act divorced. Howe bounced erratically between rage and affection, like a man hit with painful bursts of static during a long-distance call to someone he loved. He would cry out in anger, then apologize, then clench his jaw in silence. It wore him out.

We had to stop for gas, since his gauge always hovered precariously above empty. The strain of being chronically short of cash showed up all over his life—it made him a nervous driver, for one thing. His eyes darted from the road to the gas gauge every thirty seconds, a habit acquired from life on the quarter tank. Money problems had plagued him since he'd left his job as a city planner in Fort Wayne, Indiana, five years before. After a fruitless job search he decided to change careers and, at age thirty-nine, returned to graduate school at the University of Michigan. We separated the September he moved to Ann Arbor.

There were still a few kinks in the "Dissolution Agreement" we drafted, as our holistic attorney in Fort Wayne referred to our divorce papers. Before it was written down, I thought he was saying "disillusion agreement," and was impressed with his poetic sensibility. It was enormously disillusioning to break love down to its daily parts, dividing the days of our children as if their affection were a commodity that could be traded. Our two young sons, then age six and seven, made only one request during the proceedings: "Don't ever make us choose between you." They expressed this wish so passionately, I knew that being their mother also meant being an ally to their father.

Since we had a nontraditional marriage, it made sense to end it with a nontraditional divorce. We needed an elastic document, one that would grow and stretch with our continually changing lives. The divorce we wrote was designed to expire periodically, so we could adjust the provisions every ten thousand miles or so. For couples with children, there is no such thing as a "final divorce." I imagined I would be divorcing Howe for the rest of my life.

In the first stage of dissolution, we shuttled the kids between our home in Fort Wayne and Howe's cramped student quarters in Ann Arbor. The boys were cheerful but inept travelers, losing their homework assignments and baseball mitts when we transferred their kid things from car trunk to car trunk. "The best interests of the children," which they straightforwardly named as a close connection to both of us, were compromised by the 140 miles between us. Howe felt estranged and alienated, unable to capture on weekends the lost intimacy of daily life. Involved in their care since infancy, he'd spent a lot of time with the boys. The divorce shot gigantic holes through his days.

Since my work as a writer was portable and Howe's work was not, I volunteered to set up a residence in Ann Arbor for two years, postponing my move east with the kids. Phase two began when I sold the house in Fort Wayne, paid off our debts, and rented a large, three-bedroom apartment on a tree-lined street a bike ride away from their father. The kids lived there all the time, and Howe moved in whenever I commuted to my work in New York or Washington, D.C. The plan worked well for the kids, but threw us back into the same financial and household strains that doomed the marriage.

The arguments about replenishing household supplies had previously exhausted me during the changing of the guard, but no more. That was the first great silence I achieved in 1984—I'd established a temporary peace in our prolonged war over money. The terms of the truce were very simple: Howe paid what he could from his part-time income, and I paid for everything else. It was an unconditional surrender to poverty, but I had too many other battles raging that year, on too many other fronts, to negotiate further gains with Howe. By the third year of his doctoral program, with only a few pages of his dissertation on paper, I guessed it would be several more years before he earned anything resembling a real paycheck. Since our small postnuclear family was presently supported by my wildly fluctuating income as a writer, it was a frightening forecast.

ii

When the car finally pulled up to the curb in front of the New York Air terminal, I checked my watch. I had exactly ten minutes to sprint down the long corridor to the departure gate, an athletic feat compounded by the improbable load of baggage I had to haul. After three years of commuting in a monthly triangle between the kids, my work in New York, and the man I loved in Washington, D.C., I'd become a compulsive overpacker, hounded by the feeling that I was always missing something. Of course, I always was. When I was working in New York I missed the kids, and during my single-mother weeks in Ann Arbor, I missed a few deadlines. And all of the time, except for spontaneous weekends planned thirty days in advance, I missed the tender passion of Larry's arms. I missed his arms, and I missed his entire body.

Since I myself was the mad architect behind this fractured life, I accepted this pervasive missing as one of the costs for my grand designs. Eventually I planned to bring all the scattered parts of my life together into one magnificent structure. Although the dizzying commutes allowed me to maintain major responsibilities in the meantime, I'd seriously miscalculated the physical and emotional strains. Warning signs that I was severely distressed were erupting all over my body—that morning I'd awakened with a sharp report from my abdomen, and thought for a moment I'd caught the kids' flu. A virulent strain of influenza had been leveling vulnerable members of the third and fourth grades, and both kids were home sick that week. I assumed I'd caught it, since my body had a magnetic attraction for all germs. But my response to any physical or psychological assault, by 1984, was to grit it out, marching blindly and bravely into the next ambush. It never occurred to me to postpone the trip.

According to my calendar, on March 21 I was headed into a week of enormous possibilities, a week it had taken three years of thinking and striving to reach. A particularly loaded agenda awaited me in New York, inspiring a bout of packing mania. I filled three large suitcases with assorted navy-drabs, as close to Midtown business regulations as my volunteer provisions allowed; enough books, manuscripts, and paper ammunition to cover me through a week of lunches with editors; and a copious supply of pharmaceuticals, gauze bandages, and postsurgical dressings, for wounds acquired during a recent exploratory surgery. I also packed a canvas artist's portfolio with two dozen X-rays, for a second consultation with a pulmonary specialist at Mt. Sinai Hospital. Feeling uncommonly ambitious, I decided to bring the small blue vinyl suitcase containing the personal papers my brother Frank had asked me to edit for him—a chore I'd been avoiding for two and a half years. Then, because I was becoming slightly delirious during the fever of packing, I grabbed the old, purple suede, knee-length vest from the back of my closet.

It was one of many such artifacts in my wardrobe. ("You don't really get dressed in the morning," Larry said once. "You don costumes.") For years I'd collected objets d'art in each of the cities I visited on lecture tours—the Minneapolis gas-mask bag, dyed lavender, which I used as a purse; the Juneau nightshirt, with pink salmon swimming upstream below the slogan LET'S SPAWN; the ceramic Big Sur earrings; the Kansas City belt buckle; the Evansville bowling shirt; and so on. The souvenirs, all wearable, reminded me of the people and their cities—and of who I was, too, what I was feeling the day I bought it. Every time I carried the lavender gas-mask bag, for example, I remembered gasping for air before my speech in Minneapolis last month, as a low moan sounded from the interior of my rib cage. As I stepped up to the podium of the packed auditorium, I had the unshakable conviction I was about to face the final music.

The Chicago vest brought back memories of friends in headbands and African dashikis who gathered regularly in the small apartment Howe and I rented in Old Town, sitting cross-legged on the floor and plotting a revolution of peace and love. We were young and innocent, full of certain truth. Although I never wore the vest anymore, I didn't know exactly how to dispose of it—I thought perhaps it should be buried or burned, like some holy relic. In my hallucinating mind that March afternoon, I imagined that by wearing the vest without self-consciousness in Greenwich Village, I could bring those old, unextinguished yearnings up to date. So far, my Midwestern innocence had been laughable in New York: "Oh, Mary *Kay*," my *Cosmo* editor chuckled over the phone, when I described my difficulties with her assignment that week, "everything doesn't have to be so meaningful. Lighten up—you'll live longer."

I slipped the vest on before packing it, and I remembered the fun, the whimsy of wearing it. The long rows of fringe swayed rhythmically with each step, turning an ordinary walk down the street into a little dance. I imagined strolling with Larry on leisurely evenings, his arm draped affectionately over my shoulders, my thumb hooked into the belt loop at the small of his back. I pictured us sitting at our favorite table in the Riviera Café in Greenwich Village, having the celebration we meant to have on New Year's Eve, when his long-coveted transfer from Washington, D.C., to New York finally came through. It was the first critical move in the delicate transplant of two careers and two children, and it broke my heart to miss that private party last winter. On New Year's Day, I was back in the hospital again.

If I missed my flight this time, I risked my entire future, or so it seemed in my feverish mind that afternoon. With harelike speed, I jumped out of Howe's car at the curb of the terminal while he extinguished his cigarette and slowly closed the ashtray.

"You're never going to make it with all this stuff," he said doubtfully, lifting the trunk lid of his weathered red Corolla and surveying all the baggage. His shoulders hunched up against the cold March air, he warmed his hands in the deep pockets of his corduroy pants while he decided which bag to lift first. The wind tossed his dark blond hair onto his forehead, and I noticed his beard and mustache needed a trim. I was still in the habit of analyzing Howe's head, after serving as his personal barber for ten years. I'd given him a few haircuts since I resigned as wife, but had to quit entirely a few months ago. They were too difficult. Bending down close around his head, touching his neck and ears, combing the soft fine hair, then stepping back and catching the terrible pain in his sad blue eyes—it was just too hard.

"I'll have to manage it," I shrugged, as he unloaded the baggage and handed it to me, "there's no time to check it." When he didn't offer to help, I didn't ask. Rule number one in maintaining the truce was "Expect nothing." He could have handed me a grand piano to drop off at Carnegie Hall, and I'd have promised to do it. Besides, I couldn't afford a turtlelike pace to the departure gate— this was a run for a sprinter.

I hoisted the baggage to my shoulders and, risking everything, looked directly into his eyes to say good-bye. Rule number two was "Don't take on his grief," a goal severely compromised by long gazes into those sad, blue depths. He automatically reached out to hug me but checked himself midair and delivered a tentative pat on my elbow instead. It was a cool gesture, numbing my own good-bye.

That distant pat added a few more months to my calculations for the great thaw, when his anger would melt and the sprouts of friendship might appear again. After a decade of intimate touch and loyal affection, the deep freeze of divorce was particularly punishing. It worried me, this prolonged frigidity. How long could human beings exist in such icy temperatures without losing their extremities to frostbite? My determination to expect nothing relieved the disappointment of receiving nothing, but turned love into a negative. The most I could hope to feel in this emotional wasteland was the absence of pain. I headed into the terminal, trying not to take on his loneliness as part of my load.

"M.K.!" he called after me—an old, familiar salutation from a warmer past. It gripped me by the shoulders and turned me around. He was standing on the frame of the open car door, his torso appearing above the roof like a large, disembodied bust. His face was temporarily enlivened by a sudden thought.

"Don't forget about our talk . . ." he yelled across the sidewalk, reminding me of our long session at the kitchen table after dinner last night. "Just think it all over, and we'll decide when you get back." He shrugged, as if he had only a casual interest in the outcome. He was a lousy actor—his eyes always gave him away, those two neon signs of happiness or grief. Last night they were flashing unmistakable urgency, when he asked me to postpone moving the kids for one more year. He'd prepared a compelling rationale: The kids were thriving in school and had a lot of good friends in Ann Arbor; he would take a leave from his studies and work full time, resuming the financial strains he'd left to me; and it would give me a year to live as a couple with Larry before we expanded into the responsibilities of family. For the first time in three years he offered to help with our post-divorce finances and, more startling, acknowledged the fact of Larry in my life. In exchange for these recognitions, he asked for a year with the kids. It was the grand piano of his wishes.

"I'll think about it," I shouted back. He waved and said something else, too softly to reach me in the high winds, something that went with an odd, affectionate smile. The disembodied head slid below the roof and he disappeared into the car. I lost several precious seconds, stuck in the doorway until the Corolla pulled away from the curb, finally releasing the grip. It was a strangely emotional moment for me.

iii

Inside the terminal I looked for an empty luggage cart, but none was in sight. The cumulative weight of the wishes and dreams I carried was a little over a hundred pounds, about the weight of my entire body. I stumbled down the corridor, perspiring and out of breath, as if I were carrying myself on my back. The gate area was empty except for a single attendant, uniformed in gray with a little red bow around her neck, standing at the mouth of the jetway. The accordion-pleated tunnel reminded me of an oversized vacuum hose, sucking up people like large crumbs into the belly of the plane. Inside the jetway, my bags banged against the soft walls, my heart echoing loudly in my inner ear. I stepped over the threshold and through first class, trying not to bruise the seated passengers with my assorted armaments, and finally stopped, abruptly, behind a large knot of people jamming their carry-ons into overhead bins.

The instant I stopped moving, I gasped for air. With each sharp intake of breath, a flutelike blast sounded from my rib cage, long and low. The people immediately ahead of me turned around, eyebrows raised, looking for the source of the bizarre noise. The plaintive, almost subhuman moan came from a six-inch rubber tube protruding from the middle of my torso. It wasn't a simple or brief explanation, that low moan issuing occasionally from my ribs, and I wasn't about to attempt one just then. I responded by shrugging my shoulders, as if I were as baffled as they, then looked around absently, perhaps for a small child with a broken harmonica. The man in the aisle seat to my left, his ear just inches from my ribs, gave me a faintly clinical look, suspecting something fishy.

The tube was a little keepsake from an open-lung biopsy I'd undergone a few months before. Sometime during the surgery, an infection called empyema had entered the wound. I was unconscious of the invasion until a month later, when I woke up one morning and felt a lump under the wound. I lifted my nightshirt and discovered a growth the size of a halved grapefruit, stretching the tender, six-inch incision into a grotesque, moon-shaped smile. On New Year's Day, 1984, while Larry celebrated alone at the Riviera Café in New York, I went back into the hospital for surgical repairs.

A long, hard plastic tube was inserted between my ribs into my pleural cavity, draining an ominous, colorless fluid into the suction machine gurgling at the end of my bed. I was released a week later in the custody of a soft, narrow rubber tube and several feet of gauze bandage. Twice a day I had to plunge the tube with saline solution to keep it open, and change the dressings. I tried to perform this gruesome task with a steady detachment, stepping back from my horror at a body gone completely haywire.

The trouble had begun two years earlier, the week I arrived in Ann Arbor to begin the second phase of dissolution, when I checked into the local emergency room late one night with chills and a fever. The internists at Catherine McAuley Health Center diagnosed a case of pneumonia, but I recognized it was also the result of the icy climate I'd moved into. The doctors were further alarmed by my X-rays, and the mysterious dark spots at the bottom of my lungs. I was concerned but not surprised, since these shadows had appeared and disappeared before, during other periods of stress in my life. I assumed they would recede again when I got my life back under control. The problem, of course, was that my life was heading in the opposite direction. Penicillin took care of the pneumonia, but the shadows grew larger.

I resisted the open-lung biopsy for two years, because aside from the cloudy X-rays, I was otherwise symptomless. I submitted to countless blood tests and X-rays, sputum cultures and physicals, but nothing yielded a diagnosis of the shadows. My doctors were convinced an open-lung biopsy would produce an answer in seven days—ten at the outside. It always amazed me, the way men of science approached knotty problems with such precision. Unlike writers, inclined to wallow over the mystery and symbolism of a shadow, my doctors busily measured the circumferences, assigned scientific names, and expected answers within a certain number of days.

When the shadows had first appeared ten years before, for example, the pulmonary specialists at the Municipal Tuberculosis Sanatorium in Chicago performed a lymph-node biopsy and classified the condition "sarcoidosis." It was an autoimmune disorder, they told me, when a body's own defense system turns against itself. There was no known treatment—the disease simply ran its course and disappeared. In my own private exploratory probes in the sanatorium that week, I found another possible source of the scarred tissue on my X-rays. As a bride of three years, bouquet long wilted, living with in-laws during the first period of unemployment, I labeled the disorder "depression." In either case, the treatment was the same: Wait it out.

That was still my approach, ten years later, when the Ann Arbor doctors were eager to open me up again. I was unwilling to donate any more of my body to science, because I didn't believe the problem was purely physical. But suddenly, in October 1983, strange new symptoms appeared. My vision became blurry and I was flattened by a tremendous fatigue. Periodically I felt sieges of ravenous hunger, unquenchable thirst. Another autoimmune disorder emerged, more deadly than the rest: diabetes mellitus. It baffled my doctors, since there was no history of the disease in my immediate family, and I didn't fit their profile of a diabetic: over forty, overeater, overweight. I visualized my immune system, running amok during the multiple S.O.S. alerts my brain sent out, and attacking the innocent islets of Langerhans by mistake. That the tiny insulin-producing cells in my pancreas were the victims of friendly fire made the tragedy no less permanent.

Daily insulin injections and all the medical paraphernalia of diabetes came into my life, and I rebelled against the verdict that it would be with me until death. When my internist speculated that the diabetes might be connected to the pulmonary shadows— that diagnosing and treating one might relieve the symptoms of the other—I capitulated to exploratory surgery. The decision relieved my family and friends, anxious to have a name for what seemed to be draining the life out of me. But it violated everything I knew about the history of my highly psychosomatic, intensely sensitive body. I believed the shadows were symptoms of a great depression, beginning the weekend my brother Frank had left his blue suitcase with me two Novembers before, and I knew the cure for depression wasn't surgery.

My doctors were ecstatic after the open-lung biopsy. The surgeon had removed a significant slice of tissue, obtaining a perfect sample of one of the shadows. Outside my body, it appeared as a bulbous nodule, filled with a clear liquid. After seven days, the laboratory produced no cultures, and my doctors had to cancel several possible diagnoses. After ten days, even the long shots had to be abandoned, and all ambitions of presenting a brilliant paper to colleagues at the University of Michigan were dashed. With the mystery still uncracked, the hospital staff referred to me generically as the Blakely Case.

In defeat, frozen sections of the tissue were sent to the Armed Forces Institute in Washington, D.C., and to Dr. Anna Luisa Katzenstein's famous laboratory at the University of Louisiana. The pathologists described various symptoms, including those of Wegener's granulomatosis, but could not positively identify a specific infection. Various names were offered as a label— "necrotizing nodules" emerged as the favorite.

During the long convalescence in the hospital over New Year's

Eve, I had a lot of time to think about the meaning of necrotizing nodules. The ravenous hunger, the unquenchable thirst—I saw myself committing the fatal error of Salinger's bananafish, who swam into the cave and ate too many bananas, then couldn't get out. Rumor had it that someone had seen one, before he died, "with six in his mouth." I had that many passionate causes going, in almost as many cities, and knew it was beyond reason. But which of my yearnings should I cease? Not the kids, not Larry, not my family or friends. My work as a writer? The promises I'd made to Frank? My troubled friendship with Howe? Consuming too many passions, I thought, could make a rib cage explode in bizarre growths. Nevertheless, unable to contain my appetite, I ultimately took the tube.

"I can't believe this is the best modern medicine can do," I'd complained to my doctor during a checkup that week. "It's 1984, for chrissakes—we have *antibiotics* now," I said madly. The tube seemed a medieval solution to me, just a step beyond the blood letters and leeches of the nineteenth century. In those days, scholars estimate, a patient had a fifty percent chance of surviving a visit to the doctor. In my experience with modern medicine, the odds were largely the same. For three months, I traveled around the country in the company of this bizarre tubal apparatus, outraged and angry, an unamused victim of the Curly, Moe, and Larry School of Medicine.

iv

As the tube whistled its low moan on the New York Air plane, a tidal wave of dizziness passed over me, flooding my head and crashing in around my knees. Suddenly overwhelmed by the weight of my luggage, I let the straps drop from my shoulders, sending the bags to the floor with a dull thud. Losing my balance in the process, I landed clumsily on top of the largest bag. Once down, however gracelessly, I saw no immediate reason for getting up. It would be several minutes before the aisle ahead of me cleared, so I propped my elbows up on my knees, covering my face with my hands. I closed my eyes, trying to restore my equilibrium. Damply, I paid a little hospital call on myself.

Why I got on board in the first place, given my fragile physical condition, deserves some small speculation. Part of the reason, certainly, was that my early-warning system was shot. An unusually high pain threshold prevented me from feeling the first wave—Howe and I had a tense ride to the hospital the night of Ryan's birth, for example, because I'd slept through the first stage of labor. I would become aware of symptoms only when the pain reached the unbearable, head-banging stage.

The habit of ignoring subtle pain began in my Catholic girlhood, no doubt, during my thorough training as a young martyr. Suffering in silence was thought to benefit the souls in purgatory, and I imagined the longer I waited to see a doctor, the more souls I could spring. "Offering it up" was my family's formula for coping with pain—it was part of the Blakely disease. Ever since I realized the folly of ignoring symptoms, I'd been trying to reconnect with my body, abandoning the souls in purgatory and seeking earlier treatment. But when the tube was planted in my ribs that winter, I'd gone numb again.

A more reasonable person might have postponed the trip, after telltale symptoms of the flu appeared, but reason had quit the scene some time before. By 1984, I'd lost all ability to distinguish between a true emergency and an only partially disastrous one. I couldn't tell which physical signs were the result of actual bacteria and which were the product of an overemotional mind. The tremendous influence of my imagination on body chemistry was evident daily—every time I felt a blush heating my cheeks, I was impressed with the power of my unconscious mind, hauling thousands of tiny red corpuscles upstream to my face, against *gravity*, against my conscious will. A thrilling idea raised goosebumps on my neck, stage fright made me hyperventilate, and the memory of certain faces, seated across kitchen tables I've known, occasionally watered my eyes. If the body's chemistry responded so dramatically to these fleeting emotions, couldn't a dark, prolonged grief produce shadows on my lungs?

The wiring of my family's nervous system is so delicate that every one of my four siblings has broken out, now and then, in similar red alerts. My sister Gina, the last and most loved of Kay and Jerry's five children, broke out in a rash called "pityriasis rosea" before she left home. We were a family of canaries, hypersensitive to all atmospheric pressures, keeling over at the first hint of poisonous gas in the air.

I was struggling with a profound depression that year, after the multiple-megaton explosions in my personal and professional life. I no longer regarded depression as a disease, in fact, any more than pregnancy or aging are diseases. In my experience, depression was as natural, as awesome in the range of human passion as joy or happiness. It usually followed some emotional clash with the outside world, when the message "Something's wrong here" flashed suddenly on a subway wall in my mind.

It would stop me dead in my tracks for days while I drew a blank about why, how, when, what the premonition meant. But below the exterior passivity of depression, there was tremendous internal activity, as my unconscious rapidly prepared all thought systems to accommodate the arrival of a new truth. The revelations of 1984 required such stunning changes in my life, my head felt as if it were under iron scaffolding. I'd wake up in the morning after heart-pounding dreams and realize that some enormous construction had been going on all night. Awake, distracted by the requirements of the day, I couldn't see its exact form and shape. But truths were forming during these fitful nights. I could feel it, in the exhaustion that engulfed me by morning.

A depression, in my case, was always accompanied by heightened physical responses. Even ordinary events, in the spring of 1984, triggered hyperbolic reactions. A phone call from an editor produced effusive sweating, and when Larry called me late each night to tell me he loved me, I burst into tears. I was so steeled against pain and despair, so heavily armored with defenses, any message of tenderness completely unglued me. I wasn't positive, therefore, that the sudden weakness in my knees had been an attack of the flu. It might have been another necrotizing nodule erupting. Or it could have been a belated response to Howe's last words at the departure gate.

Whatever it was, my response to the flu symptoms was the same as it had been when the dentist gave me bad news, earlier that week. He examined the two molars I'd cracked after surgery, when I awakened from the anesthetic and my teeth began chattering violently. The dentist recommended two porcelain crowns, at $350 apiece. I found this screamingly funny, for some reason.

Rationality left me altogether, and I began to make a series of bad jokes: Were the crowns available in something cheaper than porcelain, say, Melmac or Tupperware? Could I register as a crown donor on the back of my driver's license, in the event of my death? Was he sure I didn't need a gum biopsy? I alone found these remarks hilariously funny, and I apologized repeatedly. But I couldn't stop laughing.

"Are you all right?" the dentist kept asking, clearly alarmed, wondering if it was safe to put his fingers in the mouth of a dangerously unbalanced woman. I nodded weakly, convulsing with black humor, tears running down my cheeks.

V

"Are you all right?" a female voice repeated. I opened my eyes and looked into the gray vest of a New York Air attendant leaning over my disorganized encampment in the aisle. The plane was moving into position on the runway and the other passengers, now all belted into their assigned seats, were craning their necks and looking interestedly on.

"Yes," I lied, "I'm fine." A Blakely, even when felled to the floor with an arrow sticking between her ribs, responds to all queries about her person with, "Don't worry about me. I'm fine." Stifling another bout of laughter, I wiped the tears from my cheeks and got rockily to my feet. Still wearing the purple vest with knee-length fringe over my sweat suit, I became aware that among the pin-striped suits all around me I appeared like an oversized elf.

"Do you need help?" the attendant asked, offering to stow some of my luggage. I needed miracles, I wanted to tell her, but surrendered the artist's portfolio containing my X-rays. I imagined them as works of modern art, in a sense—I often thought Oscar Wilde might have used X-rays to symbolize the troubled soul of Dorian Grey, had the machinery been around in his day. While the attendant headed up the aisle searching for enough space, the man seated at the end of my row stood up and lifted my other bags into an overhead bin. He then waited patiently, regarding me with high curiosity as I wedged myself into place. I dumped my briefcase and purse into the empty middle seat and lowered myself, leadenly, into the one next to the window.

I fastened my seat belt and, sensing a pending conversation from my friendly seatmate, busied myself with the contents of my briefcase. I didn't really expect to do any work. I always carried it along, in case the desire arose, but I generally daydreamed on planes. Modern air travel allowed so little time to adjust from one environment to another—passengers from Minnesota would de-plane in Florida, still wearing their parkas and looking vaguely confused. With only two hours between the frigidity of Ann Arbor and the warm affection in New York, I hardly had time to shed my layers of insulation.

I took out my journal and the folder containing notes for my *Cosmo* article and put them in the pocket of the seat ahead of me, stowing my briefcase below. I then picked up the sample copy my editor sent, advising me to bone up on the magazine's style. The instant I opened the pages, however, my seatmate penetrated the defensive shield.

"You certainly had a lot of luggage," he remarked amiably. "Are you an artist?" I turned down a corner of the magazine to look at him. He was a Detroiter, not a New Yorker, I judged—he'd been patient, helpful, openly curious, and didn't have the superior eyes of someone who knew and had seen everything. The Midwestern-ers on these flights started the conversations. New Yorkers cut them off. It wasn't unkindness, I was beginning to understand, that made New Yorkers seem so rude and brusque to heartland sensibilities. Their Eastern reserve was a kind of emotional thriftiness. They lived in a city overcrowded with bananafish— seven million human beings, pumping with ambitions and pas-sions, on one thirteen-mile island. They couldn't afford to put a quarter in every cup someone held out; they had to ration their resources.

"No," I replied, "I'm not." I tried to show by my expression that this was the end of the conversation, but I was not yet a convincing New Yorker.

"What do you do?" he continued, missing my subtle signal. I weighed the dangers of admitting I was a writer. It was always followed by a series of interested questions about what I wrote, where I was published, how I got started. All of my seatmates, it turned out, had also "done some writing" in their spare time, and were eager to explore common bonds. I didn't have any spare change on that flight, however, so I had to pass up his cup. I looked levelly into his eyes.

"I'm a proctologist," I lied flatly. There was a brief silence, in which he glanced down at my purple fringed vest, to make sure he hadn't imagined it.

"Oh," he said, his smile fading. There was no follow-up line. Apparently, he didn't practice proctology in his spare time. I lifted my magazine and pretended to read, and we both fell silent.

It wasn't a total lie—I did feel, at times, that I'd become a specialist in the anal aspects of life. And the folder in the pouch proved I certainly wasn't a writer, at least not a practicing one. That was another name for the necrotizing nodules of 1984—I had been in a severe writer's block for three months, ever since I had taken the tube. I was currently stuck on a *Cosmo* assignment called "The Riddle of Responsibility." In house, it was referred to as a "maj emo," that is, a major emotional essay of about 3,500 words, in which I was to advise the 2.8 million *Cosmo* girls how to manage their work and relationships without sacrificing too much of their joy—particularly their sexual joy.

I was blocked because I couldn't imagine offering any useful ideas to the *Cosmo* girls, when my own personal life demonstrated how to conduct a major fuck-up. So far, I had written these words: "Read Dr. Jean Baker Miller's *Toward a New Psychology of Women*. Everything else is background music." I still had 3,484 words to go, and I had run out of things to say. My typing fingers were itching imperceptibly, if at all.

"I feel like a hen who is continually expected to lay eggs," Albert Einstein once wrote in a letter to a friend, after the theory of relativity made its great splashdown among his colleagues. "With fame, I grow more and more stupid," he admitted. I understood the feeling. When *The New York Times* had published nine of my essays in the "Hers" column three years before, my writing career moved abruptly from Fort Wayne, Indiana, to New York City, where I'd been put on the Most Wanted List of national magazine editors. They mistook me for a professional writer, able to produce exactly 1,150 words every Thursday by 2 P.M. In fact I was a painfully slow writer, bleeding each word onto the page, far more influenced by lunar cycles than deadlines.

"Writing isn't your career," my sister Gina had said over the phone that week when I told her I planned to quit free-lancing and look for more reliable work. "It's your religion." In a family of seekers, my declared agnosticism was never entirely accepted. My brothers and sister persisted in seeing me as one of them, still a member of their peculiar, nondenominational, ecumenical monastery. They translated my secular behavior in spiritual terms: "Writing is your form of prayer," Gina had speculated on the phone that day. "You put words together one by one to reach the truth."

I specialized in the truth as it affected women, and it was rarely good news in 1984. There was a poster on my office wall, which I'd purchased on a trip through the Harvard Commons, containing a summary of my religious beliefs: "The truth will make you free, but first it will make you miserable." My method of writing, that year, was chaotic and exhausting. I'd sail into the dark belly of the whale, wait patiently until it coughed me back out again, then row like mad in the wake of my release. Sometimes it would take several days for me to understand what I had actually learned. Sometimes I wouldn't understand what I had written at all until after it was published and outbreaks of passion flared up among family and friends.

The elder members of my Irish Catholic family, rarely short of opinions about my life or work, would fall silent when I wrote about abortion. My feminist friends would object when they thought I was being too soft on men. Howe felt personally injured by an essay on marriage. And the longtime friend who appeared with me in an essay on divorce reported: "I cried. It was all true—it was beautifully written—but it made me cry." That was my main employment in 1984: making as many people as miserable as possible in thirty-five hundred words or less.

I would hear these cries of protest or pain whenever I confronted a difficult truth and tried to soften it, make it more bearable. This self-censorship turned my prose into indistinguishable bowls of mush. When truth clashed with love—and there was hardly a topic I could land on that didn't risk a clash with someone I loved—I leaned away from truth. The compromise left me feeling loved, sometimes extravagantly, for who I wasn't.

"ARE YOU COPING WITH TOO MUCH *STRESS*?" a headline asked abruptly, as I idly turned the magazine pages. "Stress" was in large, electrified, hot-pink letters, the same type women's magazines used for *FAT* and *WRINKLES*. I was invited to measure my anxiety level, by totaling up the "stressors" that applied to me. I checked the first five without hesitation: "Recently divorced," "Move to another city," "Major health problem," "Financial difficulty," and "Argument with a family member." I paused at six, "Getting fired from your job," since I was on the verge of accomplishing that any day now. But I didn't even need the points—I already had enough to qualify for the top category on the red thermometer illustrating the page. My score placed me in "Dangerously overloaded," a group whose circuits could blow at any moment. And I still had a whole stretcher load of points coming from the last item on the survey. Number ten, by far the weightiest stressor, was "Death of a loved one."

Francis Jude, my eldest brother, had been consumed by the most ferocious strain of the Blakely disease, responding to life with unstoppable passion. Frank was brilliant and witty, the leading madman of my four eccentric siblings, and I missed him enormously. During his brief adult life, he suffered a total of eight nervous breakdowns, serving as many sentences—voluntary and not—in Chicago institutions. Whether his wild imagination caused the stunning chemical changes in his body or the other way around, he surged with inhuman energy during his manic periods, then was flattened for months with tremendous exhaustion. He committed suicide on November 12, 1981.

His doctors diagnosed him as "manic-depressive," but Frank thought of his illness as "a spiritual fever." After his boyhood years as a Catholic seminarian, followed by an earnest search for God in the writings of Buddhist monks, Jewish rabbis, Protestant priests, and, finally, Unitarian ministers, he'd formed a nonsectarian but wholly religious view of events.

Normally reserved and shy, he was charismatic and demonstrative when he was high. He ran for governor of Illinois once, on orders from above. He broke through security at *The Sun Times* in Chicago, where he brought columnist Mike Royko the good news that he was destined to become his campaign manager. Royko called my parents, and Frank spent the rest of his campaign at the Reed Mental Health Center. The incident did prompt Royko to write a column about Frank, not endorsing his gubernatorial race, but pointing out the faulty security systems at hospitals and newspapers that allowed lunatics to roam freely about Chicago.

Although I was an avowed agnostic myself, I thought his spiritual diagnosis was as credible as anything else. Nevertheless, I felt obliged to argue with him. During his second breakdown in 1967, when he was wired with electrodes and given shock treatments at Loretto Hospital in Chicago, he reported that he'd received messages directly from God Himself. The truth arrived in tremendous jolts, he said, just as he expected it would some day. I tried to help him unscramble his brain, pointing out the difference between electricity and divinity. It was machinery, not God, that sent the sizzling jolts through his mind, I said.

"Truth doesn't fry your brain," I pointed out.

"Sometimes it *does*," he replied, wide-eyed, as surprised to report this revelation as I was to hear it. A look of sheer lucidity crossed his face, followed by sudden surprise and then vast confusion. It was a silent movie of the chaos inside his head—I could actually watch Frank losing his innocence. He shed a great quantity in the shock-treatment room at Loretto, being electrified by truth.

The treatments halted his mania only temporarily. During subsequent breakdowns, he was studied and probed, tested and drugged, interviewed and examined by some of the most famous psychiatrists in Chicago, but no one could cure him. Attempts to stabilize his moods with lithium bicarbonate failed repeatedly, puzzling his physicians. Frank himself was amazed by the constant motion inside his mind. He said it felt like his head had been clapped between two powerful hands and was orbiting around a spinning discus thrower, warming up for a mighty heave. He was eager for the final thrust, releasing him from the dizzying spins into free flight.

I was one of Frank's main companions throughout his bouts of madness, when his mind rolled out to the ends of human passion. He would hear and see things I couldn't understand, and I spent countless hours arguing with him inside the wards of insane asylums. In polite company, they're referred to as "mental health centers" today, but in the ravaged minds of the inmates, politeness was the first thing to go. Well-mannered citizens prefer to keep lunatics locked up, even the nonviolent ones, because they're frightening; they blurt out loud secrets the rest of us harbor. I watched the more stable residents of Greenwich Village, for example, make a wide circle on the sidewalk around the wild-eyed old woman in a stocking cap who stood outside Poppy's Delicatessen on Sixth Avenue every day with a poster declaring, THE END IS NEAR.

"How will it happen?" I asked her once, putting a quarter into her cup. The question threw her into temporary paralysis, as a vacant expression filled her eyes and some internal vision occupied her attention. Snapping back just as abruptly, as if some explosion had gone off behind her forehead, her arms shot up toward the sky, blackened fingernails protruding from the holes in her worn gloves. "Nuked!" she shouted, her one-word summary of the internal home movie. She handed me a pencil, the little sliver of defense she offered to believers, slim protection against the monumental destruction she imagined heading our way.

Spending time with Frank and his mad peers was disturbing, because they made the line between sanity and insanity become so murky. After an afternoon arguing with lunatics who spoke truth bluntly, I would go home and watch the evening news, where the president of the most powerful country in the world was declaring war on the tiny island of Grenada. Nobody suggested locking him up. It worried me that mental patients made perfect sense and the president of the United States seemed like a candidate for the Reed Mental Health Center. Nevertheless, I pleaded with Frank to return to reality, trotting breathlessly beside him as he paced back and forth over the grounds of Elgin State Hospital, the last stop for incurable cases. These pleas, wishing a normal life on him, came strictly from a sense of duty. In truth, I questioned the value of "normal" myself.

He would come back from his journeys into madness radically altered by what he had seen, and I understood, now, how much I relied on his expeditions. I was too much of a coward to let my own mind roll out full length, having witnessed the devastating price he paid. His manic bouts were followed by long depressions, as he struggled to apply his dreams to ordinary life. The messages he believed so ardently during his seizures would melt into doubt, and he felt his otherness with an excruciating loneliness. Para- lyzed with indecision and fear, he would sleep through those months, sometimes for twenty hours at a time. The fantastic energy abandoned him, and he lifted his thin, weakened body out of bed as if it weighed five hundred pounds. He described these terrible confrontations with his conscience as "grand mal seizures of despair." They were a regular stop on the circular course of his spiritual fevers.

The weekend before his suicide, he had visited me in Fort Wayne, coming from Chicago by Greyhound. He knew I would be devastated by his decision, and he had told me over and over that weekend how much he loved me. It was only later, when I went back over our long conversations, that I understood he was also saying good-bye. Ostensibly, he had come to deliver a suitcase full of journal notes—jottings made at fever pitch—asking me to be his "translator." The structural ideas for his grand visions were all there, he thought, but lacked fluency. I accepted the sheaf of papers, fully aware that God might appear as an electric chair in the gospel according to Frank.

He, too, was a writer, but he had abandoned very nearly all conventional forms, completely ignoring amenities with the reader in his rush to record gigantic thoughts. Some pages con- tained only a single sentence, no thoughts leading up to or away from it, like the solitary message of an obsessed placard carrier on the street. ("In the whitest light, the dancer becomes the dance," one page announced.) Frank's journal read like a series of baffling Zen koans, evidence of lunacy or brilliance.

Although it was painful to remember, I cherished that last visit together—it relieved any guilt I might have had about preventing his death. He wasn't depressed that weekend—quite the opposite, in fact. He was riding the crest of a manic high, pacing about my quiet Fort Wayne neighborhood with frenetic energy. He fright- ened the elderly widow who lived down the street, when he serenaded her one midnight on her front lawn. She was lonely, his voices told him, and he thought he had the power to spread unlimited quantities of love around.

I remember watching him through the kitchen window that Saturday afternoon, as he raked a month's accumulation of leaves with the kids. They filled a large tarp with leaves, then one or both of the kids would jump in and Frank would drag them from the far back of the lot to the curb. With a mighty heave, unexpectedly strong for his skinny, drug-shaken frame, he'd hoist the kids and leaves into the air.

The sound he emitted with each launch was a peculiar blend of karate yell and manic laugh, his voice undecided whether to expect pain or joy with the final thrust. Then he'd race the kids to the back of the yard and start all over, as if his life depended on filling the street with children and leaves. Long after the kids left the game, he was still filling the tarp, turning on the floodlights over the garage after dusk. He couldn't slow down, let alone stop.

Like the animated sorcerer's apprentice trying to hold back the flood with a broom, he raked feverishly, piercing the night with howls of aching happiness. I stood at the window, holding my coffee cup, wondering what he thought he was hauling, to where. He was exceptionally tight-lipped about his plans that weekend. But I caught him wearing his Excelsior look now and then, the one he wore when he was in the company of angels.

I knew his suicide was not an act of despair; in his own mind, he was committing an act of ultimate faith. It was a death from exhaustion, from the efforts of thinking and striving, and I was grateful he finally reached the end of his pain. This gratitude, however, didn't relieve my grief at his funeral. The pervasive missing that saturated 1984 was largely connected to Frank. Ever since this beloved madman had permanently quit the scene, a ferocious yearning had paced through my head like a caged, hungry beast.

vii

"Would you like something to drink?" the stewardess asked, rolling her beverage cart down the aisle.

"I'll have a bloody mary," I replied. "In fact, make it two," I amended, becoming aware of a tremendous thirst. I extracted some bills from my wallet and handed them to her, accepting two small bottles of vodka and a can of mix. I poured the tomato juice over the ice cubes, filling the glass to the brim, and drank it straight down. Still thirsty, I filled the glass a second time and drained it again. Unscrewing the caps and pouring both bottles of vodka over the ice, I planned to sip the liquor slowly. Instead, my glass was empty before the stewardess reached the next row. I felt a terrific wave of heat riding the length of my esophagus, and only then realized what I had done. I asked for a cup of coffee.

"You're the fastest drinker I've ever seen," my seatmate said, just opening the tab on his beer. I noticed he was wearing a second set of eyebrows on his forehead.

To steady myself, I pressed the button on the arm and reclined my seat, fixing my eyes on the slow-moving clouds below the plane. The last rays of sunset tinted them red and yellow, and a brilliant white light illuminated them from below. In the darkening sky, they appeared as pillows of light, and I half expected to see Frank sitting cross-legged on one of them, smiling crazily as he rocked back and forth, the way he had at my kitchen table during his last visit.

"What are you thinking," I kept asking, "What's going *on?*" Something was clearly up—his eyes had been on high beam all weekend, but he declined to say in perfectly intelligible terms exactly what it was.

"I'm just having my own good time," he replied, smiling provocatively but saying nothing more.

He requested his favorite meal that night, a pot roast and "Jerry's mashed potatoes," a recipe our father invented with heart-stopping quantities of butter and salt. Frank kept refilling his plate with the white fluff, reminding me of the obsessed hero in *Close Encounters of the Third Kind*. Visited by aliens, the crazed man had lost his mind at dinner one night, piling his plate higher and higher with mashed potatoes. His alarmed wife and son had watched, open mouthed, as he dropped the serving spoon and frantically shaped the mass with his fingers, forming a model of the mountain where he was destined to join the aliens. Frank stared at his potatoes with the same possessed look, but remained calm. He held on to his fork, and he steadily ate the entire mountain. I was astonished by his insatiable appetite that weekend, his rail-thin body disguising the holding capacity of a camel.

Sunday morning, I asked him if he wanted a ham sandwich for the bus ride home, and he said yes, in fact he'd like two. He asked me to hold the mustard and mayonnaise—"just put the ham between two slices of bread."

"Just plain bread?" I asked, "You don't like mustard anymore?" He used to slather it on ham sandwiches.

"I always get it on my pants," he said, with the smile of sweet, wistful surrender I'd seen all my life. His food *did* always land in his lap, because he was such an eccentric eater. Trying not to get mustard on his hands, he held a sandwich on the tripod of three extended fingers, placing his elbow on the table for support and craning his neck as he bit around the edges. It used to drive everyone in the family crazy, waiting for the delicate balance to tip and for the sandwich to drop into his lap. It happened every time. Kay, our mother, devoted her life to working out eccentric kinks in Frank's manners and clothing, but even her indomitable spirit was eventually worn down by persistent oddities. She said nothing, the last years, when he wore his navy-blue stocking cap through all seasons, through snowstorms and tornado warnings, through sweaty summers and windy autumns. That stocking cap was his lithium, he said. It muffled the voices.

These continual surrenders to his illness gave him a lean life, but he didn't see any alternatives. Instead of getting a good grip on his sandwich, he gave up mustard with ham. That's what I was thinking about when I drove him to the Greyhound station that Sunday in November—the mustardless state of his life. Trivialities usually dominated my mind in times of great emotion. When he turned around to wave good-bye from the steps of the Greyhound, it caused a zoom-lens moment, when multiple flashbulbs went off in my head. I understood I would never see him again. It seemed I should say something meaningful—how much I loved him, how I could save him.

"You forgot your stocking cap!" I hollered instead, noticing his thick black curls springing out around his head. I was Frank's barber, too. I was tempted to use a hedge shears that weekend, the growth was so wild. He reached up and touched his head, as if to verify my report, then laughed.

"You'll have to mail it to me!" he yelled back, just before the doors closed.

Two nights later, when Kay called from Chicago, the stocking cap was still in its mailer, sitting in the basket on my breakfront.

"Hello, darling," she said softly, and I instantly raised both hands to the receiver. Kay saved "darling" for emergencies—her love was made of stronger stuff, herding five children through infancy and adolescence with exacting discipline.

"Are the children in bed?" she asked quietly, and I sank into the chair next to the phone, a great ache swelling my throat, cutting off my air. I knew what she had to report. A letter from Frank had arrived that morning: "It was a beautiful letter," she said calmly, huskily, in a voice that had not yet fully recovered from an afternoon of tears. "It made us cry." She paused then, taking in an extra breath of air to hold her brief but heavy summary. "He thanked us for being his parents."

Kay had called the police, who verified the information in the letter within an hour. The coroner had placed a seal over his room at the Cedar Hotel. "Someone in the family will have to claim his effects," she said, quoting the clinical instructions from the coroner's office. We both knew whom she would have to appoint, but we didn't acknowledge it just then. His body had been delivered to the funeral home, she said, but there was no word yet about whether the casket would have to remain closed for the wake. "They're still working on him," Kay said, her strong voice almost inaudible.

Before I left for Chicago for Frank's funeral, I put the mailer containing his stocking cap in with his papers. I hadn't reopened the blue suitcase again for two and a half years. My promise to serve as "translator" was still unmet, a piece of unfinished business that weighed heavily on me.

In the vision of Frank I constructed in the clouds outside the plane, I added his stocking cap, just below the halo I imagined for him. It was an irreverent touch Frank would have enjoyed, and I began to giggle. Almost immediately, the giggles gave way to tears and I began to weep. Not quiet, discreet, window-gazing sobs, but trumpets of grief, harmonizing with the low moan of the flute in my ribs. My seatmate instantly grabbed the airsickness bag from the pouch in front of him and handed it to me, opened. He thought I'd been leveled by the bloody marys.

I tried to smile and tell him, "I'm fine!" but could form no words. Pulling a packet of Kleenex from the lavender gas-mask bag, I blew my nose—an unladylike, bulldozer heave to move the boulder from the back of my swollen throat. I was embarrassed, and I thought my addled seatmate deserved an explanation for my bizarre behavior. But I didn't know quite how to summarize it:

"My brother stopped eating mustard, and then he lost his stocking cap." I decided the damages to my self-image were irreparable, and I left the man to the inevitable conclusion that I was an unstable, inebriated proctologist in a purple fringed vest.

viii

The pilot announced the beginning of the descent into La Guardia, asking the passengers to return to their seats and fasten their belts. I wearily packed my *Cosmo* notes and was starting to put my journal back into my briefcase when I had a sudden impulse to make an entry. It was an unusual urge for 1984—the pages of my journal were mostly blank that year. During one of her prolonged writer's blocks, my friend Gabrielle Burton said her diary contained only one entry, made during a brief lift in the middle of the year: "Flossed two teeth," it said. For evidence, she taped a little piece of waxed floss to the page. There wasn't much to report during depressions, because the most productive hours were spent sleeping.

My cure for depression was to dream my way out of a blank imagination—throwing out the lines of my mind as far as I could, baited with visions and fantasies, then reeling myself slowly back in. The depressions of 1984 put such tremendous pressure on my lines, I suspected I'd hooked the big one. A clear view of the life I was trying to haul in escaped me, however, as evidenced in the blank pages of my journal. I couldn't remember my dreams.

I opened the cover and wrote the date, intending to outline my plans for the week. Instead, as the plane descended and my ears popped with the changing altitude, something inside my head seemed to disengage and shift gears. I began writing rapidly, almost hypnotically, watching rather than thinking as the words filled the page.

I have written with such speed and certainty only one other time, the morning of Frank's funeral, when I was composing his eulogy. I didn't understand where those words came from, either. My older brother Paul wondered whether I had become an instrument of some higher power. A deeply spiritual man, Paul was looking for some indication that Frank was okay, but I thought it meant he questioned my authorship. The eulogy I read that morning didn't sound much like me. God appeared in it, for one thing, and Paul knew I didn't rely on God in times of emergency. He thought I had a long way to go in my evolution—in fact, he suspected I might be evolving backward. He thought my secular involvement in the world, together with the public attention of my work and politics, made spiritual detachment all but impossible. These risky detours from my spiritual path could cost several more lifetimes, in his opinion.

Paul's assessments of the state of my soul infuriated me sometimes—it was hard to explain myself to someone speaking from such an elevated plane. He kept forgetting that I was the one who had introduced D. T. Suzuki and Lu K'uan Yu to the family reading lists, twenty years before. I used to complain to Frank that Paul thought he was the only holy man around. ("You make him feel competitive," Frank said. "You make *me* feel competitive. Maybe you can't help it," he said, shrugging his shoulders. "Maybe in this trip, you're scheduled to learn what vanity and envy are all about." He said that to me while he was locked up in Dunning, certified as crazy by an Illinois State psychiatrist.)

I didn't mind, however, when Paul questioned the authorship of the eulogy. I myself didn't understand how it had come together, though I doubted the higher-power theory. I thought my writing that morning was fueled by pure terror. Anticipating the oceanic grief that would engulf our family and friends, I tried to imagine what Frank might have said at his funeral. Only Frank would risk including jokes in a eulogy. Yet that was what had happened: I had read the words while the congregation alternately laughed and cried, releasing gigantic waves of emotion from the pews.

That feeling of terror was upon me again, as the plane descended into New York City, the island of seven million bananafish. Instead of writing the to-do list I intended, I composed the following message to myself:

March 21, 1984

FRANK: You continue this arrogance, to presume to know what only God can know. Mary Kay! You cannot reach detachment, so tangled in possessive love. You won't let go of your yearnings because you're afraid of feeling nothing. Detachment doesn't abandon love, but goes beyond it. Why do I have to keep telling you this?

HOWE: You are not responsible for either his happiness or loneliness. Leave him to work out his own peace. This means you will have to stop reading his mind all the time. Guilt is an imperfect form of love, but you use it too much. Reach knowledge without so much self-punishment. Also: Remember the conversation about Kay and Jerry at Reed. "It's none of your business" applies here.

RYAN AND DARREN: "Children are guests in the home," as you know. Remember that you do not own, cannot "have" them. This will require you to believe they love you, even long distance. Think of this year as practice for the empty nest: Could you use their nine-month school year to give birth to yourself?

OUR BODY: Start reclaiming it. Return to your yoga practice. Eat well. Sleep—by all means sleep. Rest will repair the damages. Learn peace.

The entry ended there, and my hand stopped moving as abruptly as it began. I read back over the page, completely spooked by what I'd written. It wasn't my style at all—somehow, "I" had changed to "you" except for one "our." Was this *me*? In my rational mind, I didn't believe in spirits or Martians, or the psychic explanation for the phenomenon of "automatic writing." So was I *crazy*? I felt a pressure behind my ears and swallowed hard to pop them open again. I clapped my hands over my ears, slapping them rapidly, as if a large wasp were buzzing around my head. Seeing no obvious cause prompting this flapping action, my seatmate looked politely away—stepping over to the curb, so to speak, like the passersby making a wide circle around the crazed woman in front of Poppy's Deli.

The plane contacted the runway with a double bounce, leaving my stomach hovering somewhere above New York Harbor as the engine roared with the high squeal of deceleration. It was by far the roughest flight in my three-year commute, and I wasn't quite feeling myself. Although my seat belt was still fastened securely, it felt as though I'd been bumped from my seat.

ix

It was easy to spot Larry in the small group of people assembled to meet the flight—I simply looked for the tallest, most impatient, most fully arched eyebrows in the crowd. His handsome face was always in a state of confusion in airports, radiating his sheer joy in seeing me, but dimming almost immediately as he remembered the good-bye waiting for us at the end of the week. I lurched to the end of the roped corridor outside the jetway and unceremoniously dumped my baggage into a heap. There would be help now. Of all the vows of cleanliness, courtesy, loyalty, and kindness Larry had taken as a Boy Scout, helpfulness was the one he honored most.

"Don't kiss me," I warned as he raised his arms to hug me, "I think I have the kids' flu." He kissed me anyway. Usually a reserved and careful man, he threw caution and propriety to the wind in airport terminals. Three years of helloing and good-bying had done this to him, three years of needing one more kiss, one more embrace to make the lonely weeks ahead more bearable. His arms reached out and drew me in, brushing my nose against his open collar, where a small tuft of soft dark hair curled up familiarly. I inhaled deeply, burying my face in the soft skin under his cotton shirt, warming in the open furnace of his arms.

Oh god, the comfort of those arms. I felt so happy, so *landed* in those arms, I didn't want to move. I closed my eyes and leaned against his shoulder as he planted long kisses across the crown of my head, sending little waves of electricity down my spine and grounding through my heels. ("He must have practiced it on *melons*," the love-struck star in *Pretty in Pink* said to her friend, describing such a kiss.) His warm arms melted every muscle in my body, rocking me back and forth. It seemed like several hours had passed, when I felt him gently shaking my shoulders.

"Did you fall asleep?" he laughed when I opened my eyes.

"I guess so," I smiled, coming back into focus. "I'm feeling a little woozy from the drink I had on the plane." Keeping his hands on my shoulders, he took a step back to examine my condition. Larry's critical judgment was highly developed after a fifteen-year career in journalism, dependably objective on every subject except me. Whenever he looked at me—but especially when he took the first long look after a month of separation—I saw pure approval in his eyes. Whatever my condition, I was here, and here was what he wanted most.

"So," he grinned, lifting a few strands of the long purple fringe, "who won the rodeo?" My wardrobe was frequently the target of his deadpan wit. ("So where are we going today?" he asked one evening in Washington, D.C., lowering his paper as I emerged from the bedroom in a black sweatshirt appliquéd with silver stars. "The Air and Space Museum?") A strictly Brooks Brothers guy himself, he enjoyed the outrageousness in me. I sometimes worried about the vast difference in our styles—should a man so devoted to gathering the facts fall in love with a woman who specialized in dreams?

"You don't understand," he said when I mentioned this worry to him one night. "I *rely* on your passion. You don't understand how lovable you are to me." He liked the emotional surges I brought to his calm, well-ordered life. And I certainly needed the gravity he provided for my orbiting moods.

We parked the car on Sixth Avenue, and I noticed that the old woman with the END IS NEAR poster was not in her usual place. Pencil sales must have been brisk, I thought, and she had packed up and gone home early.

"I wonder where she goes at night," I remarked to Larry, then suddenly had an alarming thought. "Was she wearing her stocking cap today?" I asked.

"I don't know," he said. "I haven't seen her for a few days."

"You *haven't*?" I said, stopping on the sidewalk. "Where is she?" I asked, as if he were supposed to be keeping track of her in my absence.

"She's probably in a shelter somewhere," Larry offered, logically. "We had some pretty brutal nights this month." It was not a day for logical explanations or normal responses, however, and I was unaccountably depressed by the news. Maybe the end she had imagined had come, I thought. But if New York City had been nuked I was sure I'd have heard about it, even in the Midwest.

"Hold on a minute," I said, and stepped into Poppy's. Sometimes, after issuing sufficient warnings and collecting enough quarters, she came into the deli and ordered a sandwich.

"Haven't seen her for a week," the Greek behind the counter said, recognizing my description immediately. "Maybe the police picked her up—she was getting loud, scaring people." She was, in fact, a frightening person. But I felt a sudden twinge of guilt for all the incarcerations my group, the sane, required of hers in the service of this fear. I pulled a twenty-dollar bill from the lavender bag and asked the Greek to make sure she got a couple of sandwiches if she showed up again.

"Make them the way she likes them," I hollered from the doorway, as the amazed man stared at the bill, then at me. "Plenty of mustard."

I had no idea whether the old woman liked mustard or not, I told Larry, picking up my briefcase and portfolio. He neither became involved in nor questioned my small, impulsive investments in the street people of New York. He'd watch me clink quarters into cups as we walked through the city—I thought of it as the tax that the takers of opportunity had to pay to the losers. I knew it was pointless to hurl even a twenty-dollar bill at the gross poverty in this city of overwhelming wealth. But these crazed people, struck dumb by the visions that obsessed them, seemed like my relatives. In my own private theory of reincarnation, I imagined everyone would have to take a turn eventually, as a frightening prophet of unspeakable dreams.

The quarters I dispensed bought me time, I supposed—by keeping the obviously crazy people going, I wouldn't have to compromise myself by standing on a street corner, baring my soul. In the human lottery of sanity or lunacy, I didn't think I had a nice, safe number in the draw. My flimsy grip on reality, in 1984, qualified me for the next round of draftees, or so I thought.

x

We walked down 13th Street and entered the Cambridge, where we sublet a large studio during our housing search in Manhattan. The location was perfect from my psychosomatic viewpoint, since it was only one block away from St. Vincent's Hospital, one of the largest medical centers in New York City.

Larry opened the door of the apartment, quickly depositing my luggage on the floor of the closet he'd cleared, then turned to me, a month's accumulation of lust in his eyes. He kissed me hungrily, the heat of his lips warming mine as our hands moved over each other's cheeks, earlobes, necks.

"Let's go to bed," he moaned softly, biting my earlobe gently.

"In just a minute," I whispered back. "I need some time in the bathroom." He held my face in his hands, looking into my eyes, reading my apprehensions.

"I don't care about the tube," he said quietly, trying to ease my self-consciousness. "I love you."

"I know," I replied. "*I* care about it, though." I always needed extra time, our first night back together, to shed my vulnerability.

Picking up the tote with my copious medical supplies and toiletries, I headed across the living room while Larry went into the kitchen for two wineglasses. I closed the bathroom door and undressed, stepping away from the mirror. Peeling the adhesive tape slowly from my rib cage, I freed the plastic bag containing the saturated gauze bandages around the tube and pitched the soggy mass into the wastebasket without examining it. Sometimes it was clear, sometimes streaked with blood, but no one could tell me what any of it meant.

I stepped into the shower, the soft red rubber tube jutting perpendicular from my ribs like a tiny hose. I held my breath and lathered rapidly, imagining battalions of tiny bacteria foxholed in the blackened cracks between the tiles in the shower stall, waiting to be sucked in. I scrubbed softly over my left side, where the skin was raw from constantly peeling off adhesive tapes. Raised welts tracked across my pale white skin, like a pink streaked trail left in the snow by a wounded army in retreat.

Nothing made me loathe the tube more than preparing to make love with Larry. Naked, it was an ugly, grotesque fifth appendage, sometimes making low moans during the heat of passion, as if another person had entered the room. It made me excruciatingly self-conscious, inhibiting the sexual pleasure I'd come to love with him. I hated the tube, the enemy of my lust.

Dizzy from lack of oxygen, I reached for the shower knob and turned off the water, finally allowing myself to take several long breaths of air. I closed my eyes and held on to the faucets with both hands for several seconds as a sudden coughing fit erupted, racking my chest with a searing pain. Head down and panting after the seizure, I opened my eyes and slowly focused on a small red object floating between my feet. It was the rubber tube, spinning like an inflated raft caught in the whirlpool above the drain.

Holding on to the shower knob for balance, I reached down and scooped it from the water.

I held it in my hand, not sure what to do with the enemy now that it was captured. A hole the width of my index finger gaped open between my ribs, where a ridge of pink scarred tissue encircled the lip of the wound. But there was no blood, no pain, no sound emitting from the empty space. For three months, twenty-four hours a day, I lived with the hateful tube between my ribs, believing my life depended on it. Yet there I stood, conscious and breathing, with the tube in my hand. I understood that there still might be some enemy troops within, that I should resterilize the tube and insert it through the open track, or the trapped infection might cause another eruption. But once I was freed, my heart ached for longer independence. I thought about loving Larry, about one glorious night without this damnable reminder of my deformity. I understood what I was supposed to do, but didn't do it.

Fuck it, I thought, tossing the rubber tube on the back of the sink. I promised myself I'd sterilize and reinsert it tomorrow.

I put on the Juneau nightshirt, with the pink salmon swimming upstream to their spawning beds. Do the beautiful salmon understand that their lovemaking pattern leads to their doom? Are they courageous or ignorant? Questions about the brain capacity of fish dominated my mind as I opened my cosmetics bag. Minutiae always flooded my thoughts in times of mortal stress.

My supply of cosmetics, by 1984, would have impressed the make-over artists at Bloomingdale's. I hadn't practiced this female ritual of face-painting for most of the ten years I lived in Fort Wayne—maternity brought its own natural glow, and becoming a feminist required the cessation of such vain pursuits. The cosmetic paraphernalia had reappeared gradually over the past three years for deeply personal reasons.

"I thought of that old joke . . ." Woody Allen's character remembers toward the end of *Annie Hall*. "This guy goes to a psychiatrist and says, 'Doc, uh, my brother's crazy. He thinks he's a chicken.' " When the doctor asks, "Well, why don't you turn him in?" the man admits, "I would, but I need the eggs."

That, essentially, was how the creams and curling irons came back into my life. In my perilous emotional condition, I was too much of a chicken to face reality without illusions. Using the artistry Miss Phillips had taught me twenty years ago during my modeling days in Chicago, I turned my wan, consumptive face into a palette of color. I brushed my long hair, pulling it up and letting it fall again, imagining Larry running his fingers through it that night. He loved the pure silver streaks highlighting my black hair. ("Is that *natural?*" women would ask, studying the unusual coloration.) I inherited my hair from Manney, my maternal grandmother, an imperious Irish beauty whose silver hair turned heads all her adult life. "It's your most gorgeous genetic flaw," Larry once said.

I emerged from the bathroom into the dim light of the living room. A small gas lamp flickered on the table next to the bed, where Larry sat propped up against the pillows, sipping a glass of wine. I lifted the sheets and snuggled up against his body, resting my head on the soft black hair of his chest. He buried his nose in my hair, smelling the fresh shampoo and humming low sounds of approval.

"You look beautiful to me," he said, stroking my head with his hand, and I wanted to believe him.

I needed the eggs.

xi

When I opened my eyes the next morning, I heard Larry's electric razor buzzing through the open bathroom door, a distinctly male morning sound, at once pleasant and alarming. Do I really want to live with a man again? The question arose, unbidden, and I quickly put it away. I'd answered it a hundred times, yet some unnamed worry continued to haunt me. I loved him—he was responsible, capable, intelligent, witty, a magnificent lover. He was patient and kind to the kids. He had a job. The only doubt I could close in on was a vague concern about his treatment of his mother. It was ungenerous, and I tended to take all attitudes concerning mothers personally. Was this single worry important enough to hold up a marriage?

Larry's childhood coincided with the most difficult years for his mother, who was nursing his father through the last stages of cancer and burdened by continuous financial worries. Duty, more than joy, was the attendant theme to his youth. By age forty-two he had dismantled his huge anger over his lost childhood with impressive intellectual logic, but the emotional hurt lingered. He remembered Christmas morning in 1954, when he opened the two large, gift-wrapped shoe boxes he'd been shaking excitedly for weeks, hearing the muted clang of heavy metal and imagining the engine and caboose of a Lionel train. Instead, he found the practical gift of two pairs of shoe trees. Thirty years later he was still unknotting the tangle such disappointments left on his psyche, trying to teach himself joy as well as duty, to play as well as to work. Happiness didn't come naturally to him; he had to study it.

When I heard this story I thought of my own sons, living with a mother deep in the trenches of a painful divorce who gave them a limited quantity of joy herself. Ryan and Darren found no Lionel trains under their tree that Christmas—in fact, there wasn't even a tree. I was back in the hospital during the holiday season in 1984; I did my shopping by phone from the general-medicine floor of the Catherine McAuley Health Center. If my sons wound up in group therapy in thirty years, there would be no shortage of unhappy childhood stories to tell.

Larry forgave his mother intellectually, but emotionally he practiced the subtle revenge of a hurt adolescent. He dutifully called her every week, but then absented himself from the conversation, answering her queries in monosyllables. She did most of the talking in the void of that nerve-racking silence, first about the weather and her hedges, then veering dangerously into the latest revelations from her TV evangelists. She didn't under-stand what she did to offend him, and he never told her. But she felt it. It made her nervous and edgy, trying to love him around an invisible, unnamed resentment.

It was the saddest mother/son dance I'd ever witnessed—and I'd observed some painfully clumsy maneuvers in my own family. Would my two young sons put me on extinction some day, in some disconnected future when we had nothing in common but the weather? Since every mother committed grievous errors against her children, I had personal reasons for desiring a general amnesty. I needed to see Larry's compassion for his mother, a human extension of me. He reminded me of Camus's passionless hero in *The Stranger*, convicted for a crime he didn't commit because the jury couldn't believe a man who hadn't cried at his mother's funeral. Larry had no tears for his mother's loveless life, and in my overemotional mind that morning in March, I thought it set him up for murder charges. I rolled over to get out of bed, impressed with the amount of energy it required.

"Jesus," I thought, "the flu bugs mean business." With great effort, I rose to my feet, breaking through a magnetic field pulling me into the mattress. The room immediately began to spin. Take it easy, I cautioned my feet, which appeared to be several stories below me. The dizziness reached my stomach, and I thought about heading for the bathroom. Not wanting to vomit while Larry was shaving, I lowered myself back down onto the bed. The cramps in my stomach relayed a clear warning: The Ann Arbor germs had occupied the whole of my intestines, and were threatening to take over my plans for the day.

Why did the flu arrive the very week we were supposed to sign the lease for our future house? Maybe it was a warning against another marriage, even the more liberal, independent, common-law kind we were planning. The week before I married Howe in 1970, I broke out in a bright red rash, inflaming my skin so painfully I stayed in the bathtub for two days. Our family doctor had never seen anything like it before, and could prescribe no relief. If committing matrimony could make me break out in a strange, unidentifiable rash, couldn't living together in sin—as Kay and Jerry would inevitably regard it when I finally mustered the courage to tell them—cause me to come down with the flu? I wasn't sure.

"Getting up?" Larry asked, coming out of the bathroom half dressed. He got into his Madison Avenue pin-stripes at the last possible minute, the distinguished uniform worn by the members of his trade, with the subtle stripes that reminded him he worked on a paper chain gang.

"I can't," I answered briefly. "I've definitely got the flu." Things had heated up sufficiently in my abdomen to prevent further conversation. I closed my eyes, trying to steady the room.

"Too bad," Larry said softly, sympathy and disappointment competing for control of his voice. It was hard enough to miss each other three weeks out of four, without spending the one together sick with the flu. Sympathy eventually edged out.

"Anything I can do?" he asked. I felt his hand stroking my hair.

"Will you call *Ms.* for me, and tell Ellen I won't be in for the editorial meeting this morning? Tell her I'll call her later, to reschedule lunch." He nodded, buttoning his coat and reaching for his attaché case before kissing me good-bye.

"Take care of yourself," he said from across the tundra of the living room. I heard the door close, and I drifted off to sleep.

I have a five-year blackout surrounding the events of the rest of the day, aside from the cardinal fact that I did not take care of myself. There were a few failed attempts. When I awakened in a sweat from a fitful dream, I got up and managed to give myself an insulin shot but didn't test my glucose or make any notation on the chart I kept. Despite several unhappy missions to the bathroom, leaning over the toilet, I was consumed by a ravenous hunger and thirst. In my fuzzy recollection, I remember downing a six-pack of club soda, and eating an entire bowl of peach Jell-O before it had gelled.

Wiping my hot forehead with a cool washcloth late that afternoon, I saw the tube on the back of the sink and remembered the promise to myself the night before. I knew I should sterilize and reinsert it, before the tract into my lungs began to close. Instead, I sat down on the side of the tub and studied it, hypnotically, hearing the melodies it had played over the last three months with its low moan. I remembered the night it whistled during my speech to the Detroit International Association for Personnel Women, and seeing the startled faces in the first row for my unexpected ventriloquist act.

It was so embarrassing, once, when Larry spontaneously hugged me on a crowded Manhattan street, and we both heard the brief flatulent sound from my ribs, like a little sideways fart. The loathsome device had killed my lust and stolen my energy, and three months of despair suddenly descended on me with a crushing self-pity. I lost several hours sitting numbly on the edge of the bathtub, debating the terms of life with the tube.

The trance ended abruptly when I heard the phone ring, sharply—the echo of several rings behind it. I tossed the tube back on the sink, casting my lot with the doomed salmon, swimming upstream to a place from which their relatives never returned. Year after year, those brave, dumb fish opted for the brief but glorious life. I limped to the phone, tiny needles stabbing my legs after the long perch on the edge of the bathtub, and finally picked up the receiver on the ninth or tenth ring.

"How *are* you?" Larry asked, relieved when I answered. "I've been calling all day." He'd used our signal—ringing once, hanging up, then dialing again. The one ring at my end said, "It's me, you can answer." Larry had to use it a lot, since I was frequently dodging editors and, usually during the same periods, creditors. I'd heard his lone ring earlier that afternoon, but couldn't lift my arm to the phone. It weighed a hundred pounds.

"I have to work late tonight," he gloomily informed me. Coming from the dark interior of his sunless office on Madison Avenue, his voice sounded as if he were calling from a small closet, with the arm of someone's raccoon coat draped over the telephone receiver. He wasn't adjusting well to the field of public relations—he missed the straightforward truth of his work as a newsman. His instinct, during briefings with clients, was to nail them to the wall with questions about public accountability. He was eligible for hundreds of newspaper jobs all over the country, but gave up the work he loved for closer proximity to the woman he loved. I always felt vaguely responsible when I heard the regrets in his voice.

It was about 9 P.M. when I heard him come through the door that night. I remember the time because I was watching the clock, fighting sleep. My eyelids were two miniature barbells. Temples throbbing, I strained to keep them up, like a weightlifter bearing a vein-popping load. The minute I closed my eyes, the same dream kept beginning: surrounded by total darkness, all light and color extinguished, I felt myself falling rapidly into a bottomless black pit. A wind roared in my ears, and I could feel the powerful drag against my body. I'd awake with a heart-pounding jolt, teeth chattering, and break out in the cold sweat of a dreamer rescued from a nightmare just in the nick of time.

I felt enormous relief when I heard Larry come in the door and call my name. Help had arrived. I could finally let go of those lids.

"How are you?" he asked softly, his cool hands soothing my hot cheeks.

"I don't think I've ever felt worse," I told him. "I must have sprung a dozen souls from purgatory today," I said, although I knew Larry didn't speak in Catholic. I wondered if the temporal offerings of an ex-believer still counted for anything. That was one of the losses I regretted most when I gave up Catholicism—pain that was once so useful became meaningless. Without the souls in purgatory, the flu was only the flu.

"I almost feel like I should check into the emergency room at St. Vincent's," I said, "but who goes to the emergency room with the flu?" Larry made no response. He sat down on the side of the bed, stroking my hair with sympathy and affection. He said nothing, but his face was wearing the good-bye side of his airport expression. His eyebrows were raised halfway up his forehead, in love and alarm. Squeezing his hand, I lowered my aching lids. The dream I'd been holding back began instantly.

The blackness closed in, and I heard the wind howling in my ears. I shivered as a stomach-dropping fall plummeted me through empty space. Abruptly, I was sucked up into a powerful drag, my heart pounding manically as an invisible force moved me with incredible speed through a long dark tunnel. A hollow thumping noise penetrated the wind, like the percussion of a small child running along a fence with a stick. I imagined I was speeding along an infinite jetway, strapped down with luggage that was banging against the soft ridged walls. A pinpoint of white light appeared at the end of the tunnel, and in my fevered mind I thought that if I could reach that light, there would be no more pain. I willed myself toward it, moving with an incredible force.

The benevolent light suddenly disappeared as the dream capriciously changed direction, and I began dropping rapidly. I swallowed hard against the rising nausea, like a flu victim, plummeting helplessly down a roller-coaster. The drop ended and I was plunged into a freezing body of roiling black water.

I shivered and gasped for air, my teeth chattering violently as I took in mouthfuls of water. Too weak to swim, I tried to grab a piece of the luggage swirling around me—Frank's blue vinyl suitcase floated rapidly past, gone before I could reach it. I caught the red rubber tube, spinning like a tiny raft above a threatening black whirlpool. I held it in my hand, above my head, as the hydraulic force of the whirlpool sucked me down.

Underwater, my eyes tearing with salt water, I struggled to hold my breath as my lungs screamed for air. A sudden, involuntary heave finally threw open my throat, and my chest seared with stinging pain as the black water rushed into my lungs, my head, the hole in my rib cage. I knew I was drowning. Gasping and choking, I felt stabbing pains in my heart. Death was near, and I hoped it would take me quickly.

I expected death to arrive with enormous moment, with immense pain or spectacular joy or, at the very least, the absence of all thought. Instead, death was slow and confusing. After I stopped breathing the stabbing pain ceased, relieving the tremendous pressure on my chest. My lifeless body floated into calmer waters. I seemed to be blind, and paralyzed, and felt the peculiar absence of pulse and air; but I still seemed to be *here*. The enormous moment of my death arrived with a trivial thought: I wondered if I had left the kids enough lunch money. I was amazed to find that without any attachment to a body, I could still think. If I was thinking, I was therefore still being, although there was clearly no life left to be in.

Sometime in the middle of the night on March 23, 1984, the slim tether lines anchoring my mind snapped, and I floated out to the edge of human life. Oblivious to the danger and alarm all around me I slept on, captured by amazing visions and hallucinations—dreams stamped indelibly on my mind, dreams I would not forget.

xii

I heard Larry's electric razor buzzing softly the next morning, like the faint whir of a chain saw several miles away. There was a sharp click followed by the dull squeak of hinges as the bathroom door opened and shut, then silence. Familiar scenes flooded into my dream in the wake of these subtle domestic noises—the soft pad of stockinged feet repeating across the hardwood floor and stopping nearby brought an image of Larry, pausing in the middle of his morning routine to look at me, to make sure I was really here. It happened often during the two years we'd commuted between Ann Arbor and Washington. I would wake up and discover him standing alongside our bed, stuck between buttons on his shirt, undecided about whether to go forward or back, wanting to shed the shirt and crawl back into bed with me. He would stand bedside for long minutes those mornings after my arrival, studying me, resisting the urge to wake me before he left for work.

That morning, I imagined him standing next to the futon in the Manhattan studio, frowning at the beginning of that debate, absently buttoning a tailed dress shirt. The white skin of his long legs paled against his blue tails and black socks. He was in that vulnerable, half-naked stage of attire, before all the armor—the suit, the belt, the eyeglasses, the tie—was in place. One of the happy aspects of living together was the frequent opportunity to bring up pressing questions while he was in that undressed state, in only his underwear and socks. Discussing serious matters with a man in his underwear made the task easier somehow, exposing any buried assumptions that wearing a three-piece suit might invite. I loved talking to him armorless.

As he dressed for work those mornings, I would lie in bed under the covers and watch, like the lucky occupant of a duck blind whose binoculars suddenly focus on a tall, shy merganser, just before it slips into the protective coloration of the reeds. I'd watch with fascination as Larry made the crossover journey from his private to professional life, folding his vulnerable self into the uniformed confidence of a Manhattan public-relations man. The end result was stunning: The passionate fool of a man I loved became distinguished, official, slightly aloof.

"What is this?" I would ask mockingly, fingering his tie. "Are you trying to pass for normal?" He used to grin at any jokes I made about his company-man disguises, but I'd noticed a change three months ago after the transfer to Manhattan came through. As the reality of the pending move dawned on him—particularly the dramatic effect it would have on the sixty-hour acreage of his work week—his usual grin evolved into a rueful grunt of assent. "No kidding," it implied. So I didn't.

Any trace of regret in his voice sent a small wave of guilt through me, since I was the sole reason he'd requested the transfer. I knew living in Manhattan posed enormous adjustments for him, a man who thrived on order, logic, efficiency, who needed peace and quiet to maintain his equilibrium. New York City was hardly the natural habitat for a man who groaned with audible despair whenever long lines at Safeway held up his evening, who opted for the sidewalk on rainy days when the buses were packed with damp commuters. The probability of a private, thoughtful man finding happiness in the city of seven million bananafish was roughly the same as that of a tall, shy merganser falling in love with one of the Flying Wallendas. I couldn't promise he'd fit into the family.

Three months after moving into the pressure cooker of the New York office, his brow wore a continuous, sweated intolerance for the heat. His work method, during the years he wrote editorials for the *Fort Wayne Journal Gazette*, was to lean back in his chair and weigh the issues back and forth, fascinated by an endless series of on-the-other-hands. In his New York public-relations firm, the decision-making quota was a breathtaking sixty per hour, right or wrong, an answer a minute. Even more regrettably, he now worked within direct range of his boss, a relentless practitioner of what Larry called "The Seagull School of Management: fly in, shit all over everybody, and fly out." Each month he received a report card, of sorts, from the firm's financial officer measuring his "billable hours" against those of his peers. Since such a system might tempt an account executive, it was a tough monthly competition for an honest man.

The peculiar circumstances of his departure from the job he loved in journalism gave him the shakes now and then, especially on report-card days. Two years before, the publisher of the newspaper where he'd worked for fifteen years—as reporter, then editorial writer, and for the last ten years as editor-in-chief—came into his office and abruptly, capriciously, fired him. It was the final act of disinheritance in their increasingly troublesome mentor/protégé relationship. Like an angry father unable to articulate his disappointment, the publisher could only provide curt monosyllables in response to Larry's dumbfounded queries about why: "It's for the best," he said.

"I never saw it coming," Larry said over and over during the next two years. *Fired* was a word he'd never imagined on his résumé after fifteen years of uninterrupted success—like the fish that never noticed its environment was wet, he'd never breathed the air of failure. He lost more than his job and income in that unexpected disinheritance. With his title he lost his ballast, his definition in our small Midwestern city. The deference from headwaiters, the clerk at the dry cleaners, the receptionist at the country club—these courtesies that he accepted personally belonged to the environment of "title." He was shocked to find that, stripped of position, he'd become invisible.

At age forty-two, he was pummeled with questions that usually ambush a much younger man, one without quite so much history at stake. Titleless, anonymous, doubting his competence at public relations, he was under siege from a common adolescent refrain: "Who *am* I?" By day, he would put the question on hold and don his company-man disguise. But at night the calm evaporated. He startled me awake the first night we spent together in Manhattan when he suddenly sprang bolt upright on the futon, face blanched, breathing fast.

"What is it?" I whispered, alarmed, scanning the room for burglars or murderers.

"God," he gasped, mopping his brow with the edge of the blanket. "I dreamed I got fired again." He was wearing his parking-lot expression, a wild, dumbfounded look I saw the first time outside my office two years ago, where he'd asked me to meet him the afternoon he was fired. Every muscle in his face was taut, trying to control the tremors around his eyes and mouth. That look of unrelieved anguish appeared often in 1984, whenever he was jolted awake by the omnipresent question: *"Why?"*

That was the query my dream put on the lips of the shirttailed man standing next to the futon, his intense brown eyes still in transition from the parking-lot tremors of the night before. I knew he wanted me to open my eyes, even before I heard him call my name.

"Mary Kay, are you awake? Mary Kay..." he whispered, hesitant to wake me after my exhausting day with the flu. He called softly at first, hoping I'd meet him halfway, awaken with as much desire as he had for me. The tenderness in his voice was joined by an alto of pain, an evocative harmony that sent a rush of passion through me. It worried me that I loved him more deeply once pain had appeared in his life, that I felt closer to him after he was humbled. It felt disloyal, as if I were glad he had suffered. The truth is, I *was* glad. Before pain arrived to temper the unconscious arrogance of his early success, he never had to wrestle with the messier human emotions. I'd never seen him really angry, for example—the highest he'd ever registered on the anger scale was something he called "surprise."

"Maybe I'm a Vulcan," he suggested once, when I commented on the tidiness of his passions. Since I'd become adept in pathos and humility by 1984, his peculiar calm sometimes unnerved me. "I'll be a rock for you to lean on," he said once, hugging me, trying to comfort me after I returned from Frank's funeral. A rock and a sandbag, we were a very odd couple.

I watched the rock disintegrate rapidly after he was fired from his job. "I'm speaking to you from the *floor*," he telephoned one night, shortly after moving to New York. He hated the futon that came with the furnished sublet. "I'm forty-two years old, and I'm sleeping on the floor. Is this progress?" he asked.

"It's for the best," I'd quoted his boss, mocking the flimsy monosyllables he'd offered to fend off the tremors of "Why?" I had to wonder if there was something in my karma or astrological chart or psychological profile that required all men I fell in love with to lose their jobs. Howe left four in the ten years we were married, and even the Vulcan was not immune to my Typhoid Mary influence. In all the years I'd known Larry as editor I'd admired him, but I didn't really love him until that afternoon in the parking lot. Maybe I couldn't love anyone who hadn't wrestled with the invisibility of no identity. Or maybe a rock was just too cold to cuddle up to. Either way, the passion and yearning in his voice that morning made me want to meet him halfway, to open my eyes and touch him, to assure him he could depend on me. But I did not. And I did not swallow when the lump gathering in my throat cut off my air, or cough when I felt the liquid filling my lungs. The messages from my brain brought no response in my body, a limp sandbag heaped on the futon. The drowning sound of my breathing alarmed Larry, enough to tip his indecision about waking me.

"Mary Kay?" he called, full voiced this time. I felt his hand on my shoulder, shaking it gently. He repeated my name several times, adding volume each time and shaking harder. There was a long pause then, as disbelief joined the growing orchestra of his emotions. It zoomed past mere "surprise" and registered somewhere around shock.

"Mary *Kay*?" he asked, the sensuousness vanishing as alarm took over. I heard several sharp intakes of air, as if he'd become suddenly breathless himself, as if he'd just been punched in the stomach. Grasping my hand, he lifted it above the futon then let it drop. He performed this test a second time, verifying that there indeed had been no muscle reaction, no human reflex.

"*Mary Kay!*" he called loudly, like a parent who spots a child extending an arm into the lion's cage. Abruptly, he lifted my eyelids with his thumbs, staring into eyes that made no contact with him. There was another long pause as he leaned over me, and I thought I could hear the percussion of a pounding heart below the fugue of his low voice.

"God," he whispered, sounding like a man who'd been shot. The tenderness and pain and alarm in his voice combined, in aching harmony, to carry his three-note conclusion: "A coma . . ."

1

THE EMERGENCY ROOM

🐾

As Larry's stockinged feet thud softly across the studio's hardwood floors, I hear the eerie, hollow breathing of a frightened man. In my dream I see a fugitive monk in loose, soft sandals fleeing down a darkened monastery hall, his face concealed under a hooded robe. Doors squeak open and small glass vials clink into a nervous palm, then a padded trot takes the shrouded monk to a wall where he taps three times.

". . . I think it's a coma," Larry told the dispatcher who answered 911, his low voice cracking under the weight of his report.

"Diabetes," he said after a pause. "Type one." He described my raspy breathing, insulin dosages, and flu symptoms, until his voice became faint and wavy, like a radio using up the last juice of its batteries. "Yes," he heaved, rallying to a question, then, "No." Another "Yes." Gaining volume briefly, he concluded: "Okay. Please *hurry.*"

The hooded monk in my dream then padded quickly down another hall and sounded an alarm, seemingly to notify the other cloistered inmates of some danger in the monastery, as Larry leaned against the button on the intercom. He held the buzzer down impatiently to rouse the doorman, the imperturbable abbott who taxed the tenants of this New York serfdom heavily. The doorman did not hurry.

"C'mon, *c'mon,*" Larry whispered, panic rising, like a bettor staked to win on a horse failing to show.

"Yes?" the doorman finally drawled, archly, clearly irritated by the rudeness of the summons.

"This is Five-D," Larry spoke curtly. "My friend is in a coma. An ambulance is on the way. If it isn't here in five minutes, come up and help me carry her to St. Vincent's." He didn't wait for a reply, given the recent history between the doorman and 5-D.

I heard soft, frantic footfalls dashing across the room, stopping briefly as a zipper whizzed and belt buckle clasped. A low grunt sounded as a hand slapped against a wall, then the steps resumed in the staccato tap of hard soles clicking across the bare boards.

The monk in my dream sheds his hooded robe and I see Larry, dressing rapidly and moving with purpose. He's wearing the grin he kept on hold for two years, breaking it out the first week we live together in Manhattan, our first chance to practice the happily-ever-after we'd imagined.

He moves speedily that February morning, more anxious than usual for his copy of the Times. *It is carrying my byline that day. The thrill of a byline should have worn off for both of us by then, but we are an untamable pair of mixed-breeds, with part ink in our blood. Any fourteen by twenty-two inch sheet of newsprint still causes our hearts to race.*

"Let's ask the doorman if he'll get a copy for us," Larry says, stopping in the middle of his shave. "There's a newsstand right on the corner," he notes, heading for the intercom.

"I don't think doormen do newspapers," I caution, on guard against any embarrassing exposures of Midwesternness. I am sensitive to such exposures, but Larry thinks it's a small price to pay if a Times *can be had.*

"I don't have a copy in your name," the doorman says, after a long, leisurely check through the stack in the lobby. When Larry explains his copy is down at the corner, on the newsstand, there is a moment of disdainful silence. "Sir," he replies with audible sarcasm, "I don't fetch newspapers." Larry is undaunted by the rebuff—whether it is oblivion or grit, I think his ability to slough off embarrassment is a gift.

"I don't believe it—he won't leave the door for half a minute," Larry says, registering a small degree of surprise. He finishes shaving and gulps his coffee, too excited to slow down.

"C'mon, put on your coat and walk me to the subway—we'll pick up two papers and you can take one home."

"I'm not dressed," I decline. "I'll get it later."

"No, c'mon." He smiles, prodding me. After our eight-year collaboration as editor and writer, he likes it when our ink-filled

hearts pump together. Those moments of being "friends to each others' excitement," the phrase Larry underlined in his copy of The Psychology of Romantic Love, *are particularly valuable during the rocky months of 1984. He is inviting me to an impromptu, come-as-you-are party, and there is just the faintest note of urgency in the invitation. It suggests how much he needs a sign he's made the right move, that his bet to win in this high-stakes New York race has not been foolish.*

"Okay." I smile, catching his excitement. I tie a belt around my nightgown and hike it up to my knees, hiding it under my coat, a trick I learned in college to cope with stray classes scheduled before noon. As we pass through the lobby—a dapper Manhattan businessman and a wild-haired, bare-legged, moccasined native—the doorman studies us. Outside the lobby, Larry laughs and grabs my hand, pulling me toward the newsstand like a mad missionary hauling a laggard convert to the altar. He puts his briefcase down and opens the paper, the thin pages flapping in the strong February wind.

"Here you are!" he says, his face lighting up as he points to my byline. He encloses me in a great bear hug, crushing the paper between us. "That's terrific," he says, kissing the top of my head, "that's just great." I reach up to wrap my arms around his neck, and feel the tie on my dressing gown loosen and drop to the ground. The wind catches it immediately and blows it down the street, past the doorman observing us from under his canopy. Although it would be easy, he makes no effort to catch it.

"He doesn't do belts either," I remark, rolling the unfolded mass of the Times *into a ball. Larry laughs and kisses me good-bye, then disappears into the subway. As I return through the chandeliered lobby of the Cambridge, my nightgown flapping about my ankles and a wadded ball of newsprint tucked under my arm, the doorman makes it clear he doesn't approve of wild-haired natives roaming through his lobby in their moccasins. I try to show by my expression that he doesn't know beans about Midwestern fashion.*

The tenants of 5-D had established themselves as the doorman's major trial this season, so when Larry delivered his urgent request that morning he signed off quickly. He wasn't in the mood for the doorman's probable reply: "Sir, I don't do comas."

After Larry's voice stopped, I was grateful for the silence that closed in. I was completely baffled—was I dead or not? I seemed to be floating between reality and a dream, dead in one but very much alive in the other. I knew I was dead in reality, because I'd tried to open my eyes when Larry first called and discovered I had no contact with my eyelids. It wasn't that the muscles resisted—there were no muscles, no eyelids, nothing at all. My command to "open" was a mere swish in the air.

Further experiments proved I couldn't swallow or move my limbs, clear my throat or clasp my hand. When Larry spoke or touched me, I heard and felt him, but couldn't speak or touch in return. My body was like a broken transmitter, able to receive but not send any messages. If I wasn't dead, I was at least blind and paralyzed, facts that would have been extremely upsetting in any other state of mind. But in the benevolent atmosphere of my dream I felt more curiosity than alarm, if I could claim any feelings at all. The absence of feeling, in fact, was the most remarkable quality of this strange sleep.

Physically, I felt no attachment to my body—not as though I were outside it, because I still sensed sound and touch—but rather like I was slowly shedding it. There was a happy weariness with this detachment, the way I felt unclasping my skis and boots after a long day on the slopes, then standing in line to return the rental equipment. It might have been alarming to discover the equipment was damaged if it were mine, if I had any desire to return to the slopes. But I had the distinct impression my body was borrowed stuff, and felt no regrets that my time was up. The phantom pains in my arms and legs satisfied any lingering desire for more.

Yet having shed my body, I still seemed to *be* here, a kind of dispossessed spirit floating through time. I existed only as thought, although it didn't seem to be exactly *my* thought. This mind I was in worked in a far more detached, intuitive, unconscious way. I knew the meaning of a sound or touch, but didn't pass through any of my usual, fitful, emotional turns on the way to that knowledge. I was thinking without having to rely on the temperamental machinery of my brain. It was completely unlabored thought, thought unbound by feelings.

I could remember my former passions whenever a sound

prompted one, but only remotely, the way rereading a favorite novel years later brings a dim recollection of a first lump raised in the throat. The pleasant detachment of my dream turned my lumps of grief into echoes of passion. When I recognized the pain in Larry's voice, for example, I was surprised to feel only a momentary twinge myself. Pain melted almost instantly under the benevolent light of my dream. My passion for Larry blended into the enormous caring between me and this light. Under its beam, I felt no pain.

Whenever sound or touch blew up a storm of images, blocking my view of the light, I felt myself sinking back into the labored thought of my own mind. Of all the broken equipment in my body, my brain was the most severely ruined. I tried to ignore its noises and jolts, but like an engine that won't stop sputtering after the car's turned off, it kept spewing out fragments of memory. Hooded monks, tender hugs, surly doorman—the director of this movie was clearly insane, jamming nonsequential scenes together and failing to identify speakers. I had no control once a scene began rolling, but again, I watched with peculiar detachment. It was as though I were sitting alone in the back of a huge auditorium for a private, unedited screening of my life. It was strange to watch familiar scenes without feeling the attendant embarrassment or anger or joy they usually inspired. My judgment of the characters themselves was altered by this odd detachment. I felt no urge to root for one outcome over another. It was a stunning shift for someone who'd spent her first thirty-six years as a driven campaigner—instead of trying to change the people who appeared in my dream, my only task was to know them, to understand who we were.

Larry's hurried footsteps approached again, stopping next to the futon. A cool rush of air swept across my naked body as he lifted the blanket. Gently, he grasped my ankle and held my foot aloft for a moment before carefully inserting it into the soft cotton fleece of a pair of sweatpants. The sober tenderness in his touch sent an echo of erotic pleasure through me, like the shiver of arousal I'd felt watching the closing scenes of *The Way We Were*. Most of my friends confessed to the same thrilling shudder, and were just as baffled by it. It was long after the first, fevered bedroom scenes, long after the lovers had revealed their best and worst to each other. The shiver came during their last good-bye, when he looks down and sees her shoe is untied, and bends down to lace it. Though the camera focused on the effect this tender gesture had on her face, every woman in the audience seemed to feel the scene in her feet.

What caused this delicious tremor rippling up from our toes? Was it the feet themselves—the awakening of hundreds of nerve endings reputed to be there? Was it the trace of pain on the lover's handsome face, the humbleness of his bent position? Or was it that he moved, unasked, to meet her needs before she spoke them; that he knew who she was and what she needed so well, he could make love to her through a shoestring? I remembered my goose-bumps the first time I watched that purely human love at work, when Larry gently raised my foot in his hand and prepared to dress me.

He knew me so well, the outfit he chose for my arrival at the hospital was the one I might have selected myself. After he tied my maroon sweatpants around my waist, I felt the soft cotton of my old blue sweatshirt coming down over my head. It was the writing ensemble that dignified my work almost every day that year—a pair of maroon sweatpants and a pale blue sweatshirt bearing the purple slogan: WILD WOMEN DON'T GET THE BLUES. That was the motto Larry chose as my greeting for the doctors in the emergency room.

"God," he whispered, breathing hard as he lifted my limp body to smooth the sweatshirt down my back. "You're just no help at all." He grunted with effort, pulling my dead limbs through something deeper than sleep, beyond even the passive reflexes of a sound-asleep child. With no resistance against the pull of gravity, my head sank like a rock against his damp, pounding chest. The soft tissue of my cheek flattened under the pressure of my bones against his. My head dropped with the heaviness of completely spent passion, as it did when I rested it against Larry's bare chest after making love and imagined sinking clear through him.

A loud, frantic banging on the door stopped him from pulling a sock onto my foot. He released my ankle abruptly, standing and running for the door. The murmuring of solemn men filtered down the hall as Larry returned, leading a small troop behind him. The quiet studio suddenly filled up with noise—beeps and alarms sounded, walkie-talkies buzzed with static, heavy equipment scraped across the floor. I watched as uniformed soldiers moved their artillery into my dream, obliterating my contact with the light. I was captured immediately.

A hard plastic mask was clamped to my face, fastened tightly with straps around my head, a reverse gas mask forcing a burst of hot chemicals *into* my throat. A tremendous pressure thumped against my chest, and I felt my heart begin to throb with sharp pains.

"ER wants a glucose reading," the man pounding me said tersely. "What kind of insulin does she take?" Deep in the background I heard Larry, voice muffled, giving information to the enemy. I pictured him bound and gagged, standing prisoner in a corner of the occupied room. A needle punctured my wrist, then another further up my arm where it was taped in place. The walkie-talkie cracked with friction as a coded message was relayed to headquarters.

"She's over eight hundred," a man reported grimly.

"Jesus," a radio voice responded. "We don't have any time at all."

The studio door banged loudly and another platoon marched in. "The police are here, sir," the doorman announced, apparently intending to notify the entire building. There was a brief pause in which I imagined Larry, still bound and gagged, exercising his remarkable gift for dismissing embarrassment.

"Sorry, sir," a young officer apologized briefly. "It's routine—we have to check out all . . . comas." He halted, his voice dropping into the field of gravity surrounding the futon. "We won't have to do a drug search," he told Larry. "The paramedic told us all we need to know. He's already signed the report." The policeman said good-bye, his bootsteps fading into the din of noises when he suddenly called back, evidently remembering a thought lost in the gravity of the futon: "I hope everything turns out okay," he said. "Good luck." His voice wavered, as if he were shaking his head slowly from side to side. "God . . . good luck," it faded.

"Okay, under her back—let's *go*," the leader directed the paramedic team, synchronizing their movements as they hoisted me from the futon. Touched everywhere, painful sensations awakened all over my body as I sank into the stretcher. I felt the hot chemicals searing the inside of my lungs, the unbearable misery of my heart waking up. My arms and legs ached dully and my throat was parched to a cracked dryness. I knew, inside the ambulance, that I was headed for the hospital. Heart beating recklessly, lungs roaring in pain, my whole being revolted against it. I wanted no part of this life, these needles and tubes, these desperate battles against hunger and thirst. I wanted out of the war, and I prayed for the light to save me.

"Something's wrong, doctor," the paramedic said, breathlessly running along the wheeled stretcher from the ambulance. "The oxygen's not reviving her." The doctor, keeping pace, leaned down and put the cold metal of a stethoscope under my sweatshirt, inching it across my ribs. "She's got a lot of fluid," he said. "We'll have to suction her."

Inside the emergency room, the gas mask was removed and a hard plastic tube jammed down my parched throat. A vacuum machine switched on and a powerful hose sucked the tender tissue inside my lung. Roaring pain crashed up and down my body. My heart squeezed, as if clenched in a tight fist. My head exploded in a burst of blinding light. I surrendered unconditionally, leaving my body in the hands of my captors. Disembodied, detached, I floated into the exile of the fading light.

The vacuum hose was extracted and replaced with the smaller tube of a respirator, the maintenance torture used between suctions. I felt only echoes of pain as my chest heaved up and down with the rhythmic pump of hot air. I was confused: What had been the crime that so enraged my captors? What grievous offense had I committed to inspire their zealous torture?

The sweatshirt and sweatpants were stripped from my body, and I recognized the loose gown of hospital prison garb being tied around my neck. A deep chill crossed my flesh as a dozen hands explored my body. They fingered the scar on my neck from the scalene node biopsy in Chicago; the scarred tissue below my navel from the emergency cesarean in Fort Wayne; the still tender wound on my rib cage from the ruinous surgery in Ann Arbor. In my dream I saw a tattooed lady, mute and still, refusing to explain the garish, purple details of her freakish life.

As the fingers moved methodically, one voice reported the location of each wound in the dull monotone of a coroner performing an autopsy: ". . . a two-inch incision above the right clavicle . . . visible keloid scarring around the abdominal wound

. . . a six-inch lateral incision and suture marks—fairly recent—between the third and fourth ribs . . ."

"Jesus," the voice suddenly halted, as strong emotion broke into his controlled recording. "What's *this*?" the doctor asked, alarmed. "Was she *shot*?"

I heard Larry explain the hole in my ribs—the open-lung biopsy, the empyema, the saline solutions, the red rubber tube. A series of questions was fired at him from different points in the room. He described "necrotizing nodules," "rheumatoid factors," and "sarcoidosis"; he supplied the dates, cities, lengths of internment and names of doctors at various hospitals; he recited the number, ages, and gender of my children. The volley of questions met with the barrage of facts Larry had collected about me over the last eight years.

"Who are you?" he used to wonder about me, especially after he'd come under siege from that question himself. Gathering facts—about my family, my children, my body—was how the journalist fell in love with me. He would ask about my calendar when he called from Washington, keeping in touch with my daily life: "What's on for tomorrow?" he'd inquire each night. I'd answer in detail, down to the last errand of the day.

". . . The post office, the doctor, and, oh yeah, I have to stop at the bank and make a withdrawal," I told him once. "A withdrawal?" he'd joked, aware of my flimsy grip on finances. "Then you'd better remember your gun."

When the questions ceased and the emergency-room team continued in silence, Larry still had a huge stockpile of information left over. Like a doctoral candidate overprepared for his orals, he had more knowledge, more fascinating insights about his subject than the questioners cared to cover. The accumulated data weighed heavily on him—he sounded drugged, overdosed on facts, when he volunteered one more, something to balance the grim picture he'd drawn: "Her hair," he said, weak and distant, discharging two last shots after the barrage, ". . . it's natural."

A pair of rubber gloves snapped off, signaling the end of the examination. The recording voice of the doctor switched from on-air formality to a weary, after-hours intimacy. A nearby observer pressed him for details on the X-rays and lab tests scheduled next. I was surprised to recognize Larry's voice—fluent in enemy code—asking, "When will you transfer her to ICU?" Had he defected, become one of them? Had he been threatened with some unspeakable torture, turning him into a willing collaborator? Who was this spookily rational, peculiarly sentimental man I loved— was he collaborator or spy?

The doctor regretted there was no room in the intensive care unit yet—three AIDS patients couldn't be moved—but a bed had been ordered for me. Larry, assimilated thoroughly into enemy culture, led a series of questions. How long would it take to bring me out of a coma, he began matter-of-factly, and I pictured his reporter's notebook poised for the answer. In any crisis, Larry's first impulse was to collect information.

"It looks like keto-acidosis and Adult Respiratory Distress Syndrome," the doctor said, then provided a vernacular translation. He described a diabetic in deep trouble, drowning in fluids produced by her own immune system. "She's very sick," he sympathized. "It might be awhile."

"Awhile" was too vague to satisfy the reporter, and he pressed for something more concrete, something to hang his lead on. What were my chances of coming out at all, he asked. The doctor was silent a moment, searching for exactly how to put it.

"I've only seen a few patients this bad," he said reflectively, then rallied some confidence. "Let's be optimistic and say fifty-fifty," he offered. I imagined Larry writing it down in his notebook, *50/50.*

After four frantic hours in the emergency room, Larry's usefulness was spent. There was nothing more for him to do until there were some test results, the doctor said, promising to call with any developments. Larry was free to go. He walked over to my bed, where he stood for a long time before his hand touched my head. He stroked my hair, my cheek, then leaned down behind the respirator to kiss my forehead. In my dream I saw myself bending down over Frank's casket, where my lips met the cold marble of his face.

Larry went to work. He stopped at the studio on the way, to pick up my calendar and phone book. At his desk, he listed the numbers of my relatives, some of whom he knew only by rumor. It was the most serious public-relations challenge he'd faced so far, calling these strangers he'd hoped to impress someday. It would be his job to report, without raising alarm: "Mary Kay is in a coma. We're looking at fifty-fifty."

2

THE FAMILY MADMAN

SHORTLY AFTER LARRY LEFT the emergency room, the staff was alerted that another ambulance was speeding down Seventh Avenue toward the hospital. The body count in New York City was heavy the afternoon of March 24, 1984, as immune systems failed on several fronts. While my body was under siege from hyperactive antibodies, the incoming prisoner had collapsed from the total passivity of his. Critical cases arrived with depressing regularity in St. Vincent's emergency room, an overworked MASH unit in Greenwich Village. The staff worked frantically to revive casualties of an oddly modern war, a social revolution in which bodies felled themselves. By caring too much, living too hard, our own immune systems turned against or abandoned us. When admissions to ER approached critical mass that afternoon, the doctor reluctantly ordered the staff to prepare me for transfer to another ward until a bed could be freed in ICU.

A pair of small, gentle hands began to massage the aching muscles in my leg, and I sensed the nurturing presence of a woman. Her strong fingers reminded me of Joan, my Fort Wayne mentor and soul mate. Despite her twenty-year seniority, Joan and I were inseparable friends. Impassioned activists in the local women's movement, we pumped each other's adrenal juices through a decade of meetings, rallies, protests and—whenever energies began to flag among beleaguered troops—we'd plan another rousing "hen convention." She would often stand behind my chair in our office and massage my neck at the end of a hard day, while delivering her grueling agenda for the next. When work and motherhood moved me away from Fort Wayne, I missed Joan. The solitary struggle to apply truths we'd learned together was laborious and lonely without her. I missed her brilliant eyes and

lightning wit, her affectionate hugs and, certainly, the hen conventions. I loved Joan, a mover and shaker who included massages
in the tough demands of friends.

The fingers stopped in one place, pressing the same flesh over
and over, as if locating the source of my pain. A needle sharply
penetrated the spot, and a sudden rush of warm liquid flooded
through me. It melted taut muscles from my feet to my head,
turning the dead weight of my limbs into airy lightness. My legs
felt as though they'd been unscrewed at the knees and were
levitating several feet above me. A strange, delightful sensation
rippled through me, lifting my scalp and drenching my head in
bright lights. The frenzied noises in the emergency room slowed
to deep, garbled monosyllables, the lethargic sounds of a forty-five
record played at slow speed.

Though the respirator continued to force oxygen into my lungs,
I felt only the pleasurable releases of the deep exhalations. The
tremendous relief of these long sighs emptied me of all resistance
and hostility toward my captors. I thought the woman who
brought this airiness, this extraordinary peacefulness, must love
me enormously. I tried to imagine who belonged to those magic
fingers—who was this friend? Was she Joan?

In the white light of my dream I saw no form or shape, but was
enveloped by a strong presence of warmth and compassion.
Happy, light-headed, I rose easily when several pairs of hands
lifted me from the mattress. I continued to rise, effortlessly,
floating through the antigravity chamber of my dream even after
my body was lowered onto a wheeled cot. Suspended in air,
tethered only by the thin plastic tubes taped to my wrists, I felt
like a slow-moving helium balloon loosely anchored to the body
below, as it bounced on the cot speeding rapidly down a corridor.

The quiet voices of orderlies mingled with the sound of glass
clinking against metal—I recognized the familiar chimes of IV
bottles swinging from the branches of tall poles. The IV bells gave
the transport the high ceremony of a church service as the solemn
entourage pushed me, the cot, the poles, and the respirator
through the hospital. There was a slight tug on the needles when
the bed rounded a fast curve and the orderlies tangled the tubes,
like two clumsy bridesmaids colliding during a tricky turn of the
bridal train. Whispering hasty directions, as if in a chapel, they
untangled the lines and hurried on.

The magic fingers held my hand through the journey, then disengaged when the cot halted at our destination. I was lifted onto another bed, where steel bars were raised on both sides and locked into place. The strong fingers went to work as the woman efficiently secured the needles in my arms with more adhesive tape, then tied my wrists to the bars with thick cotton ties. I felt her full breasts pressing down on mine, as she positioned the respirator tube deep in my throat and tightened the strap around my head. None of these actions against my liberty subtracted from my gratitude for her, the woman who brought the bright lights. She patted my shoulder when she finished her required duties; then her footsteps joined the orderlies' and receded down the hall. Her lights remained.

As the room quieted, I sensed I was not alone. The labored breathing of several others—four or five distinguishable patterns—echoed through a large, acoustically barren room. Intermittently, I heard one sigh with resignation while another snored wetly, through heavy phlegm. A second respirator pumped rhythmic echoes from the far end of the room, where a moan rose soulfully between inhalations. I pictured a small group of sickly immigrants, quarantined together on a hospital Ellis Island. I supposed we were all detainees in some kind of holding cell for ICU. Although no one spoke—breathing took all reserves of energy—I felt a peculiar affinity for these strangers. In the merciful light of my dream, forgiveness and compassion bound me together with my inmates, my captors, with everyone engaged in the war.

This power affinity—this feeling of being for everyone, against no one—reminded me of the euphoria Frank had described, two years before, during the height of his last manic passion. His eyes had shone intensely during that spiritual fever, when he told me about the amazing sensation of being absorbed into a mysterious, consuming, brilliant mind, far beyond the intelligence of his own. He had said it was the strongest pleasure he'd ever known. Floating through air in the holding cell at St. Vincent's that afternoon, I thought I understood why he'd committed his life to it.

In the absorbing white light of my dream, there was no pain, no loneliness; none of the pervasive missing that had saturated the last three years. I sensed the presence of everyone I'd loved, living and dead, embedded in that benevolent light. I recognized Gina . . .

Joan ... Howe ... Larry ... my parents ... my sons—with delirious joy, I thought I located Frank. He took the form of the inmate lying next to me, whose low whistle between breaths arrived in my ears like a small, ecstatic, "Oh, wow!"

In my mind, which had turned from solid to liquid, thoughts tumbled pleasantly through a surf of sounds. They rolled past Frank, across the ward, flooding out the door and down the hallway. Far in the distance I heard the light chatter of female voices conversing, coffee-break style, above the low broadcast of a radio. A four o'clock traffic report warned commuters about delays in the Holland and Lincoln tunnels, and I made a mental note to avoid those routes on the way home. A disk jockey sympathized with the stuck commuters in his audience—I certainly counted myself among them—and promised a soothing reverie of oldies but goodies.

The first selection was a risky follow-up to the soothing claim, as the opening strains of Simon and Garfunkel's "Bridge Over Troubled Water" carried me back to a Sunday afternoon fourteen years ago, in my first apartment in Chicago. I'd just come home from an unnerving visit with Frank, and I'd put the song on the turntable to comfort myself. In the spring of 1970, he was interned at the Illinois State Psychiatric Institute—it was his fourth breakdown, the most reckless one so far. I had been thoroughly undone after three solid hours of conversation with a lunatic.

The music wrapped me again in the old gray cardigan I wore often that spring—it was a Christmas present I'd given Jerry several years earlier, then lifted from his closet before I left home. When the lyrics began I was kneeling on the faded maroon and yellow flowers of the couch that came with the furnished apartment, leaning against the back to look out over Oak Street and Lake Michigan. It was always slippery, maintaining my equilibrium while thinking about Frank, but especially through the mind of the emotional, twenty-two-year-old, melodramatic missionary I was in 1970.

I was frustrated that afternoon because despite months of treatment, Frank was still resolutely mad. He was admitted to ISPI after Kay learned about two psychiatrists from the University of Chicago who ran the experimental program. While it was still widely believed among psychiatrists then that bad mothering caused most mental problems, Dr. Herbert Meltzer and Dr.

Ronald Moline were among the pioneers who explored manic-depression as a chemical imbalance. Their early experiments turned up evidence of faulty genetic wiring, suggesting that biology rather than socialization triggered the disease. They'd identified a muscle enzyme that seemed to play a role in manic-depression, and they had been given the ninth floor of ISPI to test their hypothesis. When Kay recognized her son's symptoms in their research—the stunning physical changes Frank underwent during his breakdowns—she called and scheduled an appointment.

To be admitted to the program, Frank had to submit to a muscle biopsy on his left calf. Kay and I, as part of the "control group," had reported to the ninth floor one afternoon to surrender blood and urine samples, ride exercise bikes for five miles, then surrender more samples. It seemed to me that from all the blood and bodily fluids my family contributed, together with the slices of lung and muscle tissue Frank and I donated to science, researchers should have been able to construct another whole Blakely.

"I'm not sure I belong in anyone's control group," I said to Kay somewhere during our third stationary mile. I felt so closely related to Frank, I suspected I bordered on manic-depression myself. Every one of my siblings lived with the fear of insanity. It seemed crazy to me, trying to retrieve him from the seduction of his madness by pedaling hard for five nonlocomotive miles. Maybe we were the lunatics in the family—I mentioned this possibility to Kay.

My mother smiled but didn't encourage a further critique of our going-nowhere ride that afternoon. The psychiatrists at ISPI offered her hope when reserves were running low, and she was determined to see the experiment through. Whenever Kay's pale blue, Irish eyes reflected her ardor for some imagined improvement in her children—whether it was a cleaner room or better grades or another home permanent despite former disasters—none of us was fool enough to try to dissuade her. She was not a woman who gave up easily, and when madness claimed her eldest, most intelligent, most sensitive son, her eyes took on the deepest blue I'd seen so far. Her smile ruefully acknowledged the absurdity of our circumstances but her eyes, those two Celtic oracles of unswerving faith, directed me to pedal harder.

My mother was a lady under all circumstances and had arrived for the physical workout at ISPI in her suit and high heels. When we mounted the exercise bikes she'd traded her high heels for a pair of paper hospital slippers, giving her perch on the seat a decidedly indoor, unathletic quality. If she felt ridiculous, she gave no sign of it. Kay's willingness to bear indignities through the successive seasons of Frank's illness aroused a strong loyalty and love for her, dormant during my long bout of adolescent arrogance. It grieved me to see her vulnerability exploited during the group therapy sessions we were required to attend on Thursday nights.

Each week Kay, Jerry, Paul, and I joined the other families with members impounded on ISPI's ninth floor for a rigorous interrogation of our pasts. My parents exempted Kevin and Gina, the two youngest siblings, in an effort to spare them a direct confrontation with the terrifying look of mental illness. They were immersed in the crisis anyway, overhearing hushed conversations around the kitchen table and witnessing Frank's bizarre behavior for themselves whenever he escaped and dropped by for a surprise visit. He always stopped home during his escapes, and included aunts, uncles, cousins, and nephews in the late-night calls he made from the hospital. Frank introduced all the members of our large extended family to how "Blakely" looked and sounded, out of control. By 1970, the madness in our family was no secret.

I hated the Thursday night sessions, when the patients and their families were collectively grilled under the harsh fluorescent lights of the locked ward. Maybe somewhere in the pasts of these humbled people there were cases of bad mothering or absent fathering or emotional neglect—what family surviving the fifties was exempt?—but I couldn't believe these human errors brought the physical changes in Frank. I knew an unhappy childhood was not the problem. If anything, my parents' unstoppable affection had postponed Frank's crisis. He didn't have his first breakdown under Kay and Jerry's roof—it happened 240 miles away, at Southern Illinois University.

Since the doctors were committed to a theory involving enzymes and brain cells, they couldn't have been counting heavily on answers from psychoanalysis. But because a cure was still unavailable through medicine, the ISPI program included weekly doses of psychotherapy. Whether obligation or tradition or just plain helplessness prompted this futile treatment, the sessions were unproductive if not outright harmful. One week, Jerry was questioned about his habit of shaking hands with his adult sons, replacing the childhood hugs. The therapist on duty that night suggested our father's formal handshakes had deprived Frank of his affectionate due. This was ridiculous, Paul and I knew.

While my father tried to practice the emotional reserve required of his generation of men, the disguise never completely covered him. I remembered a Saturday morning in June when Jerry paced back and forth across the living-room carpet in his tuxedo, anxiously rehearsing his immediate duties concerning the bride. The task of giving me away clashed with twenty-two years of loving me, and he was unable to form a single word when I emerged in my wedding dress. Instead, his eyes filled up and his face became bright red, then his smile finally appeared like a period at the end of a long, emotional speech.

I'd seen that expression repeatedly at baptisms and confirmations, basketball games and high-school plays. It was embarrassing to sit next to Jerry when one of his children was on stage because invariably, unable to hold out for the cover of final applause, he would pull out his handkerchief and alert the audience to his severely clogged-up condition. There were plenty of crosses the children of this complicated, emotional man had to bear during the John Wayne–worshiping fifties, but being insufficiently loved was never one of them. Yet in the spring of 1970, a therapist unfamiliar with this history sent Jerry home in despair. He spent the following months doubting himself, believing a dozen more hugs might have saved his son from madness.

Few participants emerged from those evenings without confessing to some charge, but the heaviest guilt was generally accepted by the mothers. During a luckless search for signs of "overmothering" or "dominance" or "aggression" in Kay one evening, the therapist appeared ready to move on to more promising candidates when he raised a question about "rejection." My mother remembered a night in 1948, when the patient was three, which still caused her some regrets.

A pediatrician had applied bindings around Frank's head during a visit that afternoon, to flatten the ears a bit. His tiny ears stuck out at what my mother thought was an adorable angle, but the doctor soon convinced her they wouldn't be so adorable when he was a young man. He suggested they would mar his attractiveness, possibly threaten his sex life. As the bindings were applied I imagine the pediatrician caught my mother wincing. That wince appeared hundreds of times as her five offspring somersaulted through childhood—when I got my hand caught in the wringer of the washing machine or one of my brothers had his head stitched in the emergency room. She usually followed the wince with a pat of sympathy, a gesture of comfort. The doctor, an authoritative man, disapproved of her soft-touch approach. He warned her of the dangers of coddling, especially coddling boy babies. There were plenty of stories back then, about young men whose lives were wrecked by homosexuality because their mothers overkissed them. Between his ears and his mother, the pediatrician believed my brother had a very narrow chance of leading a normal life.

Kay remembered being awake that whole night, listening to cries from the baby's room and wrestling with her urge to scoop him up and comfort him. It took tremendous discipline, but she accepted the punishment of the pediatrician's advice and resisted. She could still hear those cries, she told the therapist at ISPI twenty-one years later. She winced.

Perhaps that's when my brother may have felt rejected, she volunteered. How could he have known her longing to pick him up, to comfort him? How could he have known she was struggling to follow orders? Perceiving the fresh scent of guilt, the therapist probed deeper: Maybe she really did think he was homely—maybe she really was unconsciously rejecting him. My mother considered this suggestion for a moment. She looked across the room at my brother, then shook her head slowly. No, she said simply, without further explanation. Even ravaged by illness, even with something untamable coursing through him, Frank was clearly, electrically, a beautiful young man. My mother thought anybody could see that.

I made numerous solo visits to ISPI that spring, to supplement the futile investigations and confessions of nonsins that dominated the Thursday night sessions. Frank was in restraints when I arrived one Sunday morning—the result of his protest over taking medications. He loathed the drugs that made him drool on himself and garble his speech. His glazed eyes reported complete defeat on the medication front. While the nurse unlocked the bed restraints, I asked her for a two-hour leave from the ward.

THE FAMILY MADMAN

Talking to Frank on the psychiatric wards always made me anxious. When I noticed the staff unashamedly eavesdropping I became paranoid, fearing detainment for complicity in his madness when it was time to go. It wasn't easy to keep track of exactly who was insane once he began his rhapsodic soliloquies—even trained specialists, science-minded psychiatrists and nurses, would be sidetracked during intake exams, suspending their disbelief and following the wild, fascinating launches of his mind. During his third breakdown two public defenders, otherwise rational men with an undiluted reverence for logic and order, were moved to declare to a judge that Frank was not crazy but a genius. Anyone who had close contact with him risked catching a strain of his spiritual fever, but his relatives were particularly vulnerable.

I wanted to leave the ward, to have a cup of coffee with Frank without having our words scrutinized. I asked the nurse for a pass to the canteen on the first floor. She looked at me incredulously, as if I'd just volunteered to take a troop of high-strung Boy Scouts into the china exhibit of the Chicago Art Institute.

"You think you can *handle* him?" she asked doubtfully, observing my meager bulk. I looked at Frank, woozy with tranquilizers, his thin body all but invisible under the wrinkled mass of his oversize pajamas. What kind of protest had he staged that morning that made him seem dangerous? In his present condition, with roughly twenty-five percent of his mind left, the restraints on his wrists and ankles seemed completely superfluous.

"What's to handle?" I'd shrugged, choosing sarcasm over despair. Unshackled, Frank stood up shakily and performed a low bow, thanking me for his freedom.

"And to what do I owe a visit from such an important lady as yourself?" He smiled, assuming Jerry's voice and Irish way of saying. I smiled back and shook my head at his mimicry, helping him into a robe as he continued quoting our father. Sometimes he was Jerry, sometimes Henry David Thoreau, sometimes Michael Corleone—a conversation with Frank in 1970 meant taking on a whole group of people. That Sunday morning, he was Jesus Christ himself. He thought God was revealing miracles through him, spreading love around. He was infused with overwhelming power and a sense of absolute knowing. Even overdrugged with Thorazine, he could outwalk and outquote me. His Excelsior look was hard to argue with.

Over coffee, he described the great euphoria he'd felt the night before he was hospitalized. Around midnight, he went to Chicago's Rush Street district and stood on the curb in front of a club called Mother's. He began handing out fifty-dollar bills to anyone who'd take one. Under the influence of what he called "the beat, the beat, the beat," he distributed his entire savings of $2,800 to fifty-six strangers. A crowd gathered, as Frank had anticipated. The police were summoned by the bouncer at Mother's and arrested him for "creating a nuisance." It was his seond internment in jail.

The first time he was put behind bars, the year before, he'd turned himself in. Flying high despite the prescribed lithium he took daily to bring him down, he walked into the main police station on South State Street and reported to the desk sergeant that he was carrying an unregistered lethal weapon. Even if the desk sergeant was not a subtle man, he must have noticed the pure glee rising up in Frank's wild eyes. He had to know some lunatic joke was right around the bend.

"Okay, buddy, let's see what you've got," the harassed man said. The very words Frank wanted to hear, he broke into hysterical laughter.

"Okay, let's cut the funny business," the officer commanded him. "What have you got?" he repeated impatiently.

"That's it!" Frank replied, briefly containing his mirth. "My laughter! That's my lethal weapon! Look what the Chicago Eight are doing to law and order with their laughter!" He was referring to the mockery Abbie Hoffman and Jerry Rubin were then making of the Chicago courts, collecting contempt charges as if they were high-school demerits. Frank blasted the desk sergeant with a prolonged demonstration of his lethal weapon, laughing uncontrollably. The officer was provocatively unamused by political jokes of this sort. He eyed Frank grimly, then dialed security. Frank was jailed overnight for "creating a nuisance."

Though his chemistry was in an electrically charged state when he committed his caper in front of Mother's, the night in jail brought a downhill slide. Weighing maybe 130 pounds if he kept his heavy walking shoes on, Frank was a reedy, delicate man. Infused with the power of God, smiling crazily, he kept repeating "I love you" to the officer who handcuffed him. While the Chicago

police had a wide reputation for violence against political dissi-
dents, vividly documented on national TV during the infamous
'68 Democratic convention, they never laid a hand on Frank. They
didn't have to. The arresting officer locked this fragile sick man in
with two mean street fighters, both arrested for "queer bashing."

When Jesus Christ appeared in their cell with his message of
love, he was mistaken for a faggot. Two thousand years haven't
changed the way fearful men respond to revolutionary ideas—
badly beaten, eyes blackened, Frank's body was delivered to the
city hospital's psychiatric ward the next day. He couldn't walk—
his surest means of coping with his perpetual internal beat—for
several days.

"Do you love me?" he asked, grinning over his coffee cup on
that maroon-and-yellow-flower day. Since he was Jesus Christ, he
already knew the answer. He just liked hearing me say it out loud.

"I already told you twenty times," I said. " 'Yes, I *love* you.'
Jesus Christ, Frank, you've got to come *down*. If you want to get
out of this madhouse, you've got to come back to reality," I
begged. He laughed.

"I'll only go as a tourist." He grinned slyly, borrowing a line
from *A Thousand Clowns*. It was a line I used often myself—he
knew I'd recognize his application. Whenever Frank debated
siblings, he had an uncanny knack for unbalancing opponents by
using their favorite words to his advantage. He quoted J. D.
Salinger and Virginia Woolf to me, Victor Frankl and Krishna
Prem to Paul, A. A. Milne and Lewis Carroll to Gina. It was
infuriating, his habit of breaking and entering our minds, ransack-
ing our stuff. It wasn't personal—he did it to anyone who engaged
him. On the high-school debate team, he drained opponents with
his ability to recite, spontaneously, whole passages of H. G. Wells
or Thomas Carlyle or St. Paul to the Ephesians. He seemed to
remember everything he'd ever read. During breakdowns it came
to the fore at once, in disorganized exuberance.

Frank's memory was his greatest asset, his ultimate curse. One
of his hobbies, as a teenager, was to memorize the routes of all the
CTA buses in Chicago. On Saturdays, he'd ride from our house in
the northwest corner all the way to the southeast side and back on
a single transfer, without once checking a map. This love for city
travel led him to apply for a chauffeur's license, working the

summers while he was in college as a bus driver. The license was revoked during an early manic bout, when Frank impulsively changed a route. His supervisor, a sympathetic man who hated firing him, had no choice about taking Frank off the road. He had to suppose passengers on their way to McCormick Place might end up at the Lincoln Park Zoo. During his Excelsior periods, Frank believed he knew exactly what people needed: laughter, fifty dollars, zoos. His supervisor finally had to take away his bus.

During the calm periods between storms of passion he would return, spent and exhausted, to the quiet life he lived in Kay and Jerry's finished basement. We had long talks in that familiar place where years of sibling heart-to-hearters were absorbed into the walls. He would recall the whole rationale behind his madness, reproducing the exact dialogue within his head that made giving money away to strangers seem reasonable and necessary. Using two minds—the calm, recollecting rational one, and the speeding, exuberant insane one—he could map the route back through his strange behavior.

It was not memory Frank lost during madness—it was inhibition. During meltdowns, when the intellectual and emotional halves of his brain blended together, he freely crossed the boundaries between idea and action. He was willing to risk embarrassment and censure, even black eyes, to act out his compelling dreams. That courage, I thought, was the main difference between us. I also felt surges of passionate conviction, but stalled when it was time to act them out. Instead of mental illness, my nervous system responded to the pummeling of my brain with more socially acceptable physical collapses. The results were essentially the same. We both ended up confined in hospitals, though different wards, with baffling symptoms of the Blakely disease.

Despite his resistance Frank would, eventually, come down. Way down. But that Sunday morning he wanted to stay with the power. He had "the beat, the beat, the beat," he said, patting his small, fine hand over the unbuttoned front of his pajamas. He was ecstatic. It was hard not to feel happy for him, even while recognizing he was certifiably, damagingly sick. I went back to my apartment on Oak Street confused, upset, not knowing whether to hope for an enzyme or a miracle.

I donned Jerry's sweater and put Simon and Garfunkel on the

turntable to comfort myself, and instead they conspired against me. "Like a bridge over troubled water," they chanted repeatedly, "I will lay me down." The melancholy lyrics promising that one life can serve as a bridge for another—that the turbulent waters of Frank's troubled mind could be calmed by the steady resolution of mine—exactly suited my youthful, missionary zeal. The combined effects of the wistful music, the faded flowers on the couch cushion, the oblivious Sunday pedestrians strolling down Oak Street, and the image of Frank, smiling fiercely and crazily, set off such an enormous yearning, the whole of my throat was filled with a boulderlike lump. I could neither breathe nor swallow for many more minutes than even a youth well acquainted with melodrama can handle.

Once a throat has experienced such a seizure, it knows the pattern, and certain lyrics or yellow flowers or manic faces can trigger it again. It happened every time I heard the song over the next fourteen years, but especially since Frank's suicide two years before. I would quickly change the station—even I knew that a reasonable day could not be had by kneeling on a couch cushion, repeating "For chrissakes, I *love* you" to an unhearing madman. But I had no access to the knob that afternoon in St. Vincent's, tied down and blinded in the holding cell for ICU.

I expected the melody to initiate a seizure when the lyrics filtered down the hall and into the white light of my dream. But no boulders formed in my throat. Remarkably, I didn't miss Frank. In the liquid state of my brain, I thought all I had to do was roll over and wash into the mind next to mine. We would be one.

3

TWO SONS

THE ONLY INFORMATION THE emergency-room nurse could confirm when Larry called was that I was no longer there. He called the intensive care unit next, assuming I'd been transferred there, but the ward clerk on duty had no record of my admission. Worries accumulating, Larry left his office early and headed down Seventh Avenue to investigate my situation himself.

Sprinting from the subway exit across the street from St. Vincent's, he almost collided with the preoccupied man hurrying through the hospital's entrance. Wearing a sport coat with an open collar and several gold chains around his neck, seemingly en route to a happy hour somewhere in the Village, the man looked incongruously sober as he held a beeper to his ear and listened intently. Inside the emergency room a loudspeaker was announcing "Code ninety-nine." The man in the sport coat joined the small contingent in pale green uniforms heading down the hall.

It took long minutes before the harried ER supervisor could free herself to answer Larry's questions. Locating my transfer papers, the nurse looked up solemnly and announced the same wing given for the code blue. Visitors would have to wait until the cardiac team cleared out, she said—one of the patients in the ward was having a heart attack.

"Which *one?*" Larry asked, panic rising. She promised to find out and directed him to wait in the lobby. His questions mounting with alarming velocity, Larry was not a man who waited patiently for his invitation to a heart attack. He took off without a pass through the labyrinth of halls.

The clean, modern décor of the reception area changed dramatically as he entered an old, unrenovated section of the hospital.

Dark corridors led past large, depressing wards, sepia-tone images from the nineteenth century when the indigent and the contagious were crowded infectiously together. Larry pushed through the double doors of my room and halted, his breath seized by the grim atmosphere of the ward.

His stomach looped as he scanned the skeletal bodies of my roommates, their six beds parallel parked along a yellowing wall in a cavernous room. Whatever, however the decision had been made to put me in this depressing place, Larry determined to spring me—maybe to Mount Sinai, where Dr. Alvin Teirstein, one of the most respected pulmonary specialists in the city, had promised to review my X-rays again that week. Repulsed by the foul smell of my cellmates, Larry didn't feel my deep affinity for them. He was unaware that I could only be moved, now, as a group.

Surrounded by pale green uniforms, the man in the sport coat leaned over a bed at the far end of the room, listening earnestly through a stethoscope. Larry's held breath erupted in a sudden gasp as he recognized my body and sprinted toward it. High terror brought an unplanned volume to his introductory question: "What's *happened* to her?" he yelled. The stethoscope veered wildly from its methodical path and left my chest as the surprised man stood up, face-to-face with Larry's next demand: "Who are you?"

"Who are *you*?" the doctor asked, wondering how this unauthorized, emotionally unkempt man had gotten into the closed ward.

"I'm her friend," Larry said, quieting down, his voice inflicted with momentary hesitation. He mumbled his fuzzy identity, aware that *friend* didn't carry the concrete recognition of *husband*. The loaded assumptions buried beneath *husband* and *wife*, in fact, were precisely why we were both reluctant to marry again—put two people in the presence of those roles and they can't help themselves, they start acting them out. *Friend* was a resonant, powerful term of allegiance to me, but a nearly weightless word as Larry recited it to the man leading the cardiac team.

"I'm the one who brought her here—I'm responsible for her," Larry stumbled, searching for solid footing to maintain his place on the ward. Gaining only marginal ground, he abruptly switched tactics and assumed the authority of his emergency-room persona:

"What's happened to her?" he began, leading the questions with controlled volume.

"We don't know yet," the cardiologist conceded, admitting Larry to his confidence. "Her blood pressure dropped suddenly— we're not sure why. We've taken her off the morphine." He described the precarious, no-pulse moment half an hour ago, before Adrenalin shots brought me slowly back. A battery of tests had been ordered to determine whether I'd had a heart attack or drug reaction. The doctor was concerned about the fluid in my lungs—as soon as my condition stabilized, he said, I'd have to be suctioned again. I was being moved to ICU, ready or not.

Phrases of the doctor's plan filtered into my dream as the bright lights began to dim. When the woman with the magic fingers had returned to my cell awhile ago, she'd patted my arm affectionately before lifting my wrist and pressing her fingers gently against it. Suddenly, without any provocation from me, she dropped it and whispered, "Oh my *god!*" I must be in some strange, Christian prison, I'd thought. The guards prayed continuously and uttered small ejaculations during rounds.

When she first appeared I'd sensed the woman had come to bring up more lights. But I'd somehow offended her and she summoned the troops instead. She pounded the wall over my head and when it spoke to her she hollered back: "Code ninety-nine! Code ninety-nine!" Footsteps began thudding down the hall outside almost immediately. The woman, still upset with me, massaged my chest much too vigorously with a rolfing technique. A man's voice then entered the cell, calling terse orders to the troops accompanying him. Stabbed repeatedly with needles, my limbs hardened and gained weight, dragging the helium balloon of my mind to the ground. I sank from light airiness to the dark awareness of danger. My heart raced frantically as a surge of adrenaline shot through my head, cracking a narrow slit in my eyelids. Behind the bars of black eyelashes, I caught a split-second glimpse of the enemy.

They were *green!* Five or six bald green heads with soft, loose-skinned, pale green bodies! They *terrified* me.

My eyes slammed shut. The green creatures pummeled my chest without mercy, and the peacefulness of my dream vanished under the painful beat of my heart. An old anguish gripped my chest as I heard the plan to separate me from my cellmates, from Frank and Joan and Kay and Jerry, from the wonderful company of my sons. I tried to open my eyes, to plot my escape, but neither my body nor mind would follow my will. As the transport began moving me through the ward, I heard the moan of a fellow prisoner. The moan grew louder, ending in a wail, full of surrender and defeat. I imagined the suction machine taking its first victim. What had been his crime—what was mine? I searched madly for the reason.

I listened for clues from the green creatures. One of them, Dr. Kalman Watsky, introduced himself to Larry as the intern in ICU and asked about the puzzling notations in my chart. Jogging alongside the wheeled cot, Larry answered in clipped, breathy phrases as "sarcoidosis" and "necrotizing nodules" and other scientific labels dropped into the conversation. Flipping through the thick tome my chart had become, Dr. Watsky finally came to the births of my children.

"Did the diabetes appear during her pregnancies?" he asked. "Were either of the births unusually large?"

"No," Larry replied. "The second was premature—under five pounds."

"Are they healthy now? Are there any problems?" the intern asked. I thought of the therapist at ISPI searching for problems in Kay, relentlessly grilling her for confessions of overmothering and rejection.

"No," Larry lied for me. "No problems."

In truth, I'd discussed hundreds of problems concerning the kids with him, the innumerable worries that sprang from a folder on my desk called "The Children of Divorce." Burgeoning with underlined news clips and articles, the file contained dozens of headlines declaring a cacophony of expert opinions: TIME DOESN'T HEAL WOUNDS OF DIVORCE, CHILDREN FORGIVE ABSENT FATHERS, MALE READING SCORES DROP WITH DIVORCE, JOINT CUSTODY MORE STRESSFUL THAN SINGLE PARENT FAMILIES, CHILDREN OF DIVORCE RATE BETTER IN ACHIEVEMENT TESTS. I'd become an encyclopedia of facts on divorce, a tedious compendium of statistics and studies. I discussed each piece of this confounding puzzle with Larry, depending on his clear rationality.

Whenever I surveyed the wreckage of my life in 1984—the failed marriage, the financial strains, the frantic takeoffs and landings—I couldn't imagine my sons emerging from the toxic fumes with their health and humor intact. I'd called the Ann Arbor Center for the Family and become the client of Mary Whiteside, Ph.D., who shepherded me and my wounded kin through our first postnuclear years. After the diagnostic interview Dr. Whiteside, recognizing a crisis case, recommended twice-weekly sessions until some of the emergencies abated. Three years after the separation and divorce, the appropriate answer to Dr. Watsky's question was "Yes. Oh my god, yes. Plenty of problems."

While my youngest son's reading scores had gone up, the eldest's had gone down; though time had indeed relieved the children's fears about losing a parent, the specter of "stepfather" raised even more; as one study in my file predicted, the boys were compassionate and forgiving toward their father—but as another forecast, they were oblivious to the needs of "the strong parent, the one who appeared to be coping well." My charade of competence gave the kids the impression they could depend completely on me. They did, and I collapsed.

I had to suppose the crime sending me to the suction machine at St. Vincent's was this: failure to support my children. In the dissolution agreement, I'd accepted financial responsibility for the kids while Howe was in graduate school. Three years into single motherhood, with at least two more ahead, I knew I couldn't honor my word.

Continuing poverty reproached me in the grocery store, when insurance premiums were due, when a coach called to announce another soccer or baseball fee. Prompted by daily reminders, I had to confront the truth that we were poor by choice. A more stable life was available if I would turn myself in, if I would, as my parents and friends encouraged, stop writing and apply for a real job in a school or a bank. Such a surrender would bring regular paychecks and benefit packages instead of the wildly fluctuating, high-wire life we were leading. My poor health produced poor work, killing half of my essays in 1984 and providing only twenty percent of the payments. A sober review of my checkbook the morning before I left for New York proved I was failing miserably on the financial front.

Pursuing my own passion over the children's obvious needs, I pleaded guilty to the charges Dr. Watsky brought against me in the intensive care unit. Not only was I to be suctioned for the crime of nonsupport, but also separated from my children. What else could he have meant when he promised to take my morphine away? He had to mean the children. My dependence was so strong, I felt the withdrawal pains almost immediately.

As the green creatures lifted me from the cot and strapped me down in another bed, I wondered how much time I'd have to serve in lonely isolation. A whole year? That was the sentence Howe had proposed during our long talk at the kitchen table the other night. Though the dissolution agreement gave me the right to move the kids to New York after satisfying my two-year commitment in Ann Arbor, Howe had clutched as the actual date in June loomed closer. That night, he'd presented compelling reasons for keeping the kids in Ann Arbor one more year: it would stabilize their fluctuating reading scores, give them a year of visits before moving in with their future stepfather, and provide the chance for him to resume his financial responsibilities. He was asking for an equal partnership.

We discussed his plan late into the night, through five or six cups of coffee, and I couldn't get to sleep after he left. His proposal made sense—it met more of the "best interests of the children" than mine. I had to take it seriously. Yet how could I bear living nearly seven hundred miles away from the kids for a whole year? How could I assume the deprivation was any easier for Howe? How did postnuclear families regenerate happiness after the devastating split?

Maybe it was the coffee, maybe the kids' flu, maybe Howe's proposal, but I was slightly nauseated when the alarm went off the next morning and notified me it was time to get moving again. I hadn't slept at all. I rose rockily to my feet and headed down the hall to wake up the kids.

Although the boys each had their own rooms in Ann Arbor, they generally slept together. They'd been close roommates the whole time we'd lived in Fort Wayne, and were at first delighted with their new privacy and independence. Indeed, their decorating and neatness patterns reflected two divergent personalities, but after only three nights the thrill wore thin. With all the other changes they had to negotiate for the last three years, separating from each other proved one too many. My younger son invited his older brother to stay overnight, and they rarely slept alone thereafter. Even when they entertained other guests, they moved all the mattresses and sleeping bags into the same room. During a midnight check one weekend I counted six sleeping forms camped out on the floor and remembered my own youth, when kids huddled together under their desks as sirens wailed outside. Kids stick together, through air raid drills and divorce.

I walked into their room that morning with the unsteady, apprehensive step of an acrobat who'd just gotten word the nets were coming down.

Good god, they are gorgeous creatures when they sleep. Darren's long, seemingly boneless foot extends a few inches beyond the end of the top bunk, his bare toes brushing my hair as I walk by. Ryan's voluminous hair spreads across the sheets on the bottom bunk, his open mouth half buried in the pillow. The sunlight slanting through the blinds melts the lines between skin and blanket and, touching me, releases some inner valve inside. A warm liquid floods into my chest, and I long to crawl into their beds. I love their sleeping bodies.

Instead, I step to the window to let in the light. For ten years, ever since motherhood began, this has been my favorite chore of the day. This morning I take my sweet time, aware that their next ten sunrises will pass without me. Every gradation of light paints a different picture and I stop, now and then, for a longer look. More than any part of my formal education, raising children gives me the most useful information about what it means to be human. I never rush the contractions at the beginning of these motherhood days.

"Okay, bugs," I call softly from the window, attempting to rouse them . . . but not really. I like to watch them stretch and groan, pull their covers over their heads. When Darren finally emerges and sits upright in the middle of the top bunk, he has an Oliver Hardy look about him, a dazed suggestion that some divine black comedy is in the offing.

"What time is it, Mom?" Ryan asks with irritation, suspecting I've surreptitiously abbreviated his night somehow. For ten years, morning has come as a terrible shock to him.

*"It's seven forty-five," I report. "It's hut-hope-hoop-hoop time,"
I add, leaning into the bottom bunk and ruffing his abundant
hair with my fingers.*

I remembered the first time I saw that proud cowlick on the
crown of his head, at 4:30 A.M., when the nurse held up a mirror
between the stirrups and said, "See! Can you *see* it? The head's
crowning!" I saw, it came. I was conquered. From the infant's
down to the toddler's flax, I'd cut that head of hair a hundred
times. I'd combed lice eggs out of it during an epidemic in first
grade, reeling from the scent of vinegar; I'd buried my nose in its
after-bath aromas, kissing it goodnight a thousand times. If I were
King Tut listing the valuables to take into my tomb, untroubled
by cost or consequences, I'd ask for two heads of children's hair.

*"There's a lot to do today, buddy," I announce. "Let's shake a
leg." Ryan lifts his small, muscular leg and gives it a little shake.
It says: Give me a break, Mom.*

These boys never jumped to attention—respect for authority
was nowhere in their genes. But so far, they had followed my
leads. "The boys seem *fine*," Joan had reassured me, over and over,
when I brought up the worries in my Children of Divorce file.
Joan's judgment weighed heavily with me, since she specialized in
adolescents run amok. She was dean of students at Bishop Luers
High School when I met her in 1973, and though it was her
unhappy duty to expel or suspend delinquent students she was the
most loved teacher in the school.

"Adolescence is children's menopause," as author Kurt Vonnegut once wrote. Joan understood teenagers, their hot flashes of
temper alternating with slow infusions of confidence, as life
proceeded in its natural, chaotic way. I was her successor when
she resigned as dean to run for public office.

"Do you have any final advice for me?" I asked as we slouched
in our chairs in the dean's office late one June afternoon, sipping
cups of Boone's Farm apple wine confiscated earlier in the day
from a band of almost liberated seniors. She thought a moment as
she surveyed her office. It contained an impressive collection of
home-made slingshots, peashooters, and water pistols, a well-used

library of books and pamphlets from health and counseling services, and a confusion of furniture splitting the room's personality between official business and tender mercy. Her eyes finally settled on the overstuffed sofa across from her desk, where she sat with her elbows planted on either side of her plastic cup. Resting her chin heavily in her palms, an uncharacteristic melancholy crossed her face as she looked around the place where she'd soothed innumerable hysterics, detained a gang of Crazy Glue vandals, revealed essential sexual facts.

"Keep the fan on," she said finally, "or this place will smell like teenagers in no time."

I did keep the fan on, and I also adopted the band director's technique for managing surly youths. Fr. Fred was a short, Friar Tuck kind of man in his brown Franciscan robes. Fred's medieval arrogance often irritated Joan—once, during his lengthy opinion of why women were unsuited for the priesthood, Joan bluntly interrupted him: "How can you say that when you're standing there in a long brown dress?" But Fred's provocative superiority came in handy when this short, plump man headed into the parking lot to collect truant smokers, many of whom were taller by a full foot. Marching into the center of the group, he'd raise his arm and yell "Follow Me!" then turn around and stride resolutely back into the building.

"The trick," he confided after my appointment as dean, "is to never look back." Looking back not only risked turning authority to a pillar of salt but also gave the opposition a chance to argue. The "Follow Me!" approach had worked so far with Ryan and Darren, but they stood on the edge of adolescence in 1984, and I expected the revolution to begin any day.

"Have you become 'stupid' yet?" my friend Jeannette had asked during my last visit in Fort Wayne. We were sitting at a table in the Blue Mountain Coffee Company watching her daughter Erin, a twelve-year-old girl with the body of a woman bursting through, depart for the ladies' room. "Sometime last summer, I became stupid," Jeannette confessed. "My clothes are stupid, the way I talk is stupid . . . I've become a walking, talking embarrassment to her."

I laughed, remembering sociologist Pauline Bart's remark during a discussion after her lecture, "The Loneliness of the Long-

Distance Mother." Dr. Bart told the campus audience that while she was regularly invited to speak at prestigious universities and write for scholarly journals, her teenaged daughter thought she was "too stupid to cross the street by myself." The audience, full of stupid mothers, roared.

Jeannette confirmed that no amount of professional competence made up for the omniscient humiliation of "mother." She'd taken Erin to a lecture she delivered recently, hoping to gain some points against the rising tide of adolescent contempt. Her daughter sat sullenly in the audience, arms folded defensively across her chest, prepared for another assault of embarrassment. The lecture was followed by a lively discussion, but Erin's perception of her mother's performance was this: "If you had explained yourself better, there wouldn't have been so many questions afterward."

"Keep the fan on," I advised Jeannette.

After waking Ryan, I step up on the first rung of the bunkbed ladder and lift Darren's ankle. I kiss his instep—if kissing sons means raising little homosexuals, so be it. Darren's remarkable feet, from his first moment of life, were vital to his consciousness.

I saw those startling feet for the first time in the middle of the night, eight years ago, when a sympathetic nurse wheeled me from the maternity ward to the intensive care nursery. Two days after the ambulance delivered me to the emergency room, unconscious and bleeding profusely, I could remember nothing of the birth. I didn't know whether the baby was alive or stillborn, healthy or deformed, female or male.

Dulled by painkillers after the cesarean, I could hardly keep my eyes open when the young pediatric specialist who'd been called in on the emergency made an obligatory stop during rounds the next day. Standing at the foot of my bed, he recited a long list of medical details including "increased surfactin levels" and "decreasing apnea," words I didn't understand at all. He neglected to pat my arm or offer any reassurances—he never said, simply, "The boy seems *fine*." Under heavy sedation, I couldn't get my questions out when he asked if I had any. I struggled to release the one burning inside—"Will the baby *live*?"—but my efforts produced only soundless air.

"Are you at all interested in this?" the young doctor asked

reproachfully, when my drooping eyelids finally succumbed to their weight. He mistook my drugged condition for bored disinterest in his brilliant medical rescue. He left offended, without ever addressing my essential question. I was weeping in my darkened room when the sedation wore off and the night nurse came on duty.

"What?" she asked when I explained the tears. "You mean you haven't *seen* him yet? He's gorgeous! I can't believe the doctors didn't . . ." She pursed her lips, keeping the rest of her disbelief to herself. "C'mon, honey," she said softly, "we're going for a ride." She helped me into a wheelchair and sped down the dim corridors until we reached the glowing lights of the preemie nursery.

Braking the wheelchair next to a small incubator she introduced me to Darren, weighing just over four pounds, sleeping amid a tangle of wires and tubes. Stretched out under sunlamps to cure his jaundice, a tiny vacationer on a tropical island, he was an iridescent shade of pink and tan. His head was the size of a sunkist orange, with fine, high cheekbones and a delicate chin. His miniature diaper, the size of a folded handkerchief, came up to his armpits. He was tininess itself except for those enormous feet. Spreadeagled on the blanket of the incubator, his feet were as long as the calves of his legs.

The steady beep and flashing lights of an overhead monitor assured me that life was pumping along, when suddenly an alarm sounded and a panel of buzzers went off. A white-uniformed nurse looked up from her desk in the glass-enclosed nursing station, then hurried to the incubator. She flicked Darren gently on the heel a few times. The steady beep returned, and her face relaxed.

"Apnea," she explained. "Sometimes they get so tired, they forget to breathe." She patted him on the head. "He's doing *fine*," she assured me. But I carried the sound of alarms back to my room that night, worried that lack of oxygen might affect his developing brain.

Eight years later, there was nothing damaged about Darren's brain. But this dreamy boy would drift off occasionally to some remote tropic inside his mind. As he floated out that morning in March, I flicked his heel gently to keep his attention.

"Let's go, buddy," I whisper to his instep. "We have miles to go and promises to keep today."

I pick up the boys' jeans and socks and sweatshirts, the inevitable trail they leave behind as they shed their daily cocoons. The room itself is in a state of transition—every time I enter it I am assaulted by unkept promises. My friend George constructed the bunkbed frames I commissioned—the top bunk a foot higher than standard and the bottom flush with the floor— which still await my finishing touches. I promised the kids a room within their rooms, planning to sew a colorful duckcloth tent around each frame. This ambitious plan is to compensate for the room they loved in Fort Wayne, where they slept under white pillow clouds suspended from a sky-blue ceiling and a wall- length rainbow arching colorfully between their heads. The aggressive cheerfulness of that room sold the house in the depressed Fort Wayne market, the realtor said. A year and a half later, the pine boards of the kids' new bunk beds are still bare. My imagination has once again exceeded my energies. The kids sleep each night in what appears to be the construction site of an ambitious but slightly demented architect.

There had been other strange alterations in their environment that year. Several times a day, during reflective moments in the bathroom, they'd observe the bizarre medical paraphernalia, the syringes and saline bottles and miles of gauze covering the countertops. They understood "diabetes" and "empyema" only vaguely, but confronted the reality of hypodermic needles and soggy bandages directly. It repelled and fascinated them. They'd both asked to try the needles, and had given me insulin injections.

"Does it hurt?" Ryan had asked soberly, wincing as he stuck the needle into my arm. "Hurt" was still a powerful word for a ten-year-old, especially this boy who lived so close to his body, who didn't know anything about numbness yet.

"A little," I admitted, "like a pinch."

"Do you have to do this to yourself forever, Mom?" Darren had asked when it was his turn. At age eight, "forever" was how long it took for a single birthday to come, so imagining three or four decades of daily shots made him crazy with pain. I reminded him that in my case, the injections weren't so hard to take— inconvenient as they were, I preferred them to death. I thought how unnerving it had to be for two highly impressionable young boys, observing their mother with a rubber tube jutting from between her ribs, performing strange rituals in the bathroom every day. The competence I faked began in innocence, prompted by a strong urge to restore some security to their fractured lives. However counterfeit my pretense that I was doing just fine, the boys relied on it.

"Put all your laundry in the hamper this morning," I order after waking them up, carrying an armload out the door with me. "I'm doing the wash today." Whenever Howe and I switch places for the week, we try to give each other a running start on the housework. But there are always weeks the cycle halts midstage, when the kids get dressed from the laundry basket. I feel a vague reproach whenever I catch a whiff of overripe socks, a guilt unaffecting Howe. Men have no shame about housework—Joan is amazed that when her husband does the laundry, instead of putting the pocket change he finds into five separate envelopes and returning it to the rightful owners, he just keeps it. "Imagine that," she said.

I drop the clothes in the utility room and proceed down the hall to the kitchen, feeling fluish and slightly radioactive. Opening the cabinet doors in the kitchen, I take inventory and make a grocery list.

This, too, would induce a bout of self-reproach. My free-lance income gave us weeks of feast followed by draining famines. When the famines struck, I would complain if Howe didn't keep grocery lists and replenish supplies before my return. I hated the caviling that crept into my voice whenever I felt desperate about money. I wanted not to care about it. When I inventoried the kitchen shelves that morning in March, the conclusion arrived as an estimate: "Looks like about ten days left to live."

"You've got to get yourself a hard-ass lawyer and get more assertive about *money*, Mary Kay," Joan had warned, concerned about the signs of stress erupting in my body. When I hired a "holistic" attorney instead, to draft a flexible document we could change ourselves through continuing negotiations, I felt her exasperation with me. The financial agreement I signed had all the teeth of a weaning infant. My soft approach to money was one part ego—I believed that very soon my writing income would break through the poverty line—and two parts repulsion for hard-ass attorneys.

Before I close the cabinets, I glance up at the exchange charts posted inside the doors, an exhaustive list of food groups and caloric measures that have had to be memorized since diabetes came into my life. I extract a box of bran cereal and close the doors, coping with depressing realities by ignoring them. The kids appear in the doorway, fully dressed for school.

Their new self-sufficiency still amazes me. Children are so helpless for so many years—they cannot zip their snowsuits or tie their shoes, their noses run endlessly and shirt fronts are forever escaping from their pants. It's hard to stop tending them as they assert independence. When children begin tending themselves, the bite-size pieces grow to unwieldy chunks, and their wardrobe selections suggest they are unemployed clowns. Ryan and Darren have passed through the stage of prominent prints and primary colors, and now dress in their familiar gray sweatshirts and blue jeans. As usual, Ryan's baseball cap is perched over his ears this morning, the perpetual headpiece leaving a dent in his hair all around his head. He puts it on first thing in the morning and wears it through breakfast and cartoons, arithmetic and music, soccer games and back rubs. It keeps his head tightly wrapped as his family unravels, through the repeated hellos and good-byes of his parents. Like Frank's stocking cap, his baseball hat keeps the voices at a distance. I have to knock on his beak to get his attention through most of 1984.

"Oh god, Mom, do we have to eat that?" Darren groans, looking at the bran cereal as if it were a highly odiferous turnip.

"No, there's a box of corn flakes in your cabinet," I say, nodding in the direction of the lower doors where I keep the kid food and legal snacks.

"No Captain Crunch," he reports, dismayed, surveying the granola bars and yogurt raisins with equal despair.

"I hate it that you have diabetes, Mom," he says. It is not the delicate state of my health he mourns this morning, but the absence of Twinkies and doughnuts. He has the sugar blues.

I hated it, too. Having to pay strict attention to diet took concentration, and travel meant remembering to pack snacks to offset insulin reactions during long delays on runways. Small plastic bags of nonsugar sweeteners were stashed in my glove compartment and briefcase, and my purse frequently held a small cache of fruit and empty bags to collect pits or cores. Once, while Darren and I were sitting in a doctor's waiting room, a phone rang for an unnerving length of time. I reached into my purse and lifted a banana to my ear. "Hello? Is anybody there?" I asked. He giggled. I made any kind of fool of myself to hear them laugh.

"I take off for New York today," I remind them over breakfast. "Dad moves in tonight." I try to sound cheerful about the dramatic changes our lives have taken—I remember from a study in my folder that kids absorb the fears and anxieties of their parents. "The days you have to get on a plane, Mom . . ." Darren said quietly when I tucked him in last night, "I always think you're never coming back." It is an unsettling bedside confession from this spooky, contemplative Zen son—similar thoughts were disquieting me. I hugged him hard, kissing his head, promising I'd always be back, one way or another. Whatever that meant.

"Why don't we meet at the Brown Jug after school," I suggest this morning. "We have time for a pizza before I leave for the airport." I commit unabashed bribery on leavetaking days.

"Should we invite Dad to join us?" Ryan asks, looking out for the best interest of his father.

Ryan felt enormous compassion for his dad, whose broken heart was visible to anyone glancing at his sleeve. His eldest son tolerated no slights. He was upset when he'd overheard me on the phone the other day, making plans with a friend: "Okay, I'll drive—Howe was nice enough to lend me his car today."

"What do you mean, 'nice enough'?" he'd asked when I hung up, unearthing what he judged to be an insult. "Dad is *real* nice, *all* the time," he insisted. I tried to explain that's what the expression meant, but his antennae for insulting asides were turned way up and I didn't get through. He cast a sideways glance from under his baseball beak that said: Just don't let it happen again. I was jealous of the large empathy he bestowed on his father. I also admired it. Loving Ryan caused me to be more generous than I actually was.

"Sure," I agree, "I'll call Dad and ask him to meet us there at three o'clock," I say. "Maybe we'll have enough time for a few video games at the Crosseyed Moose. I have some coupons."

"I thought you hated the guy there," Ryan says, remembering the scene I created the last time we entered that establishment.

I'd presented the coupons for "Family Night," when children got double tokens if their parents accompanied them. The manager refused to honor our coupons because we didn't qualify as a family.

"If you don't have a father with you, you're not a family," he said gruffly, returning my coupons.

"Don't be ridiculous," I told him, "there are millions of families in this country that don't have a father." I quoted the statistics from my Children of Divorce file, informing him that only seven percent of Americans live in the breadwinning-father, homemaking-mother, two-school-age-children model he honored. "What if I were a widow?" I asked him, imagining that I could arrange to have Howe shot if it made a difference with the coupons.

"Doesn't matter." He shrugged. "We don't make any exceptions. If you don't have a father, you're not a family." These words incited riots in my mind. Smoldering with resentment that fathers were so well taken care of while mothers were ignored, I assaulted the man with facts from my file: the gross percentage of fathers who stop making support payments, who don't show up for visits, who forget their kids' birthdays, even their ages. I said his unenlightened policy, besides being outrageously discriminatory, didn't even make sound business sense since it cut ninety-three percent of us out of the market. I told him he was crazy.

He suggested I was the crazy person, and asked me to leave at once. After "creating a nuisance," I knew Frank would have continued provocation until someone threatened to call the police. Having witnessed his countless scrapes with authorities, however, I'd learned the benefits of a timely surrender. When I decided to go without further protest, however, I thought I was letting Frank down somehow. It was less than a year since his suicide, and I resented having to resolve every crisis alone. I was furious with him for deserting me, for expecting me to be his "translator" before he'd finished teaching me his language. Slamming the coupons down on the counter in the Crosseyed Moose, I turned resolutely around and raised my arm to signal the kids, hollering "Follow Me!"

They were outside already, naturally, having slipped out at the first noticeable sign that mother had become embarrassing. Hands in their pockets and heads drooping, they greeted me sullenly when I emerged. They hated fights—especially Ryan, who would come into the kitchen during the last year before our separation and beg us to stop arguing. Howe and I tried to save explosive discussions for late at night, after the children were asleep, but sarcasms and injuries would ooze out the next morning. The children weren't fooled. They knew we'd been fighting.

When I saw their fallen faces outside the Crosseyed Moose I felt bad and acknowledged their embarrassment. I didn't exactly say "I'm sorry," since I was boycotting that phrase in an effort to salvage my remaining self-esteem, but I came as close as my rules allowed.

"It's okay, Mom," the kids said immediately, in unison. "It's okay, Dad . . . It's okay, Mom"—that was their conclusion to far too many scenes in 1984. Small children have an immense capacity for forgiveness, granting amnesty to parents who have suffered enough. They graciously bestowed this compassion on me in front of the Crosseyed Moose, each taking a hand as we walked down the sidewalk. More than any handcuffs the police might have used, those two small hands arrested my rage.

"I still don't like the guy," I tell Ryan after breakfast. "But this isn't Family Night. These coupons are for just regular folks like us." I squat down low, knees cracking audibly, to look directly into the eyes hiding under the protection of his baseball cap. "These coupons," I say, turning the beak around to the back, "are exclusively for weirdos."

"Okay, Mom," he grins, his smile lighting up and rearranging all the freckles on his cheeks. "See you later." He hugs me good-bye before he leaves for school.

"Don't kiss me, bugs," I say, turning my cheek to them. "I might be coming down with your flu." I pat their heads instead, my routine but satisfying habit. I love to pat their hair in bed, their hands in the movies, their knees in the car. The gesture is the perfect physical accompaniment for the passion pulsating inside me, marking the beat, the beat, the beat of my heart.

4

QUEEN MARY'S HANDS

March 25, 1984

I'm on my way to New York to join Larry in his vigil at St. Vincent's Hospital: Mary Kay is in a coma there, and all I can think of is how we share, if nothing else, a certain pickiness about words, how we quote constantly to each other a sentence or phrase that sums up our experience of a writer's piece. I'm thinking specifically about one phrase from Vonnegut's *Palm Sunday,* which we both got stuck on as having quotable quality. I hear it in the sincere voice she uses for quoting the "good stuff":

> . . . somewhere in there my son Mark went crazy and recovered. I went out to Vancouver and saw how sick he was, and I put him in a nut house. I had to suppose that he might never get well again.

That is what I keep hearing in my mind: "I had to suppose that he might never get well again."

The encouraging thing about that ominous, eerie statement, of course, is that it is written in the past tense, a description of a very near miss and not of the problem itself: that for a while Vonnegut *had* to believe the worst, but that it all ended as an act of his imagination and not what he had feared.

While Gina made notes on the flight between Chicago and New York late Sunday afternoon, Larry picked up his car in the lot at Pier 40 and headed out of Manhattan toward La Guardia. It wasn't until he entered the Midtown Tunnel and realized he wouldn't be returning alone that he finally relaxed his jaw, becoming aware of the dull ache long hours of clenching had planted there. Steeled against the despairing events of the past two days, he'd been unconscious of his own pain until relief was on the way.

He'd tried to reach Gina several times Friday afternoon, counting on her to become diplomatic ambassador to my family's delicately calibrated nervous systems, but she'd been tied up in meetings all day. He kept dialing Kay and Jerry's number in Florida, unaware that they were visiting friends on the opposite coast for the weekend. Since answering machines were a step into the age of technology none of my immediate relatives felt compelled to take, he called every hour, letting the phone ring through six, then twelve, then twenty drills. On his last attempt he listened, numbly, to the shelling in his ear for ten empty minutes. Before he left his office Friday afternoon, he gave his name and number to Gina's associate in the Computer Sciences Department at De Paul University, but declined to state his message. He didn't want her returning to an orange slip on her desk that said: "Your sister's in a coma. Please contact St. Vincent."

Gina called the studio until 11 P.M. Friday night while Larry sat next to my bed in ICU, stroking my hand, holding out for an improbable resurrection. He'd interviewed the evening shift and then the night staff during rounds, hoping to obtain some small piece of good news to sweeten the bitterness of the bad. When Gina's roommate finally handed her the receiver on Saturday afternoon, Larry tried to soften the blow with the dubious consolation that while I was still comatose after almost two days, the doctors seemed pleased my condition had "stabilized."

It's hard to imagine anyone receiving the message as good news, but Gina's ears were preset to accept any word of family stability as a positive sign. Twenty-five years of peculiar medical reports and indefinite psychiatric opinions trained her to regard a "stable coma" as a good thing, given the immediate alternatives. As the youngest member of the family, it had never been Gina's role to be the worrier, much less the leader in family crises. Although she knew about my repeated hospitalizations that winter and the freakish apparatus I wore between my ribs, I'd managed to fake a dauntless bravura as effectively with Gina as I had with the kids. Her faith in my recovery was instant and absolute—she expected me to arise from the coma quickly, perhaps even indignantly, and march out of the hospital as I had two years ago, against orders, preferring to live out a case of pneumonia with a vial of penicillin tablets at home.

"When will she wake up?" she asked Larry, the same question he'd posed repeatedly the night before. The temporary stability I'd achieved was somewhere between life and death, and no one knew how long I'd linger ambiguously or which pole I'd drift toward once I started moving again. The longest coma in human history was slept by Elaine Esposito of Tarpon Springs, Florida, who left consciousness on August 6, 1941, after an appendectomy at age six and remained comatose until her death on November 25, 1978— 37 years and 111 days later. Larry didn't mention Ms. Esposito's record to my sister, and answered only with the imprecise data he'd collected in ICU the night before: "It could be a day or two, and after that, it could be longer."

The gravity of *coma* dawned slowly on Gina, as if she were inching along an expressway during rush hour hypnotized by the symmetry of the five numbers creeping up on the odometer, unalarmed by the row of nines until she faced a panel of zeros. It was not specific words from the conversation she recalled in her journal the next day, but rather a vague, dark clouding in her unconscious:

It's funny—I can't remember . . . I do know he said, *"Gina,* I'm so glad I got *hold* of you." He sounded a little desperate when he talked about trying to reach the folks, and maybe it was that he sounded just as grateful to have reached me, as if I, like the folks or one of the older kids, would know what to do. It was the first time anyone consulted me about a family crisis, expecting me to be active around it. And I was unaccustomed, boy: I think I asked him how serious it was (maybe it's this question, in fact, that embarrasses me out of remembering the words—how could I have not known, how could I have made him have to say it? "It's pretty serious. They don't know much.") In any case, he finally did jar me out of thinking I should wait until somebody else came home to take over.

Larry had proposed, reasonably, that Gina wait a few days before flying to New York: "She'll probably need you more once she wakes up," he suggested. But reasonableness was not Gina's guiding light in 1984. She didn't know why, but she knew where she needed to be. The rightness of her impulse was confirmed when she called Larry back and heard his deep relief. If she couldn't be useful to me, she knew she would be immediately valuable to Larry. The man needed help and didn't even know it.

At one time or another, Gina had surprised all four of her older siblings with her uncanny ability to "know" things we didn't, reaching her conclusions intuitively while we wired around more tedious rational tracks. ("How did you know where Mom hid them?" I asked her some twenty-two years ago, when she went directly to the tin of chocolate chip cookies stashed under our parents' bed that I'd been hunting down for nearly half an hour. Her three-year-old face drew a complete blank. "I just knew," she'd finally said and shrugged.) Intuition was so native to her thought, she was taken aback when anyone asked for an explanation of her reasoning. What reasoning? Why did it matter, to know how you know?

Sudden insights descended on her with such regularity she'd forget, occasionally, which ones came with legitimate credentials and which didn't. She'd throw odd thoughts into conversation cavalierly, as if they were widely known facts. The first time she saw Larry, for example, a twenty-second glimpse shot her brain three years ahead. He had waved to me across a crowded dining room in downtown Fort Wayne one night as Gina and I were leaving, and I waved briefly back.

"Who was *that*?" she asked in the parking lot, detecting his intensity even at twenty yards.

"My editor at the *Journal*," I said, "the owner of the giant blue pencil." After two years of weekly columns, I still hadn't produced a single page that wholly met his standards. I told Gina he was my Father Jerome, the high-school teacher who gave Frank straight A's but marked his effort "unsatisfactory" every quarter. Frank had no explanation for his failure to satisfy: "Something about me just tees him off," he guessed. That was essentially where I stood with Larry, after he'd blue-penciled several reams of my writing.

"He's in love with you, you know," Gina concluded offhandedly, as if it were an unremarkable fact to draw from such slim data. In fact I didn't know and neither did Larry, and if my heart raced at all in his presence it was generally in the opposite direction. I resented the difficulty he imposed on my work in an already trying year, when I was supporting two young sons and mourning the terminal state of my marriage. Romance was nowhere on my mind.

"You think everybody is in love with everybody," I'd said,

shaking my head. It was Gina's habit, as the celebrated last child of two senior parents and four older siblings, to regard all gestures and exchanges between people as signs of affection. It was a simultaneous gift and curse, the huge love that was poured over Kay and Jerry's youngest, funniest, most generous child. Nothing in Gina's youth prepared her for the disaffection waiting outside her tight clan.

"She must have been the most touched baby in all of Chicago," Larry remarked three years after his telling wave, sitting tieless and shoeless on my living-room rug as I threaded the last reel of family home movies. Kay's amateur camerawork often included part of a thumb over the lens or a closeup of her eyeball, but even through repeated technical difficulties Gina surfaced brilliantly in every scene.

The footage of her arrival from the hospital in 1959 began with Jerry's high-wattage grin, as he offered four similarly electrified children a peek inside the bundle of white fluff he hugged to his chest. In soundless Kodacolor we poked and patted with absorbed fascination, picking up little fingers and tickling tiny ribs. We sniffed inside the blanket and held our noses, hamming it up for the camerawoman and affecting a momentary jiggle in her grip. Gina was only a few days old when she lived this scene, her wide-open eyes curious but wholly detached from the sensation around her. Her calm, blank expression in the thick of wild affection seemed to say, "So. This is life."

Fifteen years of family history were already in the albums by the time she was born, but Gina learned to recite family legends as if she had been there. She could reproduce the exact inflections necessary for the famous refrain of Drumpety the Dragon, the hero in a serial tale Jerry unraveled nightly to his growing brood in the fifites. Drumpety was an audience-participation story and my father solicited the ingredients before each episode: A pack of wolves, a witch and a magician, two black widow spiders, three ("No, wait . . . five!") five evil dukes, Sir Lancelot, a fair young princess ("with *black* hair this time, please"), and platoons of knights from innumerable round tables. Jerry managed to stir all the ingredients together until the hapless dragon was boiling in an impossible stew, invariably teetering on the brink of a sheer cliff as a hundred bloodthirsty knights drew their swords, while an innocent dwarf or maiden or even Sir Lancelot himself stood helplessly tied to a stake in the middle of an enormous, flaming pyre, hotter and more threatening than anything encountered in *Lives of the Saints*. At this point Jerry would interrupt the story for a brief test of faith: "But did that stop Drumpety?"

"Oh, nooooooo! Not *Drumpety*!" we chanted in unison, never doubting Drumpety's talent for swift and comic rescues. Jerry's own joy in the triumph of justice every night was capacious—at the end of each episode he'd wrap all four of us in his bear hug, jamming elbows into ribs and initiating a tickling riot. These thrilling hugs waned gradually as we outgrew our childhood bodies, and Drumpety disappeared into legend. Later Jerry entertained his former fans with an occasional story or joke at the dinner table, stalling our impending departures for dates or libraries or part-time jobs, but the dependable enthusiasm of earlier refrains was by then drenched in adolescent cool: "Oh, *Dad*," we moaned with exaggerated pain, ". . . how *corny*."

A self-educated man with no university diplomas supporting the executive title he earned in a large Chicago bank, my father had mixed feelings about the calculus and Latin and literature credits piling up around him. The orphaned son of second generation Irish immigrants, he was proud of the advanced degrees his children brought home, but what did he call them now—Master Frank? Doctor Paul? "I'm still your father . . ." he asserted during arguments, as if to remind himself. Jerry never stopped loving his eldest children but their sudden maturity took him by surprise, embarrassing him out of his bear-hug habit. He conducted the substitute handshakes awkwardly the first few times he launched his genes into independence. But by his fifth child, Jerry knew his stuff.

The parents Gina inherited had fifteen years on the job and were about to start another decade of intense postgraduate work with the renowned psychologists who analyzed their eldest son. The shocking therapy at ISPI and other Chicago institutions taught my parents the fragility of expert opinions—they saw the stern admonishments of the fifties become ridiculous under the fluorescent lights of the seventies. The popular dicta of the previous era that "Children should be seen and not heard" or "Spare the rod and spoil the child" appeared as a macabre design to raise a nation of mute cripples. Was it a postwar craving for order and control that produced the joyless attitudes toward children, or were the experts guiding the baby-boom generation an especially misanthropic breed? Whatever the reason for the merciless rules, doctors intoxicated with authority issued them without inviting questions or discussion.

"Why did you follow your doctor's absurd orders?" the therapist at ISPI asked Kay accusingly when she admitted her twenty-one-year regret about not cuddling Frank the night he cried all night. "Why didn't you trust your own instincts?" he demanded to know.

"I didn't think we were allowed to," she answered humbly. "He was a doctor and I was . . . not." The odds were never even in the fifties, when being "just a housewife" commanded small respect against the giant superiority of doctors, an inequity cruelly played out again two decades later when my mother stood trial for her pediatrician's malpractice. Though the brutal examinations ultimately shed no light on Frank's illness, they did loosen the grip subsequent authorities had on my parents. My mother especially came to regard expert opinions as mere guesses about what children need: "Why" and "how" were questions my parents appropriated for themselves, and theories that no longer fit were abandoned with relief. If it had been a mistake to honor the tradition of paternal aloofness and shake the hand of his firstborn son, Jerry didn't make it again. His youngest daughter was happily encased in bear hugs for twenty-five years.

By the time Gina reached puberty, Kay had retired her vigilant defense against the sins of vanity and pride, which had diminished her pleasure in her eldest children's awards or honors by requiring a dutiful reminder against "getting a big head." It was my adolescence that collided with the period of greatest threat from vanity, the psychological disorder of getting a "big head." Kay would stop in the hallway outside the bathroom whenever she caught me primping in the mirror, her ever-present laundry basket resting on a hip as she delivered an impromptu sermon: "It's not how you look, but who you are that matters . . ." She said later she regretted never sharing with me "what a beauty I thought you were," but she recovered in time to share some thrills with Gina. What else but outsized maternal joy could have moved this scrupulously modest woman to christen her last daughter "Regina Marie," a Latin translation of the hardly humble, proudly vernacular Queen Mary?

The exceptional love and skill our parents had for Gina would have provoked an outbreak of jealousy among older siblings except for two fortunate coincidences. The rigorous program at ISPI converted Paul and me into loyal parental allies at ages typically slated for surly rebellions. My own belated strike for independence had just begun when it was halted, mid-revolt, by the tremendous allegiance my mother inspired riding her exercise bike in those paper hospital slippers. Paul was so awed by my parents' good faith that he became a self-appointed guardian angel, policing younger siblings who disturbed their peace with audible disputes: "Will you guys go fight in the basement where they can't *hear* you—can't you see they have *enough* on their minds?" It was somewhere in that decade of high defenses that we fell into the habit of "aggressive nurturance"—a term a psychologist friend identified as "the compulsion to take care of people who haven't asked for help."

The second sturdy dike holding back the natural force of envy was Gina herself: We were, singularly and collectively, mad about her. Even Kevin, eight years older and her closest sibling, had a hard time keeping up his rivalry role.

Paul was already in his teens when Kay filmed Gina's homecoming reel, capturing the first appearances of his Knocked Out look. At thirteen, whenever he got a terrific charge out of something he'd slap a hand to his forehead and roll his eyes back in their sockets. He was in a doctoral program at Virginia Polytech Institute when Gina learned to write letters (which Kay photocopied and sent to all matriculating siblings), and I strongly advised him to put on a helmet before reading them. Gina and Paul, the two great jokers in the family, took turns knocking each other out.

Frank had just become a freshman at Quigley Seminary when Gina arrived in 1959. At fifteen, before it was really necessary to shave the faint shadow he inspected regularly on his upper lip, he'd attended religious retreats warning him against lustful wanderings from the celibate path. The sinful zone on females, Frank told me once, was defined as "everything between your shoulders and your knees." That part of a woman was not to be touched, not even to be contemplated, a tremendously difficult task given the amount of reading and writing and thinking young seminarians had to do over that vast, curvaceous, forbidden area of female anatomy.

"Including my *hands?*" I'd asked him, incredulous. "What's sinful about my hands?" I pictured having to keep them over my head on future dates—in my eleven-year-old imagination, Catholicism made falling in love look a lot like getting arrested. Hands were reputed to be the worst part of us, Frank said, since they committed the most frequent sexual transgressions.

The retreat lectures made an enormous impression on Frank, still virginal and innocent at fifteen. He was already having trouble reining in his wild imagination—strange thoughts arrived, out of nowhere, whenever he went into the bathroom and closed the door. His fear of mortal sin grew so unwieldy, he would prepare for routine trips by singing loudly to distract himself, beginning with the first verse of the hymn Tantum Ergo in the hallway and concentrating on his Latin clear through to the flush. It was so heartbreaking to hear the loud dread he felt touching his own body, it ultimately diluted my reverence for the hymn. While the other sopranos in my Sunday choir obviously experienced elevation with the final amen of Tantum Ergo, I always heard the sound of a toilet flushing.

Frank was initially diagnosed by his counselor at Quigley as having a case of "scruples"—a too-literal interpretation of theology—but he thought the problem lay as much with Catholicism as his translation. After he left the seminary he urged Kay and Jerry to withdraw Gina from parochial schools, where the heavy emphasis on mortal sin made living in a human body unbearable. His own disastrous, imaginative flights convinced him that "out of body" was no place for an adolescent. He wanted Gina to stay in close touch with both her human body and her rational mind.

He recognized the seduction of her quick, intuitive leaps but cautioned her to test all conclusions against the grid of disciplined logic. He thought she should know where odd notions came from—if they arrived without clear maps back to a reliable source, they weren't to be trusted. She was barely out of kindergarten when he began quizzing her routinely with his own peculiar method of Socratic Inquiry:

"Gina, how do you know the moon isn't made of green cheese?" he asked her once while she was making a peanut butter sandwich at the kitchen table.

"Because the astronauts just brought back moon rocks, Frank, not slices of cheese," she answered.

"How do you know for certain that those rocks aren't really lumps of green cheese?" he pursued.

"Because if you took a bite out of those rocks you'd break your teeth . . . and besides, everybody *knows* the moon isn't green cheese," she said, slicing her sandwich diagonally and trying to cut the debate short. But there were always more questions— Frank never deferred to their fifteen-year age difference and let her win a verbal contest, being as tactless with young children as he was with his teachers.

"But how do we know? Have any of the scientists taken a bite of the rocks, that you know of?" he pressed further. No one regularly won debates with Frank—scoring points against him merely increased his enthusiasm and upped the ante. His badgering techniques drove older siblings into sputtering incoherence, but his youngest sister had the bald temerity to simply quit: "Okay," she conceded, "maybe the moon is green cheese. Who cares?"

My parents stuck with their commitment to parochial education but in an unorthodox move for the times, they appointed Paul and me to serve as her godparents. We were still practicing Catholics when our duties began at her christening in Immaculate Conception Church in 1959, but ten years after the shake-up during Vatican II we'd moved to other places. Her godfather, an agricultural economist working for the Canadian government, migrated deeper into Eastern philosophies, becoming interested in the possibilities of self-transformation through ego-elimination and worldly detachment, while her godmother set deep roots in Midwestern Indiana—which God had abandoned altogether—and joined the Fort Wayne Feminists. By the time Gina was old enough to read the inspirational materials we sent her, the list included *Initiation into Yoga: An Introduction to the Spiritual Life*, by Sri Krishna Prem, and *For Her Own Good*, by Deirdre English and Barbara Ehrenreich. With two devout Catholic parents, an aspiring Hindu and ardent feminist as godparents, and two ex-seminarian older brothers overseeing Gina's education, her religious beliefs were completely homogenized by 1984.

The structure of family relationships by then was a configuration of acute angles, with Gina located in the vertex between sharply diverging lines: I would invite her to the annual Halloween Witches and Amazons Coffeehouse in Fort Wayne and she'd bring me passages of *Living with the Himalayan Masters* from Paul; Kay would express frustration with Jerry's refusal to consider a hearing aid, and Gina would shout the message along to him. While disparate beliefs and opinions about acceptable decibel levels caused friction between us—Paul's unexamined chauvinism irritated me, my unspiritual political seeking offended him—Gina was able to tune in to our various wavelengths without strain.

After a long hike with her in Canada early in 1984, Paul was impressed with Gina's uncanny intuitiveness—he hadn't worn a helmet that weekend and experienced several knockouts. Her quick insights into what we thought and who we were made visits with Gina as satisfying as an intimate conversation with a wittier, more lovable version of yourself. Frank had thought she was exactly like him, I thought her exactly like me, and Gina herself found it confusing that she identified so completely with the company of the moment: "This means I have either six personalities or none at all," she noted. When she finally began unearthing her own identity in the early eighties, she had to excavate through thick layers of socialization from two official parents and four unusually involved, aggressively nurturant pseudoparents.

For nearly two decades Gina didn't mind the heavy claims made on her time and then, slowly, she did. She minded the time and she minded the mess we'd made of her native intuition, cluttering it with our cherished facts and oppressive rules of logic. It took several trial runs before she finally moved away from home—first to a dormitory on De Paul's Lincoln Park campus and back, then to an apartment near downtown Chicago and back again. She struck for independence like a yo-yo, trying to break the magnetism of family ties.

The last child who had pleased so effortlessly became increasingly difficult to understand. After collecting an alarming number of "incompletes" her last semester at DePaul, she finally quit and went to work full time. She took night classes and was only marginally committed to earning a degree—with four baccalaureates, two masters, and a Ph.D. accumulated ahead of her, she saw no urgency in framing the family name in more calligraphy.

Her procrastination worried Kay, who quickly faulted herself: "Maybe I was too much her friend and not enough her mother," she sighed when it became clear her youngest wasn't going to finish college after five years. "We just *enjoyed* her so much." Gina was twelve years old when Jerry retired from the bank in 1971, and they'd celebrated by touring Europe two years later. For the first time in their lives, after the Great Depression and World War II and forty-five years of daily responsibility had paid their dues in full, my parents had time to play. Kay felt guilty about all the fun they'd had, blaming herself when Gina eventually quit school.

"Oh, Kay," I softly chided, "You're so *Catholic*. Every good time doesn't have to have a price." I was certain that her enjoyment hadn't ruined Gina, and suggested it wasn't underdiscipline but overdiscipline behind her current grief. God knows, we all had a go at Gina. By 1984, her compulsion to capture the truth, the whole truth, and nothing but the truth blocked her ability to turn in even the simplest assignments and term papers. It was a problem I confronted habitually myself, evidenced most recently in my reluctance to abridge the complicated answer to "The Riddle of Responsibility" for the *Cosmo* readers. Gina's last letter had confirmed my hunch:

Dear M.K.,

I am just returned from my Modern Poetry class and am a little overstimulated, so you must excuse my mental spasms disguised as a letter. Fact is, I need to communicate—I just spent three hours doing a "close reading" of a Wallace Stevens poem; unlocking metaphors like a woman possessed; tracing images in their endless variation (here it's water, there it's mist; gimme a break)—and all this to hear Professor B. pronounce, oh so *casually*, that old Wallace Stevens does a nice job, doesn't he, with such a trite subject as religion? So after all this work to get at the poet's intended meaning, there was to be no discussion of theme. That's for late nights alone with Wallace Stevens's poetry, I suppose, and not for an English class—and I guess that's as it should be. But I almost imploded at the idea of religion as a theme being trite.

I'll bet he's an ex-seminarian—the comment rings of something that might be muttered between holes of golf, no?

The letter went on for another four imploding pages, railing against Professor B.'s empty swings and wondering how she was going to pass Modern Poetry without exposing her deep fondness for trite themes. She confessed that she still hadn't finished her paper on *Ariadne,* a six-pager due eighteen months ago that was now buried in the sixty-some looseleaf pages of notes she carried from class to class, library to library. The *Ariadne* term paper was her most oppressive incomplete, only a few months away from being converted into an F by the computers in the registrar's office. She'd papered my dining-room table with copious drafts the last time she visited, and I imagined the thing had now grown to become a serious contender to *War and Peace.* I understood her despair, but from my own morass of unmet deadlines couldn't offer any help. Instead, I passed along the message from my *Cosmo* editor that life doesn't have to be so meaningful: "Lighten up, you'll live longer," I wrote in my reply, but never mailed it.

Larry recognized Gina immediately among the passengers de-planing at La Guardia. Though she was eleven years my junior, a full six inches taller, and without a trace of the premature gray that began streaking my black hair at her age, he thought she looked exactly like me. She was a careless beauty at twenty-five, her clear pink skin usually makeupless and thick dark hair tied back in some haphazard arrangement, descending in appealing disarray around her face as she moved with easy grace in her tall, athletic body. She was largely unconscious of her engaging cha-risma, but it arrested new acquaintances passing through our dining room who pointed to her framed portrait and asked, "Which one is *that?*" When Kay and Jerry combined their genes to form Queen Mary, the outcome was a rare biological achievement.

Blue jeans and loafers constituted the dominant themes of the queen's wardrobe in 1984, perhaps with a man's vest or odd brooch acquired on a trip to AmVets Thrift Shop in uptown with her friend Barbara. Her style ranged from eccentric to regal, depending on whimsy more often than protocol. In an unusual concession to the sobriety of her mission in New York that March, she played it straight and arrived in a handsomely tailored suit with a tan-and-white houndstooth jacket and matching cashmere scarf. Gina was a double-take stunner when she bothered to dress up.

Catching Larry's wave, her face lit up with a full-wattage Blakely grin, established by our father as the official expression for greeting all planes and buses and carloads of relatives. Even when Jerry met my train at Union Station the day before Frank's funeral, his face still a damp map of raw emotion, his exuberant smile shot up with his hand as he spotted me in the crowd and hollered, "Hi, hon!!!" Gina maintained that our father could only speak in triple exclamation points in certain environments, particularly airport terminals and train stations. Whatever the mood of the arriving son or daughter or grandchild, it was impossible to walk directly into that boundless grin without becoming unaccountably happy yourself. This happened to Larry, when Gina dropped her bags and encased him in her bear hug.

Her solid affection for me spread out to him, providing his first direct experience with my incurable addiction to "family." To Larry, an only child, my relatives seemed an exotic, loquacious, passionate tribe. He remembered his own family reunions, populated with cousins and aunts and uncles all inflicted a heavy silence: "At parties, we sat on folding chairs along a living room wall quietly eating white angel food cake," he said. If someone spoke out of the line of duty, it was generally to ask about the weather or complain about the slow growth in the cornfields. His father was a man of such provocative loneliness, when he died at the age of sixty-six his mother couldn't name six friends to serve as pallbearers.

The absence of background chatter in Larry's childhood was still evident forty-two years later, as he conducted himself stiffly through the requisite small talk at cocktail parties or informal dinners with my friends. A self-taught conversationalist, his style with new acquaintances had the immediate warmth of an investigative journalist tracking down discrepancies in a municipal budget. But he felt an easy intimacy with my sister, a vigorous and lively reminder of me. When she spoke he heard my nasal Midwestern twang and ready laugh, but looked into eyes clearly belonging to someone else.

On the drive to Manhattan Larry prepared Gina for the unsettling scene she would encounter in the intensive care unit at St. Vincent's. Unlike a deep sleep where traces of pain or joy or even boredom on the dreamer's face provide clues to the thoughts passing behind it, the coma had erased my facial expressions altogether. Though Larry had studied my face for years—asleep and awake, with and without lipstick, hair up and hair down—I looked strangely unfamiliar to him in a coma. He found my features oddly disfigured by the absence of passion, as if I had been embalmed by a well-intentioned mortician who meticulously filled in all lines of grief or amusement to create the illusion of peaceful death. Larry tried to brace Gina for the shocking nakedness of my face. It bore the same gone spirit that made Frank so unrecognizable to me at his funeral—there were his eyebrows, his cheeks, his lips, without either his brooding gaze or electric grin. It was chilling to feel no attachment to his corpse, a body uninformed by his mind.

The coma resembled the passivity of death except for the eerie, random movements whenever the sedation wore off. I became highly agitated then, limbs thrashing in a senseless frenzy that threatened to dislodge the tubes. Larry explained that bed restraints had been applied to my ankles and wrists, preparing Gina for the disturbing view of another relative in captivity.

When they entered my isolation cell in St. Vincent's Sunday evening I was adrift in darkness, tripping morosely down a sober path in the aftermath of morphine. The broken transmitters of my brain had absorbed fragments of information that I was utterly unable to process. After what seemed like hours of labored thought, I finally concluded I was in a hospital. I'd overheard two young men standing near my bed commiserate with each other about their difficulties "living on a resident's income in New York City," and concluded they were doctors, I was a patient, and we were all in New York City. This simple calculation had taken enormous concentration, and the question "Why?" remained a mystery.

As the young doctors pulled needles out of my arms and stuck in more, they complained about inflated Manhattan rents, a topic that surfaced inevitably during any lull in a New York conversation. Since it was an immediate concern of mine I wanted to join the discussion—Larry and I hadn't come close to finding adequate space for ourselves and the kids in Manhattan, and were about to settle for a compromise in the suburbs—but discovered once again that my body wouldn't respond to my commands.

Blinded and feeling paralyzed again, I tried to remember what happened. I thought maybe I had been severely injured in the car accident—I vividly remembered the details of the collision, but in my recollection I had walked away from it. Or maybe the accident had been a dream. Facts kept changing in my mind—first I was in a prison, then a hospital, then a prison again. Initially the employees were hostile, suctioning and stabbing me; then they became incredibly kind, massaging me gently and providing magnificent light shows. At first my limbs were independent allies committed to liberating me from the oppressive tubes in my arms and nose and mouth, but now they wouldn't respond even when I willed their action. I was extremely confused—immediately after locating a truth I thought reliable, I would realize it came from the dubious visions of dreams. I doubted all perceptions in this uncertain state, so when I heard Gina and Larry enter my room I assumed it was my imagination. Their talk stopped, dropping to whispers as they approached me, and I felt Gina's hand begin to stroke the crown of my head.

"Hi, hon," Gina said, using Jerry's salutation without the exclamation points. There was an unusual flatness in her greeting, as if she had just walked into a locker room after an exceptionally draining game of volleyball. She didn't sound particularly happy to see me, yet there was unmistakable affection in the gentle way she stroked my hair. She loves me, she loves me not—contradictions were the order of the day.

"So. What's the deal here, Sis?" she asked, gaining tempo and volume as she rallied her energy. Her dependable wit returned with wry observations: "Has the wild woman come down with the blues?" she asked in mock disbelief, her hands moving down my neck and shoulders. Oh, hands, those tender hands—how could the physical hungriness of hands ever be mistaken for sin? Gina's hands carried strong currents of electricity, inciting a deep internal stirring that penetrated my engulfing loneliness.

In this dream, I imagined it had been several days since anyone had talked to me—I'd heard people talk about me, around me, over me, but until Gina arrived no one had spoken directly to me. She talked and joked and posed questions without needing any replies to carry on, a habit I'd begun with her when she was only five years old. We had shared a room for nine years between 1959 and 1968, and she was usually asleep when I returned home from a stimulating date or dismal party. I would settle down on the edge of her twin bed and ramble aloud for half an hour or more until I reached closure on the evening. Even in her sleep, Gina had been a satisfying audience. I would raise pressing adolescent questions: "Should I date him again?" or more softly, earnestly, "Do you think I'm pretty?" She rarely woke up but acknowledged my presence with unconscious grunts, which I generally interpreted as favorable responses. Gina was so sweet in her sleep, it was easy to assume her complete allegiance. My habit of nocturnal conversations worried Kay, who would remind me: "She needs her *rest.*" But unconscious dialogues became handy preparation for conversing through a coma.

Gina sat on the edge of my bed in ICU and spoke to me in the familiar shorthand we now used with each other, dropping brief quotes from former conversations to summarize whole paragraphs. I understood her meaning perfectly when she addressed me once as "the Queen of Fools"—God, she was quick with her insights into family griefs—but the tube in my mouth prevented any grunts of assent.

By 1984 Gina and I had shared so many mutual passions and experiences, in and out of consciousness, she believed we were separated only by the "very thin membrane" Salinger described between two relatives of the Glass family. It was that opaque divide she needed to cross for clear answers to her questions, and when my face admitted no entry to my thoughts she picked up my hand. She held it firmly during her steady monologue that evening, as if to detect responses through braille. She reported the conclusions she drew from this unorthodox method: "Can you hear me, hon? Yes? Yes . . . I think you can."

5

DEAR MISS X

                                              March 26, 1984

Barbara:

I'm sitting here in a friend's small apartment in New York, raging in my mind about "visiting hours" at a hospital around the corner. My sister is there in the intensive care unit, and visiting hours do not begin until 12:00—that leaves me little to do for four hours except rage against the very idea of visiting hours and, when I begin to feel unreasonable about that, write letters.

I got here yesterday afternoon and saw my sister last night. She's thirty-six years old, and I like to think the eleven years between us gives me a pretty constant idea of "what I'll be like when I grow up," but in truth it would be very hard for me to match today what she was at my age; by twenty-five she had a master's degree, had been to Europe, and, if I have my history right, had taken a job as an Andy Frain usherette to support herself and her husband while she finished her student teaching. Despite a great many health problems, her pace never slackened since. She's responsible for my only two nephews, ages eight and ten, and banged and pecked her way from a manual typewriter and a weekly column in Fort Wayne, Indiana, to being a full-fledged New York writer. I think you would like her a lot.

She'd been fighting medical experts for about two years to keep from having what she felt certain was unnecessary surgery on her lungs, and until recently, managed to stay more stubborn than she was sick. She came to New York last week to close a rental deal on a house in Connecticut where she planned to move with her friend Larry and the kids in June, but collapsed sometime Thursday night into a coma.

Larry got her to the hospital within minutes of discovering her unconscious Friday morning. Initially, she was thought to be in a diabetic coma. Larry couldn't reach me until late Saturday afternoon, and by then he knew that in fact the diabetes was only part of the problem. Her blood level stabilized almost immediately, but she's not regained consciousness since.

I could never have prepared myself for the way she looked last night. When I saw her from the doorway I fairly collapsed into Larry's arms. I sobbed for an incredible amount of time, with him assuring me, "She's so much better than she was."

She was on a respirator, a machine that clearly had no regard for her own body rhythms, and as it forced her chest wall up and down she would fight it, trying to bend her legs at the knees, moving her arms against the side of the bed, craning her neck to lift her head off the pillow. In none of these efforts did she quite succeed—she was so physically weak that I could barely believe her alive at all . . . I went in and started talking to her. And as soon as I touched her I felt better, like there was something I could do. Her hand was cold, but some warmth returned to it as soon as I held it . . .

Gina's letter to Barbara ended mid-page, without conclusion, doomed to the same unfinished state as *Ariadne*. Her writer's block, as I'd diagnosed it during our last phone call, was essentially an act of self-defense: It saved her from a direct confrontation with terrible truths, from her enormous fear of committing triteness on the page. Her "pickiness with words" asserted itself perpetually—Gina could take three or four months to complete a two-page resume and, like me, met deadlines by working until midnight and relying heavily on postal express.

Yet despite this apparently genetic intolerance for composition, she was determined to keep a daily journal while she was in New York. Clearing the coffee cups and breakfast dishes from the studio's only table to set up a makeshift desk, she opened her notebook to a fresh, blank page and carefully noted the date at the top. She stared at the brick wall across from the fifth-floor window to gather her thoughts, intending to record the strange feelings and odd sensations she'd drawn from my hand at the hospital last night.

Gina lost nearly an hour in that slim airshaft between brick walls, where the thoughts she hoped to capture with words escaped in gusty downdrafts. Since her ideas refused to come to life in her notebook she tried coaxing them into a letter, seeking the encouragement of a friendly audience, someone warm and breathing on the other side of the page. After dutifully recording the facts however, she balked, stalled by the suspicious, fishy aroma of her conclusions.

She had no hard evidence to support her belief that, contrary to all outward appearances, I was still very much alive, thinking and listening to everything; that my diabetes explained how but not why I'd drifted into unconsciousness; and that medical science alone could not bring me back to life. With no rational explanation for these hunches and no clear insight into what, if not medicine, might rouse me from the coma, she left the letter unfinished. Failing to locate an exit from her writer's block that Monday morning, a congestion of thoughts stuffed up inside her. Perhaps because she was freshly resolved to stick with the rational, the readily explainable, Gina assigned her watery eyes and aching throat to the sudden onset of a cold.

A cold, according to my own private theory, was never a purely physical phenomenon. I'd had so many in the last two years, so much time to study their symptoms and effect, I had concluded— with the full hesitancy of a long-practiced, nonsectarian doubter— that a "cold" was perhaps a spiritual affliction. I was struck by the remarkable physical resemblance between "crying" and having a "cold": the hoarse, swollen throat, the stuffed-up head, the aching sinuses. And what was the most overworked part of the body during a cold? The tear ducts, of course. The sore, red eyes, the watery seers, began a chain reaction of events. The tear ducts cleared the incessantly watering eyes, pulling the salt water down inside, sending heat waves down the throat, swelling the senses. Having a cold was just like inside-out crying. I thought a cold was actually a grief working its way through the senses, like a little physical mantra the body performs, sending a wish through the nervous system to reach the brain. The symptoms came not from an infection in the head, but from a pain in the heart. While Gina was aware of my theory and leaned toward a spiritual diagnosis herself, she nevertheless searched the medicine cabinet that morning and swallowed two antihistamines.

There was no shortage of things to do in the void of her writer's block. In the three hours she had left before departing for St. Vincent's, she extracted the appointment calendar from my tightly packed briefcase and applied herself to the chore Larry had begun Friday afternoon, canceling my appointments for the next week. He'd compiled a list of the names and numbers appearing from March 23 through March 31, filling two pages of a legal pad.

There were eight lunches or dinners with editors and prospective publishers to cancel; four breakfasts or happy hours with writers; a week-long reunion planned six months in advance with two friends of twenty years, one of whom had traveled to New York from Juneau, Alaska; two job interviews at universities; an appointment with a Connecticut realtor; and a lecture to an audience of three hundred which, regrettably, could not be notified in advance that the speaker had become resolutely mute.

Larry had flipped the calendar pages back and forth, noting the dramatic change in landscape between my life in Ann Arbor and the one in Manhattan. The weeks preceding and following the last week in March were snow white, their blankness interrupted only by doctor and dental appointments, twice-weekly visits to the Ann Arbor Center for the Family, and regular, restorative lunches with Jane, the singular friend occupying my social life. In sharp relief, my New York days were so tightly jammed with appointments and dinner parties, phone numbers and notes about which packages in my briefcase to bring to which meetings, he could barely decipher the tiny script overflowing the margins. The coma landed in the most ambitious week I'd planned so far in 1984, requiring altogether seventeen phone calls to undo. For the three weeks preceding or following, only one or two calls would have been necessary. Larry had to wonder why I collapsed so publicly.

He canceled most of my appointments and left his list with Gina that morning, who completed the remaining calls. She recognized the editors' names from my letters and anecdotes over the past three years—while she'd become a pacifist in her own war with words, taking a conscientious objector's position and refusing to write, she remained a committed ally to mine. She knew two of the names on the list personally but the others were all strangers. Taking her duties as my East Coast ambassador seriously, she weighed the most tactful approach.

How much information would I want my professional network to have? Would these New Yorkers interpret my collapse as a sign of weakness, of fragility? Would it damage my credibility among editors to become known as "the writer in a coma?" In any crisis, it was generally a joke that came to Gina's rescue: "Mary Kay won't be at the meeting today," she rehearsed. "She's in an *intense* writer's block."

Gina wondered if my professional friends required a different strategy from the one she'd needed for the calls to the family yesterday morning, when her sudden bursts into prayerful assurances or black humor were not only tolerated but welcomed. Within two calls, however, any expectations of cool aloofness eroded completely. She found herself in the thick of a passionate family of women, whose professional response to a coma was anything but guarded.

"Oh my *god*!" Ellen exclaimed when Gina reached her at *Ms.*, undoubtedly with the same vibrant empathy she'd bestowed on me repeatedly. I gave Ellen liberal opportunity to exercise compassion, first through my divorce ("I'm going to be late again, Ellen—I stayed up all last night, but the thing just won't come together. My brain is a piece of Swiss cheese, and I keep dropping into these enormous *holes*. . ."), then through my subsequent poverty ("Oh, Ellen! A guy from the electric company was just here with an order to shut me off unless I gave him a check for sixty-four dollars. This means kiting a check at Kroger tomorrow. *Please* tell the business office to spring my check as soon as possible . . .). From my continuous state of emergency I overran most deadlines, and thought Ellen was surely approaching the limit of her mercy when I called in November of 1981 with the most provocative excuse to date. "Oh, Mary Kay, I'm so sorry." She mourned with me. "Don't worry—I'll take care of everything here . . . Call me when you get back from the funeral." Remarkably, after three years of sharing the sordid and sacred details of my life, I had not yet exhausted Ellen's capacity for mercy.

"I'm coming right over," she said to Gina that Monday morning. "What room is she in? How are *you*? It sounds like you have a terrible cold. Have you eaten yet—can I take you to lunch?" There were to be a dozen invitations to lunch and dinner, for the New York response to any profound dilemma was to make a reservation somewhere and reason it out at length, preferably over Nova Scotia salmon and wine. Gina felt instantly at home in my Manhattan family, which practiced aggressive nurturance with as much zeal as our immediate relatives. She knew exactly how to speak the highly exclamatory, emphatically italicized language of the natives.

"Oh no! How awful . . ." Julia moaned, asking Gina to hold for a moment while she closed the door of her office at *Working Woman*. "How is she . . . How are the kids—do they know? How are you and Larry holding up?" Gina spilled everything, down to the tremors she noted that morning around Larry's eyes, as if a nightmare hadn't been entirely resolved by waking up. Julia's questions obviously came from deep inside information, an intimate familiarity that gave Gina a clue about why it had taken me so long to move East.

Once I'd decided to follow my writing career to Manhattan, the search for schools and doctors and housing was preceded by a three-year reconnaissance for friends. The wrenching departure from close friendships in Fort Wayne taught me an indelible lesson about survival anywhere, and I wasn't anxious to make further geographic leaps without first securing my safety nets. I believed friends were as vital to my health as insulin or vitamin C—without them, my confidence shriveled and disorientation set in. Under the suffocating blanket of loneliness in Ann Arbor my brain couldn't process even the most straightforward cues: It scrambled routine messages from my nervous system and sent platoons of antibodies on surprise attacks against innocent organs. By 1984 I had exhausted my supply of dispensable body cells—and a few indispensable ones—and knew I would need every possible advantage in the city of seven million bananafish. Before moving to Manhattan, I conducted an extensive search for soul mates. Three showed up, to my great relief, among the women I worked for.

"Do you think women reveal too much about themselves in professional relationships?" Julia asked as we were leaving the Princeton Club after our first business lunch in 1981. Three hours earlier we'd surrendered our briefcases to the concierge in the lobby, participating in the charade that no business is conducted in men's clubs. We'd walked deliberately over the motto inscribed on the threshold of the dining room, which the carpet layers had taken pains to cut around: "Where women cease from troubling and the wicked are at rest." I halted before this bizarrely hostile message welcoming the new women members, wiping my feet thoroughly before stepping back onto the plush carpet.

In fact, Julia and I commenced our troubling almost immediately—before appetizers were cleared away we'd concluded our business and had moved onto richer turf, sharing feelings about families, marriage, men, motherhood, love, and yes, of course, first date or no, we talked about sex. There was an awkward moment under the canopy outside before we parted that afternoon, briefcases again in hand and fresh lipstick applied, both of us wearing a self-conscious embarrassment as if we'd just emerged from an intimate afternoon tryst. Were businesswomen too revealing with each other? Had we trespassed against the prescribed boundaries for conversations at the Princeton Club?

"Probably," I admitted to Julia. "Thank god, no?" Why would we ever aspire to the pathological, segregated wickedness of the motto in the lobby? I thought it was a mistake to accept the corporate habit of dividing the self in two, splitting emotion from intellect, passion from reason. I'd lived the satisfaction of bringing a whole self to the job during the years I worked with Joan and her staff in the auditor's office—all forty of us had enormous difficulty splitting ourselves in two again when her term in office expired.

I'd adopted the philosophy of my friend Cathryn, a psychology professor, who determined during her last job search to be a "one vita woman"—that is, a woman who doesn't abandon vital and complicated parts of herself when they become inconvenient. Undoubtedly, her impressive credentials in psychology would have invited more invitations to interviews if she hadn't also listed her accomplishments in *Women's Studies,* which prospective employers were likely to translate as "troublemaker."

In my own work, I'd been cautioned repeatedly to omit feminist views that might "alienate our readers in middle America"—odd advice, since my own radicalism was born in Indiana. Every woman I knew there was already feeling wide alienation from her apron and apple pie, with or without the permission of national magazine editors. Whenever I accepted an assignment under those limitations, I found myself working with only half a brain.

I'd been so fervent in my belief that women should bring both reason and passion to their work, that emotions were as honorable, as necessary, in the professions as in private life, Julia finally assigned me to write about it—one of the few deadlines I managed to meet in March of 1984. On her way to her office Monday morning, she stopped in the production department to check on the art and was pleased to see the essay laid out under the prominent headline and kicker:

AM I MY SISTER'S KEEPER?

STAYING OUT OF OTHER PEOPLE'S PERSONAL PROBLEMS IS A

GIVEN OF OFFICE LIFE. BUT WHAT SHOULD YOU DO WHEN

YOU SENSE THAT A COLLEAGUE IS IN REAL TROUBLE?

The essay answered those questions with an unequivocal "yes" and "everything imaginable," including a few unimaginable changes women might affect if we gave ourselves permission to bring undivided minds to work. When she received Gina's call Monday morning, Julia was composing the bio line for the article: "Mary Kay Blakeley is a writer living in Ann Arbor, Michigan, with her two sons, ages 8 and 10. She is currently at work on . . ."

". . . A coma in St. Vincent's Hospital," Julia repeated ruefully, but without disbelief, as if her inside information made the coma finally unsurprising. My crisis had been so predictable, in fact, Julia now saw the galleys on her desk as a kind of eight-page instructional manual, describing a psychological version of the Heimlich maneuver that would come in handy for editors of writers who suddenly choke on their own words. Before hanging up, Julia offered to meet Gina at the hospital, provide a guest room for visiting relatives, and of course, make dinner for her and Larry. She wanted to roast them a leg of lamb.

The strong affection of colleagues was the most valuable benefit of the free-lance life, the one I had most difficulty giving up. During my ongoing debate with Gina about quitting, I told her the one luxury of independence I'd miss most was that I never had to work for anyone I didn't respect—at least, not more than once. After making and receiving calls for three hours Monday morning,

taking down home numbers, and promising to "call back immediately," Gina realized I'd taken such extravagant advantage of
this luxury by 1984, I no longer worked for anyone I didn't love,
actually.

The most aggressively nurturant member of my professional
family—though there was heavy competition for the title—was
Phyllis, my New York agent and fairy godmother. For the first
three years I commuted to Manhattan, X-rays and all, the guest
room in Phyllis's Park Avenue apartment was my home. Our
business meetings were often conducted in our nightgowns, in her
library after dinner, both of us committed to seeing a bottle of
excellent red wine through to the end, power breakfasts the next
morning or no. I don't remember when Phyllis and I first blurred
the line between colleague and friend—if one had ever been there,
it was a flimsy border indeed. Her affection roared out of the
starting gate with vigorous advice—about my divorce, my geographic moves, my financial future. Phyllis loved me, she loved
my work, she loved Larry, and she just hated this coma. There was
no possibility she would accept my sudden withdrawal from the
scene quietly, without animated troubling.

Phyllis was the first friend Larry contacted from the emergency
room Friday morning. There was no need to be cautious in his
despair with her—she was already familiar with the vulnerable
man behind the pin-striped disguise. Her guest room had been his
home, too, when we spent a week last December working out the
logistics of his transfer from Washington. She greeted us at
breakfast those rocky mornings after Larry's nightmares about
getting fired and my exhausting, madly unrecallable dreams, the
week we made our debut as Manhattan's fun couple. It was Phyllis
who tapped her amazing network to produce the studio at a rent
we could manage, and he knew she would help him secure the
best medical care in New York. She went to work instantly,
making calls, gathering information, and, naturally, inviting him
to dinner.

Before wrapping up her ambassadorial duties Monday morning,
Gina checked in with Phyllis. Her journal had by then become a
chaotic mass of urgent notes and messages, abandoning reflections
about her own life to make room for a detailed documentation of
mine. Like Frank's journal, the pages reflected a whole disregard

for form and order, jamming messages from separate quarters of my life together ("Drop off X-rays at Mr. Sinai. Carrie's Fri. eve.—bring red Chianti"). Of the colleagues and friends Gina had contacted that morning, Phyllis alone was prepared for her call. She read a long list of questions for Gina to investigate at the hospital, a ritual that was to be repeated daily. Eventually Gina granted Phyllis a separate page in her journal, under the label "Phyllis's Twenty Questions." My sister's frantic method of taking dictation reflected the style of a mad poet at work:

Insulin is controlling glucose—
    Is this still a diabetic coma?
    What explanation for her condition now?
Is there anything that can be done medically to bring her out?

Type alpha brain waves—how classified?
    Brain activity?
    Motor activity?

When we get the results of the CATSCAN
                SONOGRAM—what
    are we looking for?

How many various medicines?
Names?
    Heart rate?

Greenbaum said: "Normally, we'd expect some activity by now."
    Why no activity?
    Do we have a clear indication of what's
                    abnormal?

The respirator—getting her off of it? Dangerous to stay on.
    How long?

Thursday night—M.K. was not getting oxygen.
    Are we talking about brain damage?

Perhaps to unfreight the worry of the last loaded question, Gina gave Phyllis an impromptu business report. She'd noticed a thick postal express package in my briefcase addressed to Phyllis, with a nine-dollar-and-thirty-five-cent stamp affixed, as if I'd intended to mail it before I left Ann Arbor but for some reason decided against it. Should she bring it to dinner that evening? Although Phyllis guessed it contained the materials she'd requested for our meetings that week—all of which had been canceled—she nevertheless told Gina to send it immediately by messenger.

Speed was essential to the equilibrium of New Yorkers; indecision anathema to the religion of Manhattan. Although easygoing Midwesterners often found the Eastern preference for states of emergency either intimidating or moronic, Gina adapted enthusiastically. She welcomed Phyllis's spirited approach to business-as-usual, circulating my work even if the author herself refused to show up for the party.

Gina removed the material from the express envelope, saving the postage for me, and read my cover letter to Phyllis before repackaging it for the messenger. Given my critical condition, she felt authorized to conduct a thorough search for clues to my state of mind. As usual, my business letter to Phyllis turned into a six-page, semi-stream-of-consciousness therapy session with myself.

It began with a response to an editor's critique of a query for an essay called "The Politics of Pretty," about the subtle and sometimes damaging effect attractiveness had on women's relationships with each other. The editor who'd requested the proposal was "very interested" but had some major concerns about my execution of the topic, particularly if the assignment "would tempt Ms. Blakely to ramble or indulge in feminist polemics." My response was not generated by any rational, thoughtful activity in my brain, but rather by the long delayed, vehement explosion of my spleen:

March 21, 1984

Dear Phyllis,

I read Miss X's letter several times. The yellow flag has certainly been waved.

I don't blame her for being uninterested in "rambling." I, too, am uninterested in it. I would be as embarrassed to ramble as I would to be pointless, her other worry. Reading her letter, an old problem seems imminent. While one paragraph asks for "a clear message and a strong point of view," another paragraph a little later wonders if that message and view "would work for our readers." Then there is the inevitable description, a few sentences later, of "who the reader is"—those damnable demographics (90 percent married, 95 percent homemaking, 60 percent working) that are supposed to define a woman's interest and limit her scope of comprehension.

Sigh.

No, no, I can't write for women's magazines under these terms. (Actually, I think I *could* write for the readers, if only we could get past the limiting statistics and gross censorship that prohibits honest conversation.) Please tell Miss X this for me: Ms. Blakely would not be willing to write it on spec. Nor would she be willing to outline her plots in more detail—she couldn't even guarantee sticking to an outline if she were to offer one. An essay, for Ms. Blakely, goes through several outlines, several drafts, several edits, and usually the final essay is only a distant cousin of the seed idea. She is disinclined to follow a subject through the A,B,Cs of it—rather, with unladylike abandon, she generally hops on the back of an issue and rides it home, taking excursions into interesting tangents wherever they crop up. This happens, despite her good intention to be an editor's dream free-lancer—without eccentricities, without artistic peculiarities.

In addition, Ms. Blakely doesn't give a hoot about a reader's particular credentials for reading her writing. She thinks of the reader as a woman just like herself, as if she were interested in, worried about, depressed over, exhilarated by, grieving for, or amused at the same things she is, and for this reason can hardly bear to hear what editors think of us. And since the only reason for putting oneself through the agony of writing in the first place is to ferret out some small truth about life, that truth turns out to be the same whether it is published for the housewives of *The New York Times* or the housewives of *Vogue* or the housewives of this magazine. Ms. Blakely is remarkably unconcerned about whether they are wearing makeup or pantyhose when they read her essays. What she is concerned about, to an almost paralyzing degree, is whether she has thought hard enough, whether the small truth she finds will hold up outside of a magazine page, and whether she has allowed money or editors or fame to skewer her ability to see some truth.

Ms. Blakely does not want to act like a big shit, but here is her deal: Consider a question, a crisis, a celebration that should be shared with Miss X's readers. Decide if Ms. Blakely should be involved. Discuss a fee, a length, and a deadline with her agent. Ms. Blakely will then delve in, mull it over, thrash around in the library, make threats at her typewriter, and eventually produce as clean and truthful a rendering of the topic as she is able. But if Miss X already knows the answer to the question/crisis/celebration, and knows exactly what effect certain information will have on her readers, then why not write the essay herself?

You'll have to clean this up for me, P.—I just needed to have a little "Ugly Out," as Joan used to say. I think we'd better take the "Politics of Pretty" off the bidding block. I don't seem to be able to approach the subject with any objectivity these days. I hardly know where all this rage is coming from. I had a bad case of the blues when I got out of the hospital this time—I absolutely can't believe this body of mine. Last Friday, while lunching downtown with Jane, another molar cracked in half. The second one in a week! (Which means two crowns, which means two more bills in the ever enlarging pile . . .) The doctors speculated that I'd clenched my teeth so hard coming out of the anesthetic, I must have fractured an already weakened area. I must find some means of coping with stress other than gritting it out.

But I prefer even this free-floating rage to the pervasive depression. I've been reading Norman Cousins this week, who recommends laughing your way to health. Why not? "Laughs are exactly as honorable as tears," Vonnegut says in *Palm Sunday*, "Laughter and tears are both responses to frustration and exhaustion, to the futility of thinking and striving . . . I myself prefer to laugh, since there is less cleaning up to do afterward." I'm not laughing at the moment, however. Someone has to say something funny first.

I've enclosed the photos and manuscripts you requested, but have second thoughts about circulating "Dear Pope." The clerk at Albert's Copy Center read it and asked, "Did you really *send* this letter?" He regarded me with a mixture of awe and regret, as if I'd just volunteered to be the next pagan in the Inquisition. Maybe that manuscript, like most of this letter, is a private fit of madness.

I've also enclosed Jane's latest column in the *Ann Arbor News*—you'll recognize the characters here. She wrote it after visiting me in the hospital—it's about the tube and strange diseases, but mostly it's the story of our friendship. It made me cry. Every time somebody says or does something nice to me, I cry. She mentions the postponement of Kay and Jerry's trip—they wouldn't leave for Florida while I was in the hospital, waiting for a firm diagnosis. But I finally convinced them they might as well worry in warm weather as in ice and snow.

Also: your bookkeeper should expect a call from my bank. It will be a test of creative economics to make me look credit-worthy. I'm buying another car. What happened to the last one? A little, sporty, red Le Car selected me out of all potential takers on I-94, for no reason I know of in this world except there was room for one more disaster in 1984, and creamed the bejesus out of the Mazda. Miraculously, I was not hurt—I was wearing my seat belt. I watched through the windshield as the car sped irrevocably across the ice toward the guard rail, but a grand and final vision of my life did not pass before me. "At times of mortal stress," Peter Benchley once wrote, "the engine of the human mind sometimes throws a rod." The rod my mind threw was this: "Here it comes. Try not to spill coffee all over yourself."

If death knocks, it will be vanity that answers my door.

So. I'm buying another car. The real tragedy, for me, is that I must again travel the grounds of hungry used-car salesmen. And the kids were sad to lose our little Mazda, which they had christened "Ms. Maz."

Tomorrow I get on the plane, tube and all, to spend ten glorious days with L. planning our future. Only three more months of this mad commute between vital parts of my life. If I could ever get all of my happiness in the same place—my kids, my love, my work—I would be one impossibly content, smug, fat little writer.

See you tomorrow, sweetie.

> Much love,
> M.K.

While her conversations with my editors that morning might have given Gina the impression that my future in New York looked exceptionally promising, the letter to Phyllis revealed that, from my own perspective, the direction my writing seemed to be headed for was the nearest toilet. I'd confessed my deep embarrassment to Gina repeatedly, whenever I compromised an essay to fit the narrow standard considered "acceptable for our readers."

"Promise you won't buy the magazine when it comes out," I would beg her after a manuscript had been mangled in-house. "I had to sell my byline—I needed the eggs." She generally kept the promises I extracted from her not to buy the magazines, but spent an hour every month standing in the aisles at Kroger slowly flipping the pages. While Gina suffered the same scrupulous pickiness with words, she rarely agreed with my harsh evaluations. "I'm sorry they cut the part you read on the phone," she would call after her library hour in Kroger, "but I still hear you there on the page, just all over the place."

Since I'd described my writing traumas to Gina in more tedious detail than even a dedicated bibliophile would find interesting, she naturally suspected these distresses contributed in some way to my current mute condition. When she studied my calendar for the last week in March, where I was clearly destined to sign more contracts, she was convinced that the shame I felt over my writing crimes had everything to do with my sudden and complete silence.

Since she knew I regarded a cold as a physical mantra the body performed to send a wish to the brain, she wondered what gigantic message the coma was impressing on my mind. With a tremendous shudder she recognized that the mild griefs accumulating through the last two years had mushroomed into a monstrous cloud of depression. Her mind flooded with insights about who, why, what contributed to the fallout of despair.

Last week on the phone, she had argued vigorously against my decision to quit free-lancing: "In one of your lifetimes, M.K., you must have yearned to be a writer. Maybe a really *good* writer," she'd said. "From what I'm reading, I think you're stuck with those yearnings. I'm not at all sure you can give them up now—you could postpone them, if you want. But that just means you'll have to come back again, to finish the job."

She had been fervent in this singular belief last week, but when she sat down next to my bed that afternoon and picked up my hand, her faith had melted considerably. In the one-way conversation at the hospital Monday afternoon, she would plead for leniency, urging me to find a path of peace for myself.

"Okay. You don't have to be a free-lance writer. I don't know what kind of writer you have to be," she said softly. Her voice sounded hoarse, as if she had been crying. "Just come back. Just come back in this body and let's figure out who you are."

6

THE RIDDLE OF
RESPONSIBILITY

VIVID DREAMS FLOODED into my sleep all night—at least I guessed it was night, from the hushed, candlelit quality of the voices periodically drifting through my cell. I couldn't be sure though; because in the strange, dim atmosphere in which I was suspended, time had become fuzzy and unstable. Days came and went without the familiar borders of alarm clocks or the evening news, without any deliberate action from me except to keep thinking. It was erratic thought, certainly, and it didn't seem to be exclusively *my* thought. I wasn't even sure whether I was asleep or awake—I seemed to be both at once. Sounds and voices I identified as real actions, real people, would suddenly melt into the bizarre plots and characters of surreal dreams. It was as though my brain were leaking badly, bleeding fact into fiction until reality was as unreliable as a melting Dali timepiece.

I longed to press the heels of my palms hard against my temples, to get a firm grip on the looseness in my head, but this small physical relief was doomed by the cloth handcuffs fastening my wrists to iron bars. I imagined the bed restraints were part of the punishment for my offense, whatever it was I'd done to cause the woman with the bright lights to summon the guards a few days ago. My incarceration had something to do with the children, I thought, maybe something I'd written. Or the car accident I dreamed . . . I kept forgetting.

The rehabilitation program in this peculiar prison was designed to cure inmates of forgetfulness: We were forced to remember everything we ever said or did, to keep watching the same dreams over and over until we knew them by heart. There were no breaks from the relentless drilling, except once or twice a night when the images on screen blurred or stopped altogether. Prisoners had to remain stationary then, staring at a blank screen until the guards showed up to rewind the reel, so to speak.

They arrived every few hours to inspect the tubes in my mouth and arms, then would poke a needle into my thigh to keep me alert and restart the dreams. My captors were alternately kind and punishing, employing the same indoctrination method Sister Theresa used effectively with her second graders, when she bored the multiplication tables and Baltimore Catechism indelibly into our heads. It seemed brutal at the time but for years afterward I could recite the multiples of seven and the answers to "Who is God?" and "Why does He love us?" instantly, without having to think.

Visitors were allowed into my cell for long periods but my tubes and handcuffs were never removed, impeding any real conversation. And even when guests arrived, the dreams kept rolling inside my head. I could only lend Gina one ear that afternoon when she brought her stories and music—it was rude but I was desperate to finish my assignments. I was convinced my release from this paralyzing imprisonment depended on memorizing my dreams, on being able to recite them flawlessly for the final test. Why else the intense cramming?

My powers of concentration were pitiful. I memorized my life without much passion for the material. I had to know exactly what each character said and felt, but wasn't required to experience their emotions myself. This was fortunate, given my limited capacities. Since my personal opinion about the life I'd lived was irrelevant on the final exam, I concentrated solely on remembering the facts. From this detached perspective I watched myself, maybe for the fifth or sixth time, say good-bye to the kids in Ann Arbor. I saw myself sitting in the passenger seat as the red Corolla pulled up to the curb in front of a neighbor's house late that March afternoon, after pizza at the Brown Jug, after a few video games at the Crosseyed Moose—after, in effect, all postponements of good-bye had been spent.

Marie waves from the porch, holding her front door open and grinning despite the brisk, cold wind, while her three-year-old daughter creeps up behind her and slips her hand into the pockets of her mother's jeans. It must tickle because Marie starts laughing, and her pint-sized attacker immediately gets the giggles too. The small girl is invisible except for her forearms and bobbing head which, tilting sideways, appears to be sprouting from her mother's hip. From the curb I see a four-armed, two-headed, goofy-looking alien, hiccuping helplessly with the giggles. Ryan and Darren, in the backseat of the Corolla, laugh.

The boys liked to stay with Marie instead of riding with us to the airport—they preferred the lively company of her family room to the quiet adults who occupied the Corolla these days, though they were careful about exposing this prejudice. Like most children of divorce, Ryan and Darren had developed a keen sensitivity to the fragile emotions of their parents. When either one of us sank into a prolonged, moody silence without apparent provocation, it worried them. While those regrettable lapses in attention could happen anywhere—in the checkout line at the grocery store, the waiting room of the doctor's office, even on the soccer sidelines once during one of the goalie's most spectacular saves—the boys knew the preoccupied silences were guaranteed to show up on the way to the airport. The atmosphere in the car became even moodier when the kids weren't there to relieve it, but parental mood elevation was only their sometime job. Their major task, at ages eight and ten, was to be happy themselves. Under the altered circumstances of their environment in 1984, this was more difficult than they'd imagined.

I cannot return Marie's jubilant wave as I step onto the curb, needing both hands to hold the car door open while clutching a light cardigan sweater closed against the wind. During parka weather in Michigan, I am dressed for tee-off in Palm Springs.

My winter coat . . . yes, I remembered. My winter coat was in Joan's guest closet in Fort Wayne, 140 miles away. "How could you forget your *coat*?" she asked after I drove back to Ann Arbor without it. "It's February, for godsakes!" In my growing amnesia last month, I had forgotten winter was cold. My body had been numb so long, frostbite felt normal.

Darren emerges from the backseat and hugs me good-bye. The mother I play still loves to bury her lips in the boy's hair, a habit begun in infancy. Suddenly the scene shifts and I am nuzzling the downy top of Ryan's head ten years earlier, searching for the diamond-shaped soft spot on his crown.

We are on the way home from the hospital in the cozy, camel interior of our British racing-green MG, the wedding gift Howe and I gave each other in Europe the summer of 1970. Behind the wheel, Howe looks over and smiles ecstatically. His joy is so expansive I think he might leave the road—perhaps the ground altogether. He is a man of such passion that the baby, merely by wrapping two small fingers around his father's knuckle, can make him laugh until he weeps. Howe thinks this son is the most fabulous gift we have given each other so far. I do, too.

Under the soft down of the baby's newborn hair, my lips find the tender soft spot, pumping with the beat, the beat, the beat. It thrills me to touch that pulsating membrane with my lips, as close as I will ever come to kissing his heart directly. Sipping gently, I slowly drink the intoxicating essence of Ryan Blake, three days old. Something liquid releases inside me. I never expected happiness—simply human, mortal happiness—could be this powerful.

The tube in my mouth issued a congested, gurgling sound, like an excessively rude theatergoer clearing a clogged throat during an intimate moment on screen. Swallowing hard and pushing feebly, I tried to eject it with my tongue. I was panicked the tube would suck dry the reservoir of liquid happiness filling my chest. That deliriously fluid joy, so abundant ten years ago, was hard stuff to come by these days.

By 1984 it was no longer possible to drink freely from the kids' skulls—at least, not as greedily as I once did. After ten years the delicate membranes on their crowns had grown into calcified bone, much harder to saturate with kisses. Sometimes, sitting in the car or watching TV, I would pat their heads and imagine the beat pumping steadily below, but I had to ration this pleasure carefully now. Their heads were increasingly their own turf, under new ownerships that permitted only limited access to parents. They still indulged my incessant patting behavior at home, but drew the line now against displays of blatant motherhood on public sidewalks.

" 'Bye, Mom," Darren says, releasing himself from the hug before I store up a full ten-day supply of him.

"Have a good trip," he says and smiles, but with an odd resignation, as though he knows I won't. He doesn't mention his spooky premonition of the night before, when he imagined my plane flying into a kind of twilight zone from which "you'll never come back," but that thought or a similar one clearly crosses his mind. He hangs on the curb a moment, looking down as he balances on the ball of one foot, thoughtfully considering his farewell. Finally, he decides on the all-purpose, oddly secular prayer he recites during the small emergencies that crop up in his life. It's the message he received in a fortune cookie, at age six, and it still holds enormous power for him:

"Work hard and you shall be rewarded," he says.

I'd made a big ceremony of opening fortune cookies with the kids that night, when I had taken them out to dinner before the move to Ann Arbor two years earlier. I'd signed the papers for the sale of the Fort Wayne house that week and we were all a little blue about leaving the Rainbow Room. The kids tried to be brave about the impending move, eager to be back in daily touch with their father but apprehensive about leaving their friends. It was probably guilt over complicating their formative years with divorce that prompted the grand promises of frequent dinners with their dad and colorful circus tents for each of their rooms, with extra beds for hosting overnight guests. The restaurant was closing by the time I finished proposing a life of perfect harmony for them in Ann Arbor, a vision made possible by ignoring the depressing facts in my Children of Divorce file. Despite the late hour and the low drone of an approaching vacuum cleaner, I relit the wick in the bottom of the mesh-covered candle on our table and ceremoniously presented the plate of fortune cookies.

Perhaps because there were no First Communions or Confirmations in his past to compete with it, my youngest son had his first spiritual experience in Fort Wayne, Indiana, under the scrutiny of the clean-up crew in a Chinese restaurant. Darren thought his message, miraculously unbaked inside the crisped, brown container, meant he was lucky. He believed he would work hard; he believed he would be rewarded. He recited the fortune whenever he felt anxious, like a personal mantra for calming himself down before math tests or finding a friend at day camp. Darren loved peace.

That was actually the message in my cookie that night: "You love peace." I remembered writing down the date and taping it into my journal with mixed feelings—I did in fact love peace, but the fortune seemed pointless without any instructions on where to get it. I was terrified about moving to Ann Arbor, still unrecovered from the bitter hostilities the divorce unleashed. While I loved peace and pined its absence, Darren worked hard at it. Even his Halloween costume the previous year became a kind of political statement against aggression. He had made a large cardboard triangle, painted it yellow, and become a walking YIELD sign. Given our enormous blind spots that year, neither Howe nor I knew what gave him the idea.

"What kind of kid dresses up as a Yield sign?" Howe had asked, watching Darren merge cautiously with an unruly band of miniature pirates and hunchbacks clamoring down the street. He was invariably the last to open his bag on the lighted porches, a lucky position he discovered by accident when he noticed he was collecting not only his rationed treat but any surplus neighbors brought to the door. When his more aggressive companions drained ready supplies and he had to wait while the retired teacher down the street fetched more, his patience was rewarded with a double share. Unconsciously practicing the yin and yang of trick-or-treating, he simultaneously trailed behind and came out ahead. His older brother, eyeing his copious loot when they came home that night, artfully suggested they combine the booty and share everything. Darren yielded instantly, with an easy-come-easy-go shrug.

The magic chemistry of patience and generosity, mixed together, produces a magnetic field around certain people and for Darren, it was a curse against his beloved peace. Friends caught in the strong attraction were sometimes gripped with a manic possession—before he turned five he was frequently the center of hot disputes over seating arrangements in the preschool car pool.

I turned around at a red light once to issue an exasperated warning to the occupants of the backseat but stopped when Darren, squeezed tightly on both arms by two rival friends pulling in opposite directions, pleaded wildly: "Mom! It's not my fault! I'm not the one trying to be's with them—they're the ones trying to be's with me!" Wide-eyed, he looked a little fragile to have so much desire riding on him. I knew the feeling.

While the wind shivers through my open cardigan, Darren stands attentively on the curb waiting for my dismissal. His fortune cookie prayer, as I interpret it, is an earnest effort to brave the twilight zone. In this boy's secular catechism, helplessness is the major sin; hard work the hedge against despair; peace the reward. He delivers his message with so much heart, a large gratitude wells up in me. I suppose every mother sees something beatific in the faces of her children and, god knows, this mother does. The delicious liquid bubbles down the back of my throat and I feel light-headed joy.

The huge gratitude elevating me, I supposed, was my allotted measure of divine ecstasy. Though I've never received the spectacular jolts selected members of my family have been struck with, the low-level inspiration of children provided as much regular awe as I could safely handle. Clearly, Darren wanted me to share the comforting belief of his fortune. I yielded at once.

"Okay," the mother promises, "I'll work very hard. You too, huh?" Darren nods vigorously and hugs me again, then heads happily for the porch where the giggling alien and a lighter vein of conversation await him. Ryan hops onto the curb and it's immediately clear there will be no lingering crown-kissing. The perpetual blue baseball cap is firmly in place.
" 'Bye, Mom. . . . See you later, Dad," he says evenly, delivering swift and equitable good-byes that slight no one. His sober, careful farewell alerts me once more to the stunning changes in him. The self-absorbed oblivion of his prolonged boyhood is melting under the heat of divorce. Suddenly, small details are important to him. When he forgets to clear his dishes at the table, or adapt to the mood of an arriving parent and express adequate

affection for the departing one, it causes upsetting cloudbursts of
temper and tears. He thinks he can control the weather in his
postnuclear family by remaining calm and cool himself. Before
my eyes, I see the carefree young boy evolving into a guarded,
dutiful son. The transformation is as amazing to me as the baby
I watched ten years ago, pulling himself up on the ledge of the
coffee table and wobbling out of infancy on brand-new legs.

I'd caught him with a laugh as he toppled into my arms at the
end of that first solo trek, while hard lumps formed in my throat.
Those lumps would reappear continuously through the next
decade. One would expect to develop some coping mechanism for
the possessive seizures that continuously gripped me, but even
when I anticipated future stages they still took my breath away.

When Ryan delivered his careful good-bye on the curb in front of
Marie's, I lost all detachment from the mother on the screen and
a rock-hard lump jammed against the tube in my throat. I
recognized the end of his long procrastination in growing up, a
delay caused not so much by a refusal of responsibility as his deep
attachment to childhood. Funny, happy, curious, exceptionally
locomotive, he loved being a kid. He was the kind who had to be
reminded fifty times to hang up his wet towels or to put the cap
back on the toothpaste, because he'd become completely absorbed
in examining his pickled toes or seeing how far up his nose he
could look in the mirror. During the small domestic skirmishes in
the wake of these repeated neglects, his quick apologies and
cheerful repairs saved him over and over.

The beat pulsing through this boy was so easily stimulated, he
needed constant attention and a finely tuned structure to maintain
his equilibrium. It had been a disaster to send him to a school with
open classrooms and self-directed programs in first grade, which
left his mind reeling in all directions at once. He had just settled
into the new rules of another school when his family cracked
apart the next year, throwing him for a loop again. Divorce made
his life unpredictable and bizarre: wet towels on the bathroom
floor now provoked hyperbolic threats, his reading scores were
dropping, and twice this week, his mother forgot to make dinner.
Dinner! It wasn't even fun to snooker his younger brother out of
his Halloween candy last October because of a strange new

impulse to take care of him. He finally had no choice, in 1984, but to grow up. He put on the blinder of his baseball cap to keep himself focused, reducing his vision to one play at a time.

In lieu of his warm bear hug Ryan grips me awkwardly on both arms, the tentative, serviceable embrace he uses with me now. This is the worst part of 1984, dealing with the freakish tube between his mother's ribs. When I assure him "I'm fine!" he can't believe it doesn't hurt. I see his panic clearly because the new hug puts us almost two feet apart, his arms stiffening when he touches me, as if receiving painful shocks of electricity. He throws a blasé expression over his face to blanket his fear, like an undersized Gary Cooper toughing it out in High Noon. *The disguise is such a transparent failure, it's heartbreaking to watch. He can't wait to let go but is ashamed for me to see how much, and bows the beak of his baseball cap. His eyes disappear.*

This is no time for a mother to become emotional and embarrassing, but I do. My eyes begin to water and lumps engorge my throat. What brilliant words will Mrs. Cooper pass along to her son at high noon? I noisily clear my throat and attempt a light-hearted voice:

"I'll miss you, buddy," I say gutturally, sounding like an inexplicably cheerful drowning victim.

"Miss you, too," he replies automatically, as he must, duty-bound by his strict code of equal affection. I raise my hand to lift his blue beak, then hesitate. I want one more exchange directly with his eyes, but am unable to focus my own.

The tube gurgled loudly again as Ryan's blue cap blurred into watery relief. I tried to ignore the interruption and refocus the dream, afraid to miss the next critical scene, the telling dialogue sure to show up on the final test. My son was being altered in an important way, I knew, but my concentration was shattered by a sudden pain in my ribs and the unpleasant gurgling in my throat. The liquid filling my chest had reached eye level by then, and I had the sensation of drowning. I tried to cough but managed only to squeeze my eyelids, an involuntary wince that started a small rivulet of warm water coursing down my cheeks. The dream vanished completely, run afoul by technical difficulties in the projection room. Leaking badly, inside and out, I waited for help.

I remembered the last time I lost my detachment from the characters on screen, unable to focus my watery eyes in a darkened auditorium in Michigan last month. I was sitting between Ryan and Darren, trying to mop up my wet cheeks and nose before the lights came back on. The kids wanted to see *Jaws* that night but, mistakenly opting for the softer drama of human relationships, I took them to see *Terms of Endearment* instead. Just when you thought it was safe to go out again . . . Hollywood knocked on your door.

It had already been an emotionally rocky day. The laboratory report from the pathologists at the University of Louisiana arrived in the morning mail, canceling the last hope for a diagnosis and treatment of the mysterious shadows in my lungs. The check from *Vogue* was not in the mail, however, contrary to the promise I had extracted from the bookkeeper six days ago. I had thirty-seven dollars and some odd cents in my checking account.

On the weekends, the automatic teller at my bank was programmed to reject withdrawals from customers with balances lower than fifty, so I had to pay for our tickets that Saturday night with a handful of quarters and dimes I scavenged together. Since the Mazda had been totaled in the accident the previous month, the boys and I hiked the two miles into town, saving our one-way cab fare for the ride home. There was an unwritten rule that required women to travel the grounds of divorce on foot, I'd told my friend Alice when her aging station wagon broke down shortly after her separation. That way, we missed nothing of the scenery.

My cheeks heated with shame as the woman behind the ticket window counted out eight dollars in coins, while the people in line behind me softly stomped their feet against the packed snow to keep their blood moving. In the lobby I bought one large soda for the boys to share but waited until we were seated in the dark auditorium to open my backpack and hand them the bags of popcorn I smuggled in from home. The nylon crackled stiffly after the cold hike and the popcorn inside the paper bags had hardened into frozen white puffs, coated with congealed margarine. I really hated poverty.

"You know you're really poor when you have to put water on the cornflakes," comedienne Elaine Boosler once joked. I remembered the line that afternoon when I checked the supply of milk in the refrigerator, after the mail came up empty again. I figured I had one more mail drop, then it was check-kiting time at Kroger again. In my case, poverty neither built character nor rallied a fighting spirit; it made me curse anonymous bookkeepers in New York and cry over spilled milk at the dinner table.

I knew I was in trouble from one of the first scenes in *Terms of Endearment*, when a blunt but truthful mother warns the idealistic (and stoned) young Emma, the night before her wedding to a charming but irresponsible man: "You are not special enough to overcome a bad marriage." Passionately in love, Emma doesn't understand what her mother means until ten years, three children, and one delinquent mortgage later, when she faces the glaring cashier at a supermarket. The bill is forty-four dollars. Emma is about five dollars short.

"You don't have enough *money*?!" her eldest son, Tommy, moans, dying of embarrassment. Among other things, she has to take a six-pack of Clark Bars ("Mom, you promised I could *have* something!") out of the order. Her self-esteem deflating with the grocery bill, she ineffectively appeases the unhappy boy by returning a single Clark Bar to her order while the disapproving cashier and customers look on. The kindly banker who turned down her application for a second mortgage that week is standing in line behind her. He offers to pay the balance and chastises the rude cashier. It's the nicest gesture Emma's received from another adult in several years. The deep gratitude in her eyes clearly suggests that this small kindness and a few dollars will become the price of her fidelity.

Emma's humiliation in the checkout lane was enough to water my eyes that Saturday night, but by the time she was dying of cancer at the end of the movie the hydrants were wide open. Each time I blew my nose, the kids heard the tube in my ribs whistle audibly under my sweater. They kept asking me if I was all right.

"I'm *fine!*" I whispered hoarsely, waving a fresh Kleenex like a white truce flag. But another siege commenced in the end when Tommy, long deprived of candy bars, comes to say good-bye to his mother in the hospital. The smoldering anger on the young boy's face shows he can't forgive her—for arguing with Daddy and "driving him away," for not having enough money, but especially for this last, unspeakable offense of dying on him. Emma's weakened condition leaves her only a few minutes to help the resentful boy reach the words he'll need to remember having said later, perhaps the only words that will protect him from the wild grief ahead.

"Do you love me?" Frank asked repeatedly in the ward at ISPI, on the grounds of Elgin, over and over during our last weekend in Fort Wayne. How many times had I closed my eyes and remembered his manic grin lighting up as I hollered impatiently, "*Yes!* I already *told* you a hundred times! Jesus Christ, Frank, you've got to come down . . . You've got to come back to reality." Frank had to know how important those words, shouted or not, would eventually become, because he made me recite them again and again, until it was impossible to picture his face now without immediately hearing myself shout heatedly: "Yes, goddammit, I *love* you!"

Possessed with the energy of the beat, he never tired of exacting mad commitments of love from his family and friends, but how did a mother whose body was disintegrating rapidly with an invisible, mysterious disease help a young boy reach those words when his mind was stuck on Clark Bars? With the entire contents of a purse-sized Kleenex package already crumpled damply in my lap, I knew it was time to head for the ladies' room. But I had to know what Emma would do.

"Tommy, be sweet . . . be sweet," she coaxes him hoarsely, "and stop trying to pretend like you hate me. I mean, it's silly."

"I like you." The boy shrugs noncommittally, unable to cross the barricades of his resentment. Emma sighs, knowing she will have to carry him the remaining distance. She props herself up weakly on one elbow and addresses her final words straight into his eyes, as if wiring around unhearing ears and resistant lips to sear an indelible message directly on his brain:

"In a few years, when I haven't been around to be on your tail about something . . . you're gonna realize that you love me. And maybe you're gonna feel badly because you never told me. But *don't*. I know that you love me. So don't ever do that to yourself, all right?"

"Okay," the boy says unconvincingly.

"Okay?" Emma asks again, with spirit, wanting to hear some passion to assure her the message took.

"I said *okay*," Tommy repeats, with enough heat for the words to be branded permanently in his head. Her job over, Emma kisses the boys good-bye.

I was Emma for weeks afterward. I imagined myself dying, with only a few minutes left to find the right words to comfort survivors after my death. Extracting a genuine "I love you" from a boy struggling in the turbulent wake of divorce was at least as difficult, it seemed to me, as hunting sharks in a leaky boat. And possibly, just as consequential. Despite rehearsing graceful exit lines for myself through many imagined deaths, my live performance three weeks later on the curb in front of Marie's was clumsy and awkward.

I was suddenly unsure of my part in this drama—was I dying or not? If so, I played an exceptionally vigorous corpse. Doctors who met me first through my X-rays could hardly believe the lively, highly colored patient they eventually greeted in person. I'd felt slightly fluish all day, but who died of the flu? Yet the premonition lingered.

And if I were actually slated for the twilight zone in the next scene, as it were, was it really in the best interest of my ten-year-old son—working so hard to keep his emotions under wraps with his baseball cap—to deliberately unravel his cover? I knew it hurt like hell to lose someone you loved; did it hurt less if you never acknowledged affection? Was Ryan's distance that afternoon a declaration of turf, a privacy I was bound to honor—or was it inexperience with grief, a handicap that called for help? I couldn't get an accurate reading from his face, shielded below the blue beak. With only minutes left before departure time, I took a chance. I lowered my hand from his cap, leaving his cover intact, and placed it under his chin. I applied no pressure. The beak came up slowly and a pair of opaque eyes, determined to be disapassionate, greeted mine. That was the scene coming up in the dream when my equipment failed, the one I most needed to review.

"I love you," I remembered saying, knowing exactly what his response would have to be. This boy who insisted on fair play, who called even the unintentional fouls between his parents, operated from a code of decency that obliged him to meet all comers halfway.

"Love you, too," he replied, naturally. I then freed him from our stiff-armed hug and he ran for the porch.

I waved good-bye to the boys again as the Corolla pulled away from the curb. Frank no doubt would have given in to the impulse to roll down the window and holler once more for the record— "Do you love me?" He had no shame about causing public embarrassment. The lumps engorging my throat rendered me mute but, already guilty of trespassing on their turf, I wouldn't have said more anyway. Perhaps that was the crime I'd committed against the children—some deficiency in my good-byes to them. Because I wouldn't risk embarrassing them, maybe I hadn't given them enough words.

Or maybe I'd given too many. As Dr. Whiteside pointed out during our session that week, I had an unfortunate habit of requiring everyone I loved to feel exactly as I did. Practicing passion by committee may have kept my own in check, but it didn't leave anyone else room to move around. The pattern was certainly manifest on the curb: I promise to work hard but you must, too; I'll miss you if you miss me; I love you, "Love you, too."

The impulse to persuade, to manipulate agreement, was legitimate for a writer to indulge, but a mother, given her enormous power over the most vulnerable human beings, had to be careful with it. So perhaps that had been my crime—an inappropriate use of "Follow Me!" What's more, I gave the order without any idea where I was going.

7

THE 500-PAGE DIVORCE

THE TUBE IN MY THROAT gurgled noisily as I drowned from the inside out. Floating blindly in the dark, mind fogged, I knew I was in serious trouble. This same peculiar liquid sensation had rippled through me once before, eight years ago, just before I lost consciousness the night Darren was born. My swollen body dissolved rapidly into a pool of blood that night, forcing Darren into independence two months before he was due.

Twice during the summer of '75, I'd experienced a phenomenon my obstetrician identified as "breakthrough bleeding," a symptom of placenta previa. In my second pregnancy, the embryo implanted low in my uterus—the last stop, as it were, before the final exit. Since the placenta grew into the lower area of my womb, the embryo had to occupy the second floor, so to speak. From the very beginning, Darren's approach to life was singularly unorthodox.

Bursts of fetal growth or movement put pressure on the delicate placental tissue, causing it to tear and break with profuse bleeding. It was completely painless bleeding, with no forewarning, like the sudden drenching at the end of a pregnancy when the amniotic fluid breaks out of the sac before birth. The first occurrence produced only light spotting, alerting me to the condition. But the second episode happened while I was sitting on the floor of Alice's family room, planning lectures for the women's studies class we taught together, and soaked her rug with nearly a pint of blood.

Fortunately the carpet was deep red and Alice the kind of friend who wasn't unglued by biological accidents. Among my feminist friends in Fort Wayne, it was politically incorrect to feel compromised by any aspect of female biology. We were cultivating pride, a radical change for a generation of women who grew up thinking of our sexual organs as the remote and shameful "down there"—as in, "Don't touch yourself down there." The deep alienation we had to overcome was clear that semester when a guest speaker, a local midwife, brought a speculum and medical dummy named Ginny Vagina to class. It took one of the women, a fifty-six-year-old mother who had given birth eight times, almost an hour to come up to the front of the classroom, hold the doctor's instrument in her own hand, and have a look "down there."

She was fairly certain her religion forbade looking directly at a cervix, even a plastic one, but these were revolutionary times. By the summer of '75 the Boston Women's Health Book Collective had sold more than a million copies of *Our Bodies, Ourselves,* fathers were finally being permitted into hospital delivery rooms, and the home birth movement was well underway. The widespread challenge to old taboos occasionally inspired acts of overzealous enthusiasm—in her research that summer Alice uncovered a recipe for "Placenta Stew," invented during a celebration after a home birth somewhere in Montana. ("Can you *believe* it?" She laughed, reading the ingredients over the phone. "It's supposed to be high in protein.") Looking at the raw material on her rug that afternoon, it was hard to imagine how anyone had been remotely tempted to think of stew. But neither could we quite comprehend, after mopping up the rug and then me, how there could be anything left inside to nourish the baby. Despite repeated obstetrical assurances, I worried about brain damage.

It wasn't labor pain that woke me in the middle of the night two weeks later, but a warm, sticky fluid soaking the sheets. I got out of bed and hurried down the hall to the bathroom. As the fluorescent lights slowly blinked on, I was confronted with the bloody evidence of a massive breakthrough. My legs were two red rivers, flowing over a clotted red delta at my feet and seeping into the crevices of the white tiled floor. I wiped up the blood with a bath towel, then layered several more on the floor and laid down on my back, elevating my feet on the side of the tub to stop the hemorrhage.

Red streaks trickled down the porcelain surface below my dripping legs, but the bleeding didn't stop. In minutes, the towels under my back were saturated, soaking my arms and head in a warm liquid pool. As I bled unstoppably in the middle of the night on August 28, 1975, my dominant thought was this: Would I have time to clean up the bathroom before I passed out?

Give me good housekeeping or give me death—it was humiliating, the trivial thoughts that flooded my mind during mortal emergencies. Closing my eyes, I tried to calm down. I breathed deeply to relax tense muscles. I even prayed: "Keep your head," I whispered, patting my swollen abdomen and speaking for both of us, "Just please keep your head." My habitual method of coping with disaster, including traumatic breakthroughs, was to surrender vital parts of my body but by all means hang on to my head. Generally, by keeping my head and shouting "I'm fine!" I managed to convince myself that I was—at least, until a damning X-ray or critical lab scan betrayed me.

I rolled over on my side and got dizzily to my feet, intending to wake Howe, but my knees buckled with the first step. Grabbing a towel bar behind the toilet to break the fall, my wet hand slipped and dropped me heavily on the seat. Dazed and confused, I watched the water in the bowl turn from pink to dark red as the color drained out of me with alarming speed. It was immensely disorienting to bleed profusely but feel no pain, as if the stream flooding through me were from someone else's wound. I shivered with the spooky feeling of being possessed. The room began spinning, and I felt my mind unravel.

I slid from the seat onto my knees and crawled into the hall, making it only halfway to the bedroom before my arms collapsed. I called Howe's name as the lights went out. A wind began to howl and I lost consciousness.

Thirty minutes later, as the paramedics lifted my stretcher and rolled it into the ambulance, I became fuzzily aware of the sounds and motion around me. In the few seconds before the doors slammed shut, I saw Howe standing on the dark street, red lights flashing eerily across his tense face, holding eighteen-month-old Ryan tightly in his arms. Awakened abruptly by the live nightmare outside his nursery, the baby frowned sleepily and rubbed his eyes, blinking uncomprehendingly at the jerking movements under the strobe lights. He squinted narrowly into the dim interior of the ambulance, staring at my face under the oxygen mask. "Mom?" he asked.

Truth dawned with wrenching agony as he recognized me and

understood I was being taken away. His eyes and mouth exploded in wide open protest. "Mmmooooooom!" he cried, dropping his pacifier to the street and reaching out frantically with both arms. The doors clanged shut before I could wave back and assure him "I'm fine!" For years afterward, I would remember his agonized expression whenever I heard the piercing sound of an approaching ambulance. The siren always reminded me of the soulful wail of a child crying:

"Mmmooooooom . . . Mmmooooooom . . . Mmmooooooom!"

Two days after the ambulance delivered me to the emergency room, I was awakened from a drugged sleep by an intense, throbbing pain in my abdomen. I shivered in the aftermath of a chilling nightmare—then wondered if the visit from Howe and the pastor of St. Mary's had been real. I remembered some urgency about choosing a name. Howe held my hand and said we had to make a decision right away; Father Tom was going to baptize the baby in the hospital that morning in case . . . just in case. Howe said we could have another ceremony later, with all the relatives, if the baby . . . if we wanted to. They were deliberately vague about the facts prompting their visit, trying not to alarm me, and they assured me everything would be taken care of if I could just give them a name.

It should have been a simple task, but when I went to the cabinet in my head where such information was usually stored, I discovered everything had been rearranged. After liquefying two days earlier, my brain had apparently resolidified in another shape. It was as if a new tenant had moved in since I'd vacated my mind and changed all the furniture around to suit her own tastes. Even the fixed truths had shifted—I had trouble recognizing the multiples of seven and had to think hard about "Who is God?" and "Why does He love us?" Instead of answers I found only more questions: "Why 'He'?" "Who am *I*?"

Nothing was automatic. Howe and Father Tom had had to wait long minutes while I thought ponderously over the answer to their simple question. They had smiled indulgently and leaned closer when I finally whispered a response, as though they were straining to understand a person with a speech impediment. I remembered the enormous effort it took to draw each syllable through the sore muscles in my throat, but I couldn't remember what I'd said. What name had I given them from my unraveled mind?

Christened in his incubator, sans godparents, Darren Oliver—whom I'd intended to name Oliver Darren—slept through his first induction to the faith. I had just awakened from my own drugged stupor, trying to recall what happened, where I was, when a stranger in a white lab coat suddenly materialized next to my bed. Using a language I could barely comprehend, he had given a lengthy clinical description of the baby's condition and then asked, clearly irritated with my dull response: "Are you at all interested in this?"

My son was only two days old—I hadn't even met him yet—and I'd already established myself as a bad mother. It was an easy label to acquire, especially in the contemptuous atmosphere of hospital and psychiatric wards. I was at first enraged by the pediatrician's arrogant judgment, but a young mother's fury lasts only as long as her self-esteem. Mine petered out in a matter of minutes. In truth, I had a hard time identifying myself as a terrific mother, given my immediate circumstances: I'd left one child crying in the middle of the night and couldn't remember the other one's name. Far more damaging still, I could claim none of the nurturant feelings a mother is expected to produce upon birth. Any maternal impulse in me was buried under the weight of a tremendous, free-floating fear.

My confidence was badly shaken by the time I met the rumored son in person, when the night nurse wheeled me down the hall into the preemie nursery. He was indeed as gorgeous as the nurse had promised, but looked far more fragile than I'd imagined. At four and a half pounds, how had this tiny creature commenced such a horrific flood? Since my own strength was completely drained by the ordeal I wondered how he, inexperienced in even the simple task of breathing, could possibly come through it without permanent injury. Still and mute, straining for oxygen, he made no response to my touch. Unable to make contact, I wasn't sure how to love this son.

"Fathers and teachers, I ponder 'What is hell?' " Dostoyevsky asked, then answered: "I maintain that it is the suffering of being unable to love." I tried desperately to locate my affections for this tiny being, but the closest I came was a warm sympathy for his desperate struggle to breathe. But I couldn't call what I felt love. It seemed impossible to love him when I had no idea who he was.

All night, I worried about brain damage. I worried about Darren's brain, more than his heart or eyes or hands, because I equated thinking with survival. Why was thinking so much more important than feeling or seeing or doing? Thought, as I'd suspected and Frank had insisted, seemed to be the only immortal thread of human existence. That hunch was confirmed two days earlier when I'd lost all feeling and physical sensations, but continued to think. I didn't know where I was going when the room spun out and my mind unraveled, but I was definitely going somewhere, and at a terrific speed.

If you didn't have a brain, if you didn't manage to keep your head through these traumatic births, how would you know you existed? How would you know you were loved? Knowing who you were, what was true, why you were here—this knowing was all that survived when a body expired. Knowledge, it seemed to me, was the only redeemable part of being human. While I wrestled with these existential questions on the meaning of life, Howe had no doubts about his feelings. For two days, he stood by his son in intensive care and loved him beyond reason.

"You saw him last night?" he asked when he arrived the next morning, beaming broadly through his blond mustache and beard. "Isn't he *great*?" His spirits were soaring. The doctors had assured him of my total recovery from the trauma and the baby, well, there was no more bad news that morning. No bad news, for Howe, was incredibly good news. He helped me into a wheelchair and pushed me through the halls to the preemie nursery, where we spent our first hour together with our newborn son.

There weren't any moments of weepy joy as the baby curled tiny fingers reflexively around his father's knuckle—this son resisted all such playful gestures, having no spare energy to flex muscles that didn't contribute directly to breathing. Nevertheless, Howe's visible affection at the incubator was impressive. He marveled at the shock of dark hair covering his small head, petted the soft fuzz on his legs, laughed at the enormous Ichabod Crane feet. He loved Darren immediately and unconditionally, imagining himself the father of the most beautiful baby in the nursery. He actually felt *lucky*.

I was amazed. Brain damage was nowhere on his mind. His love was so large, he was oblivious to what a handicapped child might mean for his life—from the first moment he laid eyes on his second dreamy son, Howe's bonding was complete. While I sat in my wheelchair, wounded and worried, his father simply opened his heart and welcomed him. It seemed to me Darren was wished into life by the sheer force of that joy. God, I loved Howe for that.

I admired his passion for the kids, and I loved the huge affection he showered on me. For our first five years together, I thought that love was all I'd ever need from him. Until that morning in the intensive care nursery, I hadn't recognized the fatal difference between us: Consumed by love, Howe was oblivious to the attendant responsibilities; preoccupied by duty, I failed to show any noticeable affection. Painfully polarized between love and duty, we approached the first crisis in our small family from opposite directions. Although neither of us understood it at the time, that polarized pattern would eventually erode the marriage.

The magnetic attraction between us had been so strong, it overshadowed the small frictions that erupted now and then. Although we joked about his turtlelike pace and my manic frenzy whenever we were under stress, the pressures so far had been manageable. After a series of effortless victories when we both earned graduate degrees, acquired professional jobs, and celebrated the almost painless birth of a healthy son, we had no reason to believe life wouldn't always be wonderful.

Marriage, so far, was all about love—we hadn't yet encountered the complicated economic or legal implications buried beneath "I do." Love came easily to us; it was money that threw us, and threw us terribly. When we added our love for children to our love for sports cars and European trips and the freedom to pursue personal dreams, we didn't realize it was a trade. It was preposterous to admit now, but we didn't think love involved any compromise.

The truth invariably arrives several years after you need it. A lifelong love affair with a man of Howe's passions—if a Catholic could permit herself such a choice—would have been the healthiest arrangement for a woman with my propensity for worry. I should have become a "friend to his excitement," a partner to his affections but not his finances or personal obligations. I'd enlisted in marriage and motherhood without understanding the full ramifications of "for better or worse." After Darren's birth the summer of '75, we headed almost immediately into worse.

I left my position as dean at Bishop Luers to work at home, writing for the local paper and teaching part time at the university—rewarding work that paid almost nothing. After the mayor lost his reelection and most city employees active in his campaign had resigned or were dismissed, Howe spent an anxious year waiting to be fired before he, too, quit his job. By 1978, the children had two full-time parents but no one to pay their bills, a minor hitch from our naïve point of view. We'd walked to the edge of security before with splendid results, experiencing the kind of early success that gives risk-takers a false sense of the odds. We didn't calculate the influence a recession could have on our future until we'd cashed the last unemployment check. Without comprehending the depths, we began wading into poverty.

The months of lean living we had marginally prepared for turned into grueling years. Joblessness begot poverty, which begot depression, which begot inaction, which begot guilt, which begot anger—usually at each other. Learning to fight was a tough skill to acquire late in a marriage, and our uncoached bouts resulted in some serious injuries. Firing hundreds of words at each other we struggled to get the marriage back on track, exchanging innumerable promises and entreaties over coffee at the kitchen table. An unemployed man and a free-lance writer have plenty of time, if nothing else. Perhaps it was the sense of abundant time, the comforting guarantee of " 'til death do us part," that made us dull to the danger of an irreparable split.

Under mounting debts the differences between us became even more pronounced—stress slowed Howe's pace to a standstill, while it accelerated mine to frenzied action. Much of my nonstop agitation was directed at him: "Only the powerless need to nag," a character in *The Women's Room* declared. Nagging a man into action was about as effective as sizzling the madness out of a manic-depressive—no amount of pleading with my loved ones to "come back to reality" made the slightest difference. For better or worse, I became silent.

Bound by our marriage vows and commitment to the children, we wound relentlessly around the track of unemployment, depression, poverty, and anger, like two processionary caterpillars compelled by instinct to follow the silken thread laid down before them, even when it offered no food. The noted entomologist Jean Henri Fabre was stunned by the lengths processionaries were willing to go to follow family tradition. In one experiment, he manipulated the trail of the leader to form a closed circuit around the base of a pine tree, wanting to see how long it would take the starving family to break rank and aim for the needles he'd placed just a few inches away. For seven consecutive days and nights, he despaired to watch them wind exhaustedly around the same pointless route hundreds of times, blindly obedient, missing the obvious. Even though he was "already familiar with the abysmal stupidity of insects as a class," the entomologist said it was depressing not to find "any gleam of intelligence in their benighted minds."

The physical world presented myriad lessons about the compulsive instincts that drove us to death. Nature seemed unnecessarily cruel to its most loyal species—the salmon, driven by lust, swimming upstream to their fatal orgy; the pine processionaries, victimized by their impulse to "Follow Me!" giving up food to stick with the family. The laws of nature prohibited independent thinking—if it wasn't instinct, then the salmon and processionaries had to be Catholics. Maybe fish felt guilt, and welcomed punishment for having too much pleasure. Maybe divorce was out of the question in the benighted minds of the processionaries.

It was for me, until I finally understood that " 'til death do us part" was a form of suicide. I felt a keen sense of failure backing out of my vows, but as Mary McCarthy explained in *How I Grew*, "it really happened that someone you loved could exhaust your capacity for suffering." I knew if I didn't break rank, the path I was on would lead to lifetime dependence on Valium.

Still, I balked at the decision to divorce whenever I read the grisly details of a custody battle in the newspaper, or listened to the misery of friends going through it. They were intelligent couples, compassionate people who nevertheless found themselves consumed by anger and revenge, and I didn't think I was exempt from the emotional fallout they couldn't escape. Divorce was structured by lawyers and judges to be an antagonistic ordeal—I thought there had to be a more humane way to end the suffering without putting on boxing gloves and annihilating each other in court. I wanted to divorce in gradual stages, to live apart for a year and then, keeping our heads, write our own terms for divorce.

We separated the year Howe was accepted into a doctoral

program at the University of Michigan. That summer, finding it too painful to face the impending break over coffee every day, I left Fort Wayne with the kids and spent the summer months at the home of friends in Denver. I sent dozens of letters to Howe—it was easier to write than speak over the phone and risk picturing his sad blue eyes when I heard his voice. In my letters, I pleaded with him to help me imagine a "good divorce." ("Please, Howe, don't let divorce be something that happens *to* you, like a bad car accident or getting fired. Please plan it with me, think with me, anticipate how you want to shape your fatherhood.") Howe wanted no part of a "good divorce"—he wanted more time to save the marriage. He thought agreeing to plan a divorce with me was akin to drinking hemlock.

Since he didn't participate in the planning, each step took him by surprise and became an occasion of pain. Although the first stage of divorce was already under way, he was hurt and angry when he noticed I'd taken my wedding band off that November. After ten years of wearing it, asleep and awake, I felt naked and vulnerable without it. Whenever my thumb reflexively tapped the base of my ring finger and found the crater of tender skin instead of the solid gold band, I felt my despair all over again.

While I'd removed the wedding band, which symbolized the institution of marriage, I decided to keep wearing the emerald engagement ring, the symbol of commitment and love. I wanted to believe it was possible to eliminate the suffering but salvage our relationship—to step out of the ruins of our marriage, separate the legal and economic obligations, and still maintain an affectionate friendship. Since an engagement ring on the left hand represented a forthcoming marriage, I moved mine to the right as a reminder of a past one. After ten years, two children, and innumerable vows exchanged over the kitchen table, it seemed to me we were still very much engaged—always would be, as long as we shared a passion for the children. When Howe responded angrily to the disappearance of my wedding band, I tried to redress the grievance by explaining my complicated ring theories. But promising to be a "friend" to a man who really wanted to hear "wife" invited contempt.

The first year Howe was in Ann Arbor I remained in Fort Wayne, writing the ideal divorce agreement. Divorce became my full-time job. I composed twenty-page letters explaining myself, making proposals, gripped by a strong need for understanding. I described our divorce as an "unmarriage," or "positive disintegration," the term Kazimierz Dabrowski assigned to the period of accelerated change before every global development. "It can bring a dark night of the soul," Dabrowski maintained, but these painful periods were "essentially healthy and creative . . . permitting us to make new and original approaches to reality." It was high-minded stuff, the contents of my letters to Howe. But whatever language or theories I invented to soften the hard reality of divorce, he interpreted each message I sent this way: "I don't love you anymore."

Change, even when anticipated, was terrifying. After a decade of living together, it had been easy to lose track of ourselves in the habitual "we" of marriage; divorce separated us back into the "me" and "he" of us. Legal papers altered our identities from "husband and wife" to "petitioner and respondent." The petitioner invariably has a year or two head start on the respondent—more time to own mistakes and forgive yourself; more time to absolve guilt and shame and finally, get on with life. Howe thought the changes in our relationship were coming at breathtaking speed. I saw the long distance we had to go to restore the affection we'd once had, and thought we'd never get there.

I kept writing more letters, explaining myself through five hundred pages, convinced that if we could reach some understanding it would eliminate the huge anger that kept ambushing us. That same year, I heard about a brilliant young psychologist in the Midwest who was working on a manuscript about the need to be understood, proving it was an even stronger human need than the desire for sex or power. The book was never published—the young man was subsequently diagnosed as manic-depressive and his research turned out to be a product of his imagination. But the theory made enormous sense to me. I thought anyone who could offer enlightenment on the overwhelming need to be understood could outsell *I'm OK, You're OK*, maybe even the Baltimore Catechism. It was depressing that the only theory to come out of psychology that made any sense to me was invented by a madman. I certainly felt driven by an insatiable need for understanding, while at the same time my desires for sex and power were almost extinct.

I was so desperate for Howe to recognize that I still loved him and would continue to be his ally, I volunteered to sell the house and pay off our debts, move with the kids to Ann Arbor, pay their expenses while he was in school, and commute to my work in New York. He never had to ask for these accommodations to his needs, and therefore never had to acknowledge them. Had I made the offers because I felt guilty for breaking my vows, or was I trying to divorce him without his noticing?

In either case I discovered that aggressive nurturance, at its most extreme, was a form of vanity. The promises I made were once again beyond my capabilities. My assuming his share of the financial responsibilities only made him oblivious to them, while I began to buckle under. My weight dropped rapidly that year and the emerald ring kept slipping off my finger in the shower. Each time I put it back on, my hope that love would survive this punishing divorce became dimmer and dimmer.

After moving to Ann Arbor I checked into the Ann Arbor Center for the Family and paid Dr. Whiteside sixty dollars an hour to use her Kleenex. She watched me cry for an hour twice a week—after six months, the most detailed information she had about me was how many ways I could blow my nose. "If you get the damn hurt, use it," Hemingway once told Fitzgerald—use it to know who you are, why you're vulnerable, what you need to do. Pain was invariably a route to change—it wasn't the only route, god knows, but it certainly seemed to be *my* route. Learning to let go through the agony of divorce was even more difficult than letting go through death. Death, for all its irrevocable consequences, was swift and clean. Divorce, or "the little death" as Vonnegut called it, involved dying over and over again.

I was sure that if I were a widow, I'd remember the good times with lasting affection; as a divorcee, I was still arguing about money, where to live, who should do the laundry and grocery shopping. Death ultimately provided dignity while this ongoing series of little deaths seemed to cancel it. When I wasn't wishing Howe dead, I was evidently trying to kill myself. In the three years since the separation, I'd had two car accidents, three hospitalizations for mysterious diseases, and a bike accident that knocked me unconscious.

I'd awakened in the street last month to face a circle of concerned neighbors leaning over me, offering to call an ambu-

lance. They were alarmed by the deep wound over my left eye—I
saw the blood but didn't feel any pain. "I'm fine!" I said, gathering
up the groceries that had thrown my balance. A neighbor offered
to drive me to the emergency room, recommending that I get
stitches for my eye, but I declined. The wound kept reopening—in
fact, I felt a warm stream running down the left side of my face
even now. Someone was dabbing it.

I became aware of noises in the hall and felt enormous relief
when I recognized the sound of the guards making morning
rounds. Help had arrived. Women's voices filled the corridor,
calling each other by name as if they were all members of a
friendly service sorority. It was an uncommonly cheerful prison—
given the grim nature of their work, it was surprising how often
they managed to make each other laugh. The women usually
came in groups and spoke in a kind of shorthand to each other.

"I don't like the sound of this congestion," the woman dabbing
my wet cheeks said. "She may not be getting enough oxygen.
Better call Dr. Greenbaum—she seems to have a lot of fluid
again." A pair of crepe soles squeaked quickly from the room. A
warm cloth moved over my face and neck, removing the sticky
runoff around my leaking eyes. The woman untied the cloth
handcuffs and untaped the adhesives around the needles in my
arms. Was I being released? I tried to get up, to show I was worthy
of parole, but my limbs wouldn't respond.

A warm soapy cloth moved over my arms and legs, then a dry
one, then fresh adhesive tape was wrapped around the needles and
my wrists were retied to the bed rail. I felt the woman's strong
fingers knead a squishy muscle in my thigh and then cold wet
cotton swab the spot. A needle penetrated the tingling skin and I
knew what came next. I was *not* being released—I had more
dreaming to do.

"We'll have to put another heplock on her arm." Another voice
wavered as the images began filling the screen again. "Dr. Greenbaum . . . ordered a new antibiotic . . . to start today." Another
needle pierced my arm and more tape was applied. A stinging
liquid began dripping into my arm. Did she say hemlock? Had
Howe's fatal vision of divorce been right after all? With despair, I
watched as the Denver dream began to roll, the nightmare that
filled my sleep over and over the summer I left Fort Wayne. It was

the last one I remembered before I stopped dreaming altogether three years ago.

I am steering down a narrow alley in the Audi, the rusted brown car Howe and I are driving into the ground that summer. Without any forewarning, the front seat cracks and falls forward onto the accelerator. I cannot control my speed, only the direction, as a small child steps into my reckless path. The boy sees me but remains frozen in place, as if all responsibility for avoiding a terrible accident depends on me. I reach for the brake but it has fallen through the bottom of the rusted car frame. The only way not to hit the child is to veer sharply into one of the brick walls on either side of the alley. Heart pounding, I aim for the left wall. In the split second before the crash, I have a chilling thought. It is not about my imminent death but the fact that I have no car insurance. I wonder how I will pay for the damages.

Suddenly, I am standing outside the car. The front end is smashed in all the way to the steering wheel. I am covered with blood but feel nothing. Looking back down the alley to where the child was standing, I see a form lying face down. I run toward the motionless body, but it keeps receding as fast as I advance. Running harder and harder, the sharp stabs in my ribs finally drop me to the ground. When I open my eyes, the motionless form is lying right beside me. I turn the body over and, like a chilling scene in an Alfred Hitchcock movie, the figure turns out to be a doll with a china face, cracked but smiling wickedly, with two ice-cold blue glass eyes staring in opposite directions.

The alley fills up with these grotesque, broken dolls—I can't step anywhere without my foot falling on one. I'm desperate to escape from the spooky alley of dolls. An old woman in black who witnessed the whole accident walks silently toward me. She sees my horror but does not seem to feel horror herself, as if she were accustomed to living in a graveyard of broken dolls. I ask her how to get out and she points to the brick wall.

There is no door, no windows, but I finger along the bricks and am suddenly, inexplicably inside a room. I look for a phone, thinking I should report the accident. But I'm sure when I explain my side of the story the police will not understand me. I am almost relieved when I find no phone—the room is empty except for a bowl in the middle of the floor with broken pottery in it. The old woman appears again and points, wordlessly, to the pottery. I know I am supposed to get rid of it, that it is connected to the broken children outside. My heart starts pounding again, for I know I have almost no time to save them.

I look around for a place to hide the shards—the room has no wastebasket or garbage can, and I have no pockets. I have no choice, and put the sharp pieces into my mouth and begin swallowing. Though I can feel nothing, I know I am ruining myself inside. I keep swallowing until I come to the bottom of the bowl, where long slivers of glass shimmer in a thin layer of water. I know drinking this mixture will ruin me for sure, but it is the only way for someone without insurance to pay for the damages. It is pointless to have swallowed the rest of the pottery without swallowing the glass too. I pick up the longest slivers and put them in my mouth. My fingers become bloody and I feel liquid trickling down my throat. Then I hold the bowl in both hands and drink the rest. The peculiar liquid sensation—the precursor of birth or death?—passes through me and I shiver violently.

I awoke with a start from that nightmare in Denver, my heart pounding loudly in my ears. Ryan was standing next to my bed and shaking my shoulder. At age seven, he was wrestling with his own nightmares—it was the month before he transferred to a new school, where he was sure all the friends had already been taken, the same year his parents had begun behaving strangely. By day he managed to keep his fears at bay. They got him at night, in his sleep.

"Mom, I had a bad dream," he said, shaking me awake. "Can I sleep with you?" I lifted the covers and he crawled in, curling his back into the crescent of my body. Wrapping my arms around him, I rocked and kissed him.

"I'm sorry, bugs," I soothed. "What was it about?"

"Falling . . ." he said, the tremors of fear gradually leaving his voice. "I was falling . . . and couldn't stop." He described the same nightmare he'd been having all week.

"Well, you're okay now—it was only a dream," I said, hugging him hard. Still not recovered from my own dream, I searched for more solid assurance of our safety. I rejected the prayer that came to mind, the one designed to lull children to sleep. I thought the line about "if I should die before I wake" was too close to home for both of us. Whose brilliant idea was it to remind children of death every night? Since prayer failed, I looked to the movies for inspiration. I remembered his favorite line in *Superman*, when the hero swoops through the air and catches the terrified Lois Lane as she's plummeting from a skyscraper. We'd repeated their brief conversation dozens of times.

"Don't worry, miss, I've got you," I said into his ear, doing my best imitation of the man of steel. He recognized the line with an amused grunt and immediately recited the next line: "You've got me?" he said, mimicking Lois Lane's astonishment, "Who's got *you?*" I felt his ribs shake with a satisfied laugh, and he was soon breathing in the deep, slow rhythm of sleep. I kept stroking his hair softly, not yet ready to close my own eyes again.

For an uninsured woman contemplating divorce, "Who's got you?" was a more relevant question than he imagined. That night, I wished I had the gift of faith. I wished I could pray. I would have petitioned St. Jude, the patron saint of hopeless cases. Instead of religion, I borrowed lines from Hollywood and depended on Superman to relieve the philosophical dilemmas that terrified me in the middle of the night. It was a compromising position for a feminist to find herself in.

"Mary Kay," a woman called, gently patting my arm. The guards had begun addressing me by name and describing what they were going to do next. "There will be some pain," she informed me, and she seemed genuinely sorry about the tortures she was ordered to perform. "We have to suction you. It will only last a minute," she assured me.

Another suctioning? How many counts of delinquency had I been charged with? Before I could brace my unsolid body, I heard her switch the vacuum machine on.

My chest heaved up instantly as a powerful hose sucked the liquid from my lungs. I felt the slivers of glass and pottery scrape across the soft tissue in my throat. The broken pieces I'd swallowed without any feeling were removed with roaring pain. The hose gurgled loudly until my chest was sucked dry and the machine eventually clicked off. The plastic tube was resecured in my mouth, pumping hot chemicals through the open path to my lungs and stinging the exposed tissue inside. When the pain finally subsided, I noticed that my bed was moving.

I was rolling down a long corridor under a steady pattern of lights, growing bright and fading against my closed eyelids. My bed was parked next to some machines, humming like the old tickertape printers in a newsroom, while two or three people discussed elaborate plans for me. Then the most amazing thing happened. A woman started giving me a home permanent!

This was the weirdest goddamn prison! After they suctioned your lungs, they frizzed your hair! I could hardly believe it when a woman began to section my hair, parting it into exact degrees of longitude and latitude, and then applied a thick, cold paste to my scalp. I remembered the most loathsome permanent of my youth, when I sat for two hours in the basement of a neighbor's house, wound up tightly in curlers and fuming damply under a smelly plastic apron.

She's leaving me under too long. If she doesn't come back down soon I'm going to look like Bozo. I told Mom this was a bad idea. Last time Mom fried my scalp with that Toni, I had to wear a babushka to school to hide my hair, springing out at right angles. She promised me this neighbor knew what she was doing—she used to be a real beautician. I hear her baby crying upstairs. I think she's forgotten I'm down here. If she's not back by the time I count to ten, I'm gonna take these rollers out myself.

"It's a little tight," she says, finally returning to unwind the curlers. A little tight?! I feel a stiff Brillo pad around my head. I'm totally kinked! "It will soften in a few weeks," she says nervously and hands me a mirror. I hand it back with pure hatred and give her the money from Mom. I think I'm in the middle of a vicious hair-bending conspiracy. She says thank you. I keep "you're welcome" to myself and march madly up the stairs.

Walking the six blocks back home, I rehearse what I will say to my mother. I think of all the dirty words I've heard on the playground at school, but I don't know exactly what they mean. This is no time to be unclear. While I smolder down the sidewalk, the neighbor calls and warns my mother of the vast unhappiness heading her way.

"I hope you're satisfied!" I holler as I slam the door. It's as

insulting as I can be. My mother is stunned. Talking back is strictly forbidden in our family. She used to threaten to put a bar of soap in our mouths as the punishment for back-talk, but I am too big for that now. Before she knows what she's doing, she slaps me across the face. Horrified, she looks at her hand and then at me. In fifteen years, she has never slapped one of her children across the face. A home permanent plunges us into the depths of mother/daughter rage. We are both undone by the monstrous size of my vanity.

So, was it vanity that put me in this prison? Why else would the punishment require a home permanent? It had to be vanity, the "big head" Kay cautioned me against throughout adolescence. "Maybe you can't help it," Frank had said when I visited him in Dunning. "Maybe in this trip, you're scheduled to learn what vanity and envy are all about." Aggressive nurturance was the form of vanity I indulged most, taking care of people who never asked for my help. I could see now, from my present paralyzed position, that it led me to make promises I couldn't possibly keep.

8

IRREGULAR BRAIN WAVES

DR. DENNIS GREENBAUM, chief of Critical Care Medicine at St. Vincent's Hospital, wore his weighty title with such unassuming authority a stranger in the intensive care unit might easily mistake him for the janitor. Larry was at first skeptical of the short, soft-spoken man whose hospital uniform consisted of a plaid sport shirt and loose-fitting trousers, with a stethoscope stuck casually in his back pocket as if it were a handyman's screwdriver. On the few occasions he did deign to wear a white lab coat, he resembled the crafty Lieutenant Columbo in his rumpled trench coat, disguising a quick, observant mind behind a slow grin and furrowed brow. Curly brown hair sprayed out in undisciplined wisps around his head, either the deliberate statement of an eccentric nonconformist or the unplanned style of a man whose life allowed no time for barbers. In Greenbaum's case, a judgment wasn't immediately clear—the first impression he made on strangers invariably fell somewhere between jokester and genius.

Larry had checked him out, of course. Still wondering if I should be transferred to Mount Sinai, he called Dr. Alvin Teirstein, the renowned pulmonary specialist who'd examined me there last month.

"She's at St. Vincent's now?" Teirstein asked when Larry reached him from the emergency room. "That means she'll be under Greenbaum when she's moved to ICU," he mused aloud. "It doesn't really make sense to transfer her anywhere else. You can't do any better than Dennis Greenbaum. He's awfully good . . ." he told Larry, then paused for a private, lengthy recollection to himself. "*Awfully* good," Teirstein concluded. "He's one of the first doctors I'd consult if we ran into trouble here."

After three months in New York, Larry automatically translated "awfully good" into "extremely fast." Accustomed to the frenetic pace in the emergency room he found it almost painful to slow down in ICU, where the unhurried chief moved leisurely from crisis to crisis, coma patient to coma patient. This one had AIDS, that one diabetes, and if or when these patients recovered there were always more bodies waiting to fill their beds. Greenbaum approached his work with the measured pace of a marathon runner, conserving energy for the long haul. Reaching the finish line, in the coma business, was often just the beginning. After recovering the bodies of his patients, he then faced the laborious task of healing their minds.

In Dr. Greenbaum's theory of survival, if you placed yourself in the center of human grief, if you worked with the most severely injured and wanted to be at all useful to them, you had to take measures not to catch the pain yourself. His main defense was a wry blend of self-effacing humor—"laughs are exactly as honorable as tears"—and he shared it liberally with the small troop of young interns and residents rotating through ICU with him. Intermittently during my dreams, I heard the low mumbling of an approaching army when suddenly a voice would erupt in a rise and send warm streams of laughter down the hall. Like an urban witch doctor casting a spell of immunity around his vulnerable staff, the chief of ICU relied heavily on wit to fend off despair.

His medical brilliance, ready humor, and long endurance made Dr. Greenbaum a valuable ally to his desperately ill patients, but in my case there was another quality that made him indispensable: He had a high tolerance for emotional relatives. He not only tolerated the extravagant passions of the family and friends who came onto the ward with me—he aided and abetted them. Whether or not he anticipated the happy effect it would have on my dreams, Greenbaum immediately granted Larry's request and suspended visiting hours for Gina and him. By Monday afternoon, a note authorizing their presence on the ward was posted prominently in the nursing station. Larry and Gina soon became adjunct staff members, arriving for shifts as early as eight in the morning and staying as late as midnight.

Their presence supplied the missing elements in my relationship with the staff, the essential ingredients of human bonding.

Without voice or gestures, without facial expressions, a coma patient has all the personality of a slab of raw meat. Trussed up in tubes, dressed in a hospital gown, and identified with a plastic band wrapped around my wrist like the paper cuff on a lamb chop, one had only to imagine the respirator tube in my mouth as a sprig of parsley for a clear picture of my charisma. Although the staff treated my meat tenderly, Larry and Gina brought the absent spirit back to my flesh. They asked questions and provided vital information about my history; they smiled and expressed gratitude for kindnesses; they grunted or moaned in response to probable pain. There is something contagious about human caring—when an anonymous patient becomes the object of great love, it spreads.

The women who worked the night shift noticed Larry's singular devotion as he gazed into my face with unbroken concentration through his first long vigil. Jessyca, a staff nurse, was moved by his silent longing as he held my hand for hours, recognizing immediately what it meant to my life. She must have experienced some version of *The Way We Were* shudder—women are so susceptible to the thrill of being loved without having to ask. "She's a lucky woman," Jessyca remarked to Gina. "She has a wonderful man."

The day shift noted my improved color and appearance since Gina arrived Sunday night. Between readings and monologues, she amused herself by combing and restyling my hair ("M.K., let's go punk today—whaddya say?") and performing other little grooming vanities a staff has no time for. Gina unsterilized the décor of my room, adding music and books and a lounge chair from the lobby. She brought conversation, telling stories and responding to questions as she thought I might, often with a joke. Most significantly, Gina brought faith—her belief in my survival was absolute, unshaken even when all evidence pointed in the opposite direction.

By Wednesday morning, insulin had lowered dangerously high glucose levels and strong antibiotics flooded into my veins through multiple intravenous tubes, closing in on the various enemy camps identified in preliminary lab tests and X-rays. Dr. Greenbaum expressed "surprise" to Larry that the Ann Arbor doctors who inserted the drainage apparatus in my ribs had prescribed no antibiotic protection to safeguard against unwanted traffic through the tube, the medical equivalent of a four-lane highway welcoming bacteria into my open wounds. After three months of unrestricted immigration, five distinct colonies—including the prodigiously reproductive pneumonia family—had settled into my lungs.

"She must have been one strong woman," a resident observed after reviewing my chart, asking Gina how I'd managed to board a plane six days ago carrying all that cargo.

"I'll bet she was a real fighter," a nurse added as she injected a second dose of Valium into my arm, when the first shot failed to calm my thrashing limbs.

"What do you mean, *was?*" Gina asked, alarmed. "She *is*. My sister *is* a fighter."

Gina's pickiness with words asserted itself prominently on the intensive care ward—she asked the staff to please watch their use of past tense and recommended addressing me in the friendly second person rather than the impersonal third: "Don't say 'she' when you talk in her room. Don't exclude her from the conversation—she can hear. Use her name, 'Mary Kay.' My sister is a very intelligent woman—words matter to her. She's a writer." Gina believed that being a writer had as much to do with my mute condition as being diabetic or having pneumonia. Trusting the staff to revive my body, she imagined her responsibility had to do with reaching my soul.

Although there were no substantial changes in the lab reports by midweek, everyone perceived subtle improvements in my condition. The piece of meat had become a person. While I was still unquestionably sick, I had become "lucky" and "colorful," perhaps even "lovable." I was a person with a past and, given the number of calls and letters flooding onto the ward with my arrival, someone with a great deal of affection in her future. When a heavy toll of long distance calls from Florida, Indiana, Illinois, Michigan, Colorado, Kansas, California, and Canada began to frazzle the harassed clerk in ICU, Larry and Gina organized all the branches of concern into several telephone trees. They fed detailed messages into a forest of trunks each day, planting strategic information and harvesting a crop of fervent wishes.

"Who *is* she?" a hospital messenger asked curiously, dropping a large cache of mail on the table in my room. "She's my sister,"

Gina replied absently, naming the most prominent interest she had in me at that moment. The young man looked puzzled. "The guys in the mail room thought she was some kind of celebrity," he said.

Without any effort from me, a rumor spread around the hospital that I had been a winner, a magnetic label that attracts loyal support from complete strangers. In the killing fields of ICU, where so many losers come to battle with death, the sudden possibility of a winner excited the staff. They jumped on my bandwagon eagerly, even as it appeared to be barreling recklessly toward the cliff's edge.

"The whole staff meeting was devoted to her this morning," Jessyca told Gina Wednesday morning. "I know you're terribly worried, but if anyone can save her, Dr. Greenbaum can. We all believe she's going to make it," she said. Faith, that magic elixir sustaining my family, infected the rationally bound minds of the hospital community. Along with the heavy regimen of prescription drugs injected directly into my veins, the ICU nurses poured a litany of prayers into my ears: "Lord, we got to do somethin' about this girl," a nurse whispered in husky, black vernacular, as her gentle hands untaped the tight adhesives around my mouth. "I'll need a new respirator mouthpiece," she called over her shoulder to someone standing behind her. "She's chewed up another one."

When my blood chemistry stabilized and I failed to awaken, Dr. Greenbaum ordered another round of lab tests, EKGs, and X-rays, doubling the already heavy traffic of white coats through my room. Since Gina sometimes had to wait outside while I hosted other guests, she called the nursing station before coming to the hospital Wednesday morning to find out when I'd be free, so to speak. The nurse reported that, unfortunately, more fluid had collected in my lungs overnight. The first order of the day was another suctioning.

While Gina knew the suctionings improved my oxygen intake and provided critical fluid samples for the lab, she hated witnessing them. The first procedure she watched was agony for her. She felt the vacuum hose penetrating her own throat as it was forced deeply down mine; then came the rush of unbearable pain when the switch was thrown. She held my hand tightly as my chest heaved up violently, overwhelmed with helplessness when she watched my dispassion explode in sudden anguish. The youngest family member, never having served on the front lines before, Gina felt her inexperience keenly.

"Oh god, what time?" she asked when she learned I was to be suctioned again. "I should be there for her . . ."

"It's already done," the nurse said, "and she's doing fine." Because I was still heavily sedated, however, the EEG had been postponed until later that morning, a procedure that would take several hours. Dr. Greenbaum thought it would be useful to have a detailed map of the mind he was trying to contact and consulted Dr. Mary McLarnon, a neurologist. My body would be in Dr. McLarnon's custody most of the morning, the nurse told Gina, since her staff needed my head through several cycles of printouts.

"An EEG? Is that painful?" Gina asked, embarrassed by her naïveté in hospital language and rituals.

"Oh no, no," the nurse assured her. "She'll hardly feel anything." Several electronic sensors would be pasted to my scalp at strategic points and it would feel, essentially, "like twenty small fingers taking her pulse," she explained.

"She'll be in very competent hands," the nurse promised. "Dr. McLarnon is a terrific neurologist. I think you'll like her a lot." These assurances together with the soft consonants of Mary McLarnon's name comforted my sister. If the secret territories of my mind had to be opened and explored, she was glad the leader of the expedition had some experience thinking with an Irish brain herself. Since I was unavailable to visitors all morning, Gina decided to use the time to rehabilitate herself. By Wednesday, her batteries were beginning to run down.

"Hi, hon, I'm back," she called happily when she entered my cell late that afternoon, decidedly recharged. "What a day!" She'd met Ellen for breakfast and, after a satisfying heart-to-hearter, they walked back to the *Ms.* offices in Times Square through the icy March slush. Ellen noticed Gina's loafers were soaked and suggested they shop for some boots. Shopping, for Gina, was not a matter of serious business, crossing off a list of urgent errands; it was a fascinating trip to the private museums of American culture, full of costumes and gadgets to try out, the more unfamiliar or offbeat the better.

"We found this *fabulous* store!" she exuded. "I'll take you there when we spring you from this place. *Great* shoes. I bought a pair of boots—bright yellow!" There was a brief, excited rustle of cardboard and tissue paper followed by two flat thuds as a pair of shoes dropped to the floor. Then the squeaky notes of new crepe soles played across the linoleum until they stopped on a high note, next to my bed. I pictured Gina wearing her successful-hunt smile, looking down at two glowing yellow neon feet. "I wish you could *see* these numbers," she sighed, regretting the shortcomings of her audience. I could certainly imagine them.

"The weird-shoe affliction evidently runs in your family," my friend Carolen said once after meeting Gina, standing exceptionally tall in her imported Japanese sandals. A pair of wide platforms perched on two parallel wooden bars under the heels and toes, the thongs had to be more or less mounted rather than casually slipped on. A person of my coordination risked serious injury in the contraptions, but Gina, an accomplished Tae Kwon Do instructor, moved gracefully in them. She liked the feeling of walking on air: "This way, you never step on a crack and break your mother's back." She laughed.

My own penchant for odd footwear was famous in Fort Wayne, since Joan loved to introduce me at local hen conventions by describing the way I looked the day we met in the Luers faculty lounge: "Here we are in the middle of a serious women's revolution, and what kind of help does Chicago send us? A cream puff in a powder-blue pantsuit and white shoes, with red apples appliquéd on the toes. Apples with a *bite* out of them!" By the time I was making speeches at political rallies I had long retired the apple shoes, but they'd been enormous favorites of mine. I'd probably never have bought them if Gina hadn't taken me off course before I left Chicago, stopping at a bizarre little boutique she found near Rush Street. Her enthusiasm for the odd, the deeply eccentric, was catching.

"Look at *these*, M.K." She'd smiled in the boutique that day, pointing to a pair of bright yellow-and-black checked shoes, squared at the toe with four small leather tires sewn to the sides. "Aren't they *great?*" It wasn't practical to remind her there weren't many places a grown woman could wear a pair of taxicabs on her feet—it wasn't the kind of thing she cared about. Grinning broadly, she tried them on and looked in the mirror, immediately breaking into a spontaneous little dance of shuffles and slides, an inspired performance somewhere between the Andrews and the Pointer Sisters. Gina had the whole showroom laughing—she was dazzling.

"I always know how to find you two," Kay said once after tracking us down in Marshall Field's, when we were late for an appointed rendezvous with her outside the Walnut Room. "First I check shoes, then hats, then head toward the laughing." Gina was an inspired mimic with a hat. She would drape a beret low over one eyebrow and drop her lids, affecting the German accent and sultry pout of Marlene Dietrich; then she'd change into a soft felt hat and turn up the brim, becoming the sheepish, loose-limbed Norton of *The Honeymooners*. She and Paul had both perfected convincing impersonations of Art Carney and Jackie Gleason, directing each other ("No wait, like *this*!") and cracking up. Her melodrama and comedy, so far, had been limited to private performances in our family room and in various millinery departments around Chicago. But that Wednesday in March, Gina hit Times Square.

"New Yorkers . . . they're outrageous, aren't they?" she remarked fondly, like a woman falling in love. She described wandering down Broadway after dropping Ellen off at *Ms.*, fascinated by the people and conversations on the street.

"You'd never have to feel weird here," she said, probably thinking of taxicab shoes, "because someone else is bound to be weirder." She'd inhaled the scents and caught the undertow of the sidewalks, feeling the currents of desire and longing. For anyone who needs to lose her innocence in a hurry, New York City is the place to come. Manhattan was composed of "strangers who have pulled up stakes somewhere and come to town, seeking sanctuary or fulfillment or some greater or lesser grail," E. B. White wrote about the City, "the concentrate of art and commerce and sport and religion and entertainment and finance." But he warned newcomers: "It can destroy an individual, or it can fulfill him, depending a good deal on luck. No one should come to New York to live unless he is willing to be lucky." Normally, I would have passed these cautionary words along to Gina, but my own luck in New York left me speechless.

After imbibing the pleasures of the City, my sister's spirits were further elevated during a long lunch with Susan and Carrie, two friends who had been part of our family since childhood.

"I really love those two—AGOGs, for sure," she said warmly. In the private lexicon between us, AGOG meant "a great old gal," the honorable title we conferred on friends committed for life. Carrie and Susan were definitely lifers.

We'd been close friends since our sophomore year in high school, serving as confidants through twenty some years of algebra classes and senior proms, beer-soaked parties and honorable mentions; we'd bolstered each other through broken engagements and eventual weddings, two separations and one final divorce; we'd grieved the ultimate tragedies of madness and death, celebrated the amazing miracles of pregnancy and birth. Somewhere in there, without formal vows or ceremony, we recognized a rare fidelity.

Now separated by four thousand miles, a number of small children, and three full-blown careers, we didn't taken reunions for granted. We had to plan them well in advance, save money and vacation time, excuse ourselves from families and then travel, sometimes as far as Juneau, Alaska. While we postponed or relocated these visits occasionally, it was unthinkable to cancel one—we'd become too dependent on these week-long fixes of uncut friendship.

I was especially in need of their delirious relief in March of '84, when I boarded the plane for La Guardia with my cumbersome baggage, with my freakish tube and inscrutable X-rays and unfinished deadlines. I saw my life coming apart like a handknit sweater, with a thread caught in Ann Arbor and unraveling all the way to New York City. Since my vulnerability was certain to be exposed during the critical interviews and meetings ahead of me that week, it was a relief to know I didn't have to hide my nakedness with Susan and Carrie.

We knew each other in the raw, through all the awkward, ridiculous stages of growth in the last two decades. However famous or important we'd become by the time the eighties rolled around, each of us in charge of a large staff or tremendous budget or complex family, when we looked at who we were together we remembered that only twenty years ago, one of us had driven an open convertible down Route 1 from San Francisco, stark naked, thinking seriously about changing her name to Rebecca Wildflower. A more cautious woman now, Ms. Wildflower only bloomed in certain environments, once a year or so in New York or Fort Wayne or Juneau. But her act was still something to see. I loved these friends for their incredible smarts and fierce affection, but I loved them most because they gave me the giggles.

Susan was en route from Juneau, laying over in Chicago to visit her parents for the weekend, when Larry called Carrie in New York with the coma report.

"Oh god, how will I tell Susan?" Carrie mourned. "She'll just be *wrecked* by this." For more than twenty years, neither one of us could bear wrecking Susan with bad news. Her immense gift was for pleasure, for cultivating joy—it was Susan who usually masterminded the unparalleled good times. "Whenever you get back from dinner with Susan," Gina observed years ago, "you always look like you've just had a week's vacation." When tragedy unbalanced her, it was particularly unnerving to witness the drain on that great, expansive face. After all plans for cocktails in the Rainbow Room and tickets for *Le Cage Aux Folles* were scrapped, Susan needed a recuperative day with Carrie to rally her spirits. Before standing sober watch at St. Vincent's, she had to rearrange her mind entirely.

"They'll be here tomorrow," Gina assured me. "This is hitting them hard," she reported softly, patting my head. "They love you—said to give you a big hug." She leaned over and attempted to deliver one but was impeded, as usual, by the respirator.

"When are you going to be *finished* with this thing?" she asked, feigning impatience, sounding exactly like our mother when she observed an unhealthy dependency developing in one of her brood. "This is a crutch you can live without," Kay had admonished me once, emptying a loaded ashtray at the bridge table. My mother's willpower was legendary in our family. She loved coffee but drank only one cup each day to my five or six, never smoked, and managed to enjoy herself through decades of baby showers, first communions, Irish wakes, and New Year's Eve parties on one whiskey sour per event. Her only weakness that I remember was an addiction to chocolate Heath Bars, which she bought by the six-pack and stashed in an obscure corner of the pantry. None of the children were allowed to touch them. It drove us nuts because she made them last for months, taking a bite or two at a time. But she learned to live without even that small crutch when, midlife, she developed an allergic reaction to chocolate. We could always tell if she had a relapse because she'd get laryngitis for a day. She hadn't touched Heath Bars for years.

My willpower in the face of strong cravings, on the other hand, came from the recessive genes in the pool. Every Irish family I know has at least one relative in the deep end, an addictive personality who jumped in after the siren call of pleasure and had been treading water ever since. I lived with the constant hum of desire—for coffee and cigarettes, for friends, for laughs and hugs; for hen conventions and their adrenaline highs; for babies and children and love and sex. I had acquired so many crutches by 1984, I could have opened a Western division of Lourdes. Only a few days ago, a single shot of morphine sent me to unprecedented heights of desire. I craved more.

The brilliant light that filled my head had enveloped me in such powerful love, such magnificent peace, there was no pain in that magic stratosphere. If I had a body at all, it was one without borders—the blinding white light blurred all distinction between where I left off and the benevolent presence began. It felt as though my body had been lifted from a damaged delivery package, unwrapped from its torn skin and frayed nerves, shaken gently to loose the clinging packing matter, and then held up to a warm, welcoming light.

Outside the wrappers of my body I discovered that I, too, was a being of light. Everyone in that dream was a filament of light—though blended indistinguishably into one, I had the distinct impression of one as many. Though I felt none of my familiar body sensations as a being of light, except a few tingling patches of skin where the tubes still clung to me, I was unquestionably "present"—happy and loved and, oh god, *brilliant*. Way beyond the "Oh wow!" brilliance I'd experienced sporadically before, the intelligence of the light was complete and laborless. There was no chasing after more thoughts, putting them through the wringer of doubt, worrying about contradictions and fallacies. All wisdom was there in an instant. I had never experienced such peaceful intelligence. Naturally I yearned to use it again—as soon as possible, at whatever cost.

Since the lights disappeared a few days ago when the green

creatures began pummeling my chest, I'd been floating in a depressed gray cloud over my body, reconnected by more wires and tubes. Forced to dream unceasingly, I yearned to escape. In my dimly lit imagination, I thought if I could free myself from the tether lines attached to the dead weight below me, the magnificent light would welcome me back. One by one, I'd surrendered my bodily attachments: I didn't desire any food or water. I no longer had the urge to pee. I didn't even have the impulse to breathe anymore. Only the fragile lines in my arms continued to hold me, easily broken if I could detach from the thick, oppressive tube in my mouth. It was the last significant anchor weighing me down.

Over and over, I tried to clench my teeth and bite through the hard plastic, but instead my knee would jerk or my cheek would twitch. Or nothing would happen at all. The repeated message to "chew!" produced no more than a random response from my body. All communication was scrambled by the broken machinery of my brain. My head and jaw ached from the monumental effort required to make a small hole. Exhausted, I'd have to rest, floating numbly in the gray dimness. I'd return to the job later only to find the little trench I'd dug was gone. I'd have to start grinding all over into the new, hard plastic.

In addition to the exacerbating communication problems between the parts of my body, my concentration was completely shot. Every voice or touch sent my mind reeling in its wake, rocking thoughts back and forth in time. The incessant dreams, colorful and compelling, distracted me from the singular task of lifting the last anchor. I seemed to have no willpower against interruptions—Gina's monologues absorbed me entirely.

Her excitement that afternoon triggered old cravings. She read the return addresses and I wanted to read the mail. I wanted a hug from Carrie and Susan; I wanted to be lucky in New York; I wanted to see Gina in her fabulous yellow boots. I wanted to save the children, kiss their soft spots, pat their heads. I wanted to be understood. Loading up with the weight of these wants, I felt myself sinking back into the humming desires of body. Distracted, all work on the tube would cease.

"So . . . any news from Dr. McLarnon?" Gina asked, moving to the foot of my bed and lifting my chart. She flipped the pages rapidly, speed-reading, like a civilian intruder worried about getting caught with classified information. She knew patient charts were regarded as hospital property, off-limits to unauthorized personnel and curious visitors. Even patients themselves were discouraged from trying to understand them, and except for those familiar with the *Merck Manual*, most didn't. Larry was the only lay person I knew who held a hospital chart as if he were entitled to the information.

When he visited me last October after my surgery in Ann Arbor, he read my chart aloud and quizzed my doctors about what the words meant. He even *wrote* on it, once, editing it after a verbal explanation because "the writing wasn't clear." Fifteen years of blue-penciling clumsy jargon and needless obscurity made him more indignant than intimidated when my chart made no sense to him. But Gina became depressed. In the margin next to the emphatically underscored "No morphine!" she was tempted to write her own unorthodox orders for reviving coma patients: "No past tense! No impersonal voice!" But her confidence in these theories was shakiest when she held my medical chart in her hands.

"I wish I understood neurology," she mumbled, flipping the pages. On the way to my room she'd met Dr. Watsky, her favorite among Greenbaum's interns, and asked him if he'd seen the results of the brain scan. Uncustomarily, he hedged. The tests were "unusual," he said obliquely, "unlike anything we expected." The brain-wave patterns were highly "irregular," exceptionally long on alpha waves but short on beta—or maybe it was the other way around. Gina didn't follow the exact details, but her mind leapt intuitively to a conclusion: Dr. Watsky was deeply alarmed.

"I told him not to worry," Gina reported from the foot of my bed, still flipping pages. "Irregular brain waves are probably *normal* for you, M.K.—you've been 'irregular' your whole life. 'Don't worry about her brain,' I said. 'It's her strongest organ.' " While her delivery may have been genuinely earnest when she spoke those words to Dr. Watsky half an hour earlier, it was notably flat when she repeated them to me. She sounded absorbed, becoming quiet for long periods as the pages kept turning.

" 'Necrotizing nodules . . . positive rheumatoid factor . . . high sedimentation rate . . . infectious empyema,' " she read absently, as if speaking from behind the spine of a gripping novel and only marginally aware of her audience. " 'Pneumonia . . . possible fungi' . . . Jesus, Mary Kay," she sighed finally, replacing the chart.

"Jesus," she whispered again, "no wonder your brain waves are a little irregular." She heaved another sigh, issuing the last of the energy she came in with, and moved away from the bed. I heard her sniffle several times as she rummaged through her purse, keys and coins clinking dully, then listened as she blew her nose at length. It was a three-Kleenex seizure, at least.

Without consent of my will, without understanding the danger it posed to my escape plans, I envisioned her face at that moment. It bore the same terrible look I'd witnessed on other faces I loved, when some unexpected revelation wrenched away their innocence with traumatic pain. That look haunted Frank, electrified by truth in the shock treatment room at Loretto; Ryan, eighteen months old, staring into the grim interior of an ambulance; Larry, outside my office the day he got fired; Susan, returning to Chicago for the funeral of her most loved friend; Howe, stopped on the staircase the night he recognized the inevitability of divorce. So many scenes of grief. I never understood why ascetic monks thought they had to manufacture the artificial tortures of self-flagellation and burning coals to reach enlightenment, when human life presented so many opportunities for real pain. All they had to do was report to the ninth floor of ISPI for a year's supply. Why invent fake pain when there was already plenty of the real stuff to go around?

Rocked by depair, few people returned from these emotional assaults without a perceptible limp, without some tic or tremor or deeply blue eyes telling their history. I never wanted to see that devastating pain on Gina's face—her innocence was so lovely, so beautiful and inspiring to the rest of us, the whole family tried to shield her from depressing realities. It was an impulse that served her wrongly for twenty-five years. Despair came anyway, and with particular cruelty, when the house of cards collapsed abruptly in St. Vincent's that afternoon.

The heartbreaking blows into her handkerchief subsided eventually, and the room became eerily quiet. I halted my grinding work on the tube and listened hard, trying to locate her in the gray dimness. Was she all right? Without sounds I had trouble picturing her—or maybe I was afraid to imagine what her face looked like without its beautiful innocence. After a penetrating silence, I picked up the soft pad of new crepe soles squeaking slowly across the linoleum, like the hollow steps of a weary dancer leaving an empty auditorium after the show was over. They stopped at the head of my bed and Gina stood still for a long time, stroking my hair but keeping her thoughts to herself. She lifted my hand, then, and pressed it against a wet cheek.

"But did that stop Drumpety?" she finally asked, hoarsely, with the distinct inflection of doubt as she recited the cherished family line. "Oh noooooo . . ." she moaned, as if her breath were escaping through a narrow fissure in her airtight faith, leaking into a vacuum of misery she'd never anticipated. "Oh noooooo . . . not *Drumpety*."

9

THE REPORT ON ALPH

✎

"I'd be extremely flattered if you'd write a story exclusively for me sometime . . . Make it extremely squalid and moving," she suggested. "Are you at all acquainted with squalor?"

I said not exactly but that I was getting better acquainted with it, in one form or another, all the time, and that I'd do my best to come up to her specifications. We shook hands.

"Isn't it a pity that we didn't meet under less extenuating circumstances?"

I said it was, I said it certainly was.

"Good-bye," Esme said. "I hope you return from the war with all your faculties intact."

On the slim chance that I still cared about words as much as she did, although strong doubts had already begun to infiltrate her solid faith in that conviction, Gina chose her readings Thursday morning with a particular theme in mind. My siblings' first reaction in any crisis—whether it was being rejected as homecoming queen or facing the possibility of brain damage—was to reach for the books that had relieved them before, turning the pages until they found the passage that soothed or explained. Frank went to Camus and *The Stranger*. Gina went to Salinger's *Nine Stories*.

Usually a dramatic oral reader, Gina could impersonate a whole cast of characters with her uncanny mastery of regional accents and inflections, but that morning she couldn't seem to shed the heavily nasal tone of a deeply depressed Midwesterner. Her cold had obviously worsened. Her voice cracked noticeably while she read "For Esme—With Love and Squalor," a short story about the wish a young girl sends to a badly shell-shocked soldier, drowning in despair in an Army barracks. Thirteen-year-old Esme has sustained heavy damage from the war herself, and has tried to shield her vulnerable five-year-old brother from the full, grisly details. When she introduces him to the American G.I. she befriended in a tearoom one afternoon in Devon, England, she apologizes for the young boy's peculiar behavior. "He misses our father very much," she explains, then adds cryptically, "He was s-l-a-i-n in North Africa."

A few weeks after D-day the soldier, a writer in civilian life, sinks into an immobilizing depression. Having witnessed the kind of barbaric violence a man never forgets, he doesn't know how to bring this altered self back home, how to live again among the faithful correspondents overseas whose major grief during the war had been the shortage of cashmere yarn or the service falling off at Schrafft's. He can't bear to finish the letter from an older brother in Albany after he reads: "Now that the g.d. war is over and you probably have a lot of time over there, how about sending the kids a couple of bayonets or swastikas . . ." The wounded man sees with nerve-racking clarity that the savage violence against un-counted millions would come down, in the end, to souvenirs.

The passage Gina read over and over was when the emotionally distraught veteran opens Esme's letter, almost lost in the mail after a dozen canceled APO addresses, and feels redeemed by her innocence. An overwhelming gratitude washes over him when he realizes that at least one young survivor, who's experienced incredible losses during the war, has emerged with no trace of cynicism. By accepting Esme's simple, straightforward affection he's finally freed from his psychological paralysis and the "suffer-ing of being unable to love." A welcome drowsiness, the first cessation from the grimness of war, suddenly comes over him.

"You take a really sleepy man, Esme, and he always *stands a chance of again becoming a man with all his fac—with all his f-a-c-u-l-t-i-e-s intact."*

That was the wish foremost in Gina's mind as she read to my unconscious form Thursday morning. She wanted me back from the war, whole and together. Noting my blank face and depleted energy, she didn't think I had all the time in the world to reach this strategic objective. While the promised sleep of the story's conclusion would restore the soldier's sanity, she couldn't shake the conviction that the deep sleep holding me was steadily draining mine. She knew that if my dreams, like hers, had become a grim review of the nightmarish facts surrounding my existence, then getting up and carrying on was becoming that much harder.

"Mary Kay, wake up . . ." she called, as she did each morning after her reading. "Let's go, Sis—we haven't got all day here," she said, affecting the exasperated voice she used as my young roommate twenty years ago, when she faced the formidable task of rousing me every day. She shook my shoulder firmly, like she had then, as if the whole problem were that I'd forgotten to set my alarm again and overslept for seven days. Earlier in the week, she imagined at least a minimal response to her wake-up calls, interpreting my twitching cheek or clenched fist as a sign that I'd heard her. But the only movement she saw Thursday morning was the steady pumping of my chest, in passive surrender to the torture of the respirator. It looked to Gina like I'd quit the war completely.

"Mary *Kay* . . ." she whispered again in her own deep voice, no longer kidding around. "It's been *seven* days . . . What's going *on*, hon?" she asked, issuing a thick, watery sigh. "What can you be *thinking*?"

Until yesterday, she thought the only two outcomes of the coma were that I would live or die, and had no trouble depositing her considerable faith in the former. But a third possibility presented itself Wednesday afternoon with the neurological report, a devastating alternative she hadn't yet considered: Part of me might die, while the rest of me continued on. Once the thought occurred to her, it was impossible to dismiss. Now when she looked at the vacant expression on my face, when she observed my jaws grinding mindlessly or my knees jerking randomly, she had to consider the possibility that my comatose body might be all the sister she had left.

The evidence of abnormal brain waves kept her awake most of the night. If my brain were irreversibly damaged, she knew she would take care of me, she would feed me and change me and touch me with as much tenderness as our history compelled her to feel. But tending my empty shell would be a perpetual reminder of the mind she missed; yearning for the rest of me—the part she loved most—would be almost more painful than losing me altogether. She felt the tremors that must shake the sleep of loved ones when Alzheimer's strikes, helplessly watching a cherished mind become gradually boarded up until finally, nobody's home when they call.

She had to suppose I might not remember significant moments of our past, that I wouldn't recognize her as the sentimental flower girl who watered her bouquet during my critical moment at the altar or the ecstatic godmother who taught my first son how to dance the boogaloo even before he could walk. She realized there might be no more giddy shopping trips, no more hugs or laughs or jokes. If my brain were permanently damaged and she had to learn to love me as a vegetable, wouldn't she have to let go of such recollections herself? Wouldn't it be easier to cease remembering, and therefore yearning?

Yet another stretcher-load of Gina's innocence was carried out of ICU that morning, when she recognized the uncompromising way disease claimed its victims. She saw how the devastating symptoms of certain illnesses, alcoholism, say, or senility or AIDS, overpowered who or what a person had been in the past and became the dominant fact of the present. When Frank had his first breakdown she was only four years old, and she understood now that she knew him primarily as a "manic-depressive." Who else had he been before disease redefined him? She was mortified that she didn't really know, that she hadn't thought to wonder. Through the eyes of the hospital staff she saw that I was now mainly "the coma case"—it was an effort for them to imagine me in any of the lively, engaging roles she described. It troubled Gina that after seven days in ICU, her own grasp of me was slipping badly. When she closed her eyes and thought about me last night she, too, had pictured a mute and lifeless coma case.

Daily routines were welcome distractions from her overwrought thinking, and Gina stuck resolutely to hers. After the readings and monologues designed to rouse me failed again that morning, she picked up her notebook, with a fresh installment of "Phyllis's Twenty Questions," and tracked down Dr. Greenbaum for her daily tutorial in critical care medicine. On March 29, 1984, she made the following entry in her journal:

No morphine. Very high doses of Valium. Greenbaum said she must remain sedated—when she gets agitated and thrashes around she doesn't get enough oxygen.

Pressure on oxygen—reducing it slowly. Problem from sarcoid and cavities—G. fears lung wall blowing out from pressure. Must reduce if "we want her to recover with some situation she can live with." More problems if lung wall gets too soft—not enough pressure means not enough oxygen.

Adult Respiratory Distress Syndrome—still has some symptoms, but responding very well to treatment for pneumonia and infections.

Diabetes was severe—but under control now with insulin.

No more test results neurologically for another 24 hours—and even then they won't tell us much about her mental state. G. says what we observe is a more important indicator of how she's doing. He does see acuity, but says: "She can stay like this for awhile."

On the face of it, Thursday's report was an improvement over Wednesday's, but Gina was hardly cheered by the news that I might "stay like this for awhile." The more calm I became in my Valium haze, the more disturbing she found it. Given the givens of my life, she thought "agitated" was a perfectly healthy response. From her lay point of view, she thought I needed my anger even more than oxygen—maybe I was supposed to ride this one out, breathlessly to the end. She didn't share this hunch with Dr. Greenbaum, however. Launching an unorthodox, emotional theory about a coma to the chief of Critical Care Medicine, without feeling ridiculous, required a lot of confidence. Gina was running on empty.

After recording the medical data in her journal she faced the next item on her daily agenda—it was her miserable duty to notify the family of my condition every day. Although she invariably began with the "good news," such as it was, she knew that dropping "the possibility of brain damage" on my parents and siblings would have the same effect as pulling the pin on a hand grenade. In the last seven days, she'd encountered her immediate relatives with their defenses down, before they had time to carefully conceal their pain from her. Without their disguises, she discovered a vulnerability she'd never seen before, admitting her to new levels of intimacy, but also anxiety. The baby of the family was now in charge of grief management—and her reports from the hospital aroused more than she knew what to do with.

She generally called Paul first, her soul mate in the family. He was the most reliable, though not necessarily most grounded, seer and adviser—particularly on matters concerning the folks. When she had to break the news of my coma last Sunday, he was the first one she called:

"Hi, Paul, it's me," she said when he picked up the phone in Ottawa last weekend.

"Hi, Gene!" he exclaimed, surprised to hear from her. Long-distance phone calls were a step into the twentieth century my family made only with difficulty. The telephone in our house was an instrument of business, to be conducted swiftly and with respect for incoming calls. Whenever one of the kids had been camped out on the kitchen floor under the wall phone Jerry had invariably appeared in the doorway and pointed to the clock, pantomiming a message that time was money. For the fifteen years all seven of us lived together, on and off, we learned to talk fast. My father had established a five-minute rule after he spent three unsuccessful hours one afternoon trying to penetrate the busy signals of his five children, finally having to call a neighbor to deliver an important message to our mother. He had taken a firm stand against long-winded conversations and never wavered.

When my immediate relatives had the urge to reach out and touch someone, it was generally done through the less expensive and more leisurely method of the postal system. So Paul instantly suspected something was up. "How *are* you, Gene?"

"Fine, fine . . . I'm fine! How are you?" she stalled, squandering a precious minute.

"What's wrong, Gene?" he asked, ignoring her words and listening to her inflection instead.

"It's Mary Kay, Paul." Gina delivered the details of the coma, recognizing from the drop in his voice that he was wearing the flip side of his Knocked Out look. This brother so devoted to achieving spiritual detachment had an enormous quantity of human emotion to transform—by 1984, his face was still such a clear reflection of glee or despair, even his young nephews could tell during poker games whether he held aces or deuces.

With exactly two years between us, Paul was my closest confidant throughout childhood. He was smart and funny and had the same incredible blue eyes, simultaneously intense and easy to talk to, that our mother had. During our college years, we took over the Ping-Pong table in the basement and set up our typewriters, passing term papers and works-in-progress back and forth across the net. Paul was the inspiration behind my early quests for truth, first through Catholicism, then Zen and other Eastern philosophies; and he was my steady companion through the most rigorous lessons of love, when we looked madness in the eye on the ninth floor of ISPI and vowed to see it through, however terrifying the exorcism became. He was such an important and affectionate brother, his approval was one of my first addictions. After twenty-five years of continuous indulgence, the withdrawal pains of the last few years had been excruciating.

A seemingly unmendable break began with the social upheavals of the seventies, when I joined the women's movement and Paul identified with the resistance. Becoming a feminist brought intense alienation from all previous learning, including the learning I acquired in my own family. My appearances during holidays and family reunions were cataclysmic events, when I clashed noisily with honored traditions. One Thanksgiving I sat down with the men in front of the TV after dinner, even though football bored me, and proposed it was their turn to do the dishes . . . for the next twenty-five years. I took exception to any joke at the dinner table that offended my new sensibilities—a one-liner could invite a forty-five minute lecture on the evils of racism or sexism. I was neither subtle nor skillful in my campaign for change. I conducted an all-frequencies assault on my family's ears.

Those were the years the word *feminist* rarely appeared in print without "strident and hysterical" somewhere in the same paragraph. Even when feminists spoke softly, however, we were perceived as strident and hysterical, because that's how most people received the idea that men should do their own ironing. The most serious issues brought the most heated rejection—when Susan Brownmiller revealed unwelcome truths about rape in *Against Our Will*, she was accused of being a "man-hater" and writing a book that was unkind to men. Apparently, the women's movement was the first revolution in history that was supposed to accomplish its goals without hurting anyone's feelings. "Man-hater" was a difficult label for a peace-loving woman to wear, but I didn't see any choice. The only way not to hurt anyone's feelings was to remain silent. Silence, for a writer, was a kind of death.

It was my first experience with the terrible choice between telling the truth or being loved. I found it far easier to open the newspaper and read a hostile letter-to-the-editor from an Eagle Forum member in Fort Wayne than to sit down in the polite silence that surrounded me at the family dinner table. Peace was achieved by limiting the conversation to topics we could agree on, which left us with the time and the weather—and even the weather could invite a controversy about why hurricanes were named after women.

Paul coped with the maelstroms by adopting a Zen-like detachment, refusing to argue or become engaged in my passions. His implacable serenity infuriated me, thwarting my enormous need to be understood. "You seem like a jerk to me," his composure seemed to say, "but you are who you are, and have an obligation to do what you do. I accept this jerkness in you, but refuse to get involved in it." Feeling chastised by his silence, I became even more inept in my communication with him. Ideas I expressed articulately—sometimes even eloquently—to audiences all over the Midwest became clunking and irritating monologues to Paul. Jerkness was in me, all right, in direct proportion to my need for his approval. To salvage my dignity, I established a cool distance of my own.

It was almost five years since we'd had a heart-to-hearter or come anywhere close to admitting "I love you," but Paul did not achieve complete detachment. A week after Gina returned from a visit in Fort Wayne and relayed her intuitive hunches about the grim state of my finances, a packet of checks arrived in the mail from Canada, with a brief note wishing me well in my writing career. "One hundred dollars, U.S. Funds," postdated every other Friday for the next six months, kept me alive at Kroger that year. I thanked him for his unsolicited generosity, but his finely calibrated conscience would not admit any gratitude. Since he knew I railed against a man's presumed superiority, and he himself was confused by the twists and turns in our relationship, he thought adding gratitude to money would only complicate the equation. The next packet of checks came with a note asking me to receive them anonymously, as it were, without any thanks that might disturb his detachment and mess him up again in the pleasure of gratitude. By 1984, we were exchanging favors without acknowledging affection, an uneasy truce that left us both wanting. But his detachment was utterly shattered when he was hit with the grenade of my coma.

"Geez . . ." Paul said, speechless when Gina finished her report. "Geez," he repeated over and over, the monosyllable in our family vernacular that meant: "I got a D on my midterm" or "Look how she butchered my *hair!*" It was the only word that came to our lips when all seven of us huddled together on the couch in the bluish glow of the TV, watching the news the night John F. Kennedy was assassinated. "Geez . . ." we said between our tears when our beloved Irish Catholic president was slain. We meant, "How could this *be*?"

Gina had been counting on Paul to volunteer to call the folks, but it was clear he was in worse shape than she was. Instead, she asked him to supply reinforcements, to check in with them later that night after she made the first assault. Dialing their number in Florida, she prayed Kay would answer the phone. Jerry was not the member of the parental team whose face you wanted to picture while talking about comas.

Nobody answered the phone in Punta Gorda, however, all afternoon. Since Gina had to leave for New York the responsibility fell back on Paul, who promised to keep trying. He called their neighbors and, unable to locate them, finally contacted the sheriff of Punta Gorda, who posted a note on their door, instructing them to call him for an important message. It was the local sheriff who eventually made the first assault. They called Paul immediately and when Gina finally reached them late Sunday night after she returned from her first visit to St. Vincent's, they had barely recovered their defenses.

"Hi, hon!!!" Jerry shouted, as he always did long distance. "Do you have any news about Mary Kay? How are *you*?!!!" There were certain phrases my father delivered from his field of exclamation points that demanded in-kind replies.

"I'm fine!!!" Gina shouted back, then remembered that she was not. She adjusted her voice down several octaves and said, "Yes, Dad, I have some news."

"Okay! I'll get your mother," he said automatically. In our parents' division of labor Jerry handled the greetings, the "Hi, hon!"'s, while Kay managed the news. Amidst the combustible Irish passions in our family, Kay was the layer of asbestos containing the flare-ups, the level-headed leader who restored equilibrium. Gina was intimately familiar with the multiple expressions in our mother's blue eyes, but she'd never before seen the look that her clairvoyant machinery spun out as she spoke to her late Sunday night. Gina thought she heard the sound of defeat. This was not the mother she knew.

She was stunned when Kay seemed willing—even grateful—to yield her position as leader in the crisis to the baby of the family. It would not have been so amazing if Gina had factored in how almost two decades of madness could diminish a mother's claim to power, if she had witnessed the shock and despair that crossed those eyes every Thursday night at ISPI. But Gina and Kevin were excluded from the dramas the rest of us enacted on psychiatric wards, based on Kay's determination to guarantee them a happy childhood. By March of 1984, almost two and a half years after the suicide of her firstborn son, Kay's blue eyes no longer held the conviction that she would fix things. She promised to pray for me, but she couldn't promise to come to New York and stop this coma.

Kevin was the last sibling she notified, her closest in age and nearest rival. Fourth in the birth line, Kevin had the toughest position in the family. There was a seven-year space between him and his oldest brother, next to whom Paul and I were tightly aligned, and an eight-year space between him and his youngest sister. The triumvirate ahead of him set an oppressive record of overachievement, while the baby behind him charmed the socks off of everyone, so Kevin settled into the role of family fuck-up. Somebody had to do it.

He was a nattering teaser, particularly to his sisters, and I spent most of my adolescence demanding that Kay "*do* something about this *beastly* child." Histrionics were my specialty, even as a youth.

"Be patient." Kay would smile. "He'll mature some day." But even Kay's mettle could be rattled by his exuberant goofiness. While she was peeling potatoes at the kitchen sink one afternoon, she listened to Kevin needling Gina until he had her close to tears. My mother's general philosophy toward all disputes was to let the warring parties "work it out," but this flare-up showed no sign of settling down.

"Kevin!" Kay exclaimed, potato peels flying in the air as she slammed her hand down on the counter to get his attention. "For years, you and Mary Kay were at each other's throats, and now it's you and Gina! What do you think that *indicates*?" She steeled her eyes in his direction, waiting for the humbled acknowledgment that look always inspired.

"I dunno." Kevin shrugged, genuinely baffled. "Maybe Gina gets it from Mary Kay."

His ingenious explanations made him the most quotable member of the family. Throughout elementary and high school, his teachers reported during parent conferences that high scores on his aptitude tests proved he "wasn't working up to capacity," and Kay and Jerry tried valiantly to rescue his potential. He was grounded and curfewed and sentenced to solitary confinement more than the rest of us collectively, but these strategies made almost no difference in his grades. One evening he came down to the basement where Paul and I were studying, flopped down on the couch next to the Ping-Pong table, and offered a resigned view of his fate: "You guys are really lucky," he sighed. "You were born with the will to study."

His own will awakened shortly after college, when he scored high on a civil service exam and became a federal bank examiner. Hard work was rewarded with a successive string of promotions, and falling in love matured Kevin almost beyond recognition. Everything had changed by 1984. He was a husband and a father, a graduate student on his way to an MBA, and an important executive with a bright future in the banking business. The family fuck-up was now an intelligent counselor and financial adviser to his eldest sister and the benevolent personal loan officer to his younger one.

Paul thought Kevin was a simultaneous reincarnation of Jerry—a serious family man of intense loyalty, whose corny bank jokes kept moans rolling at family dinners after our father retired. To Gina, however, the changes were not all joyous. He'd gone and grown up without her. The only Peter Pan left in the family, Gina hated it when Kevin pulled sibling rank on her—whether he actually did or she merely thought he did, she was touchy about the air of maturity a solid income and growing family provided. Her personal loans from him were as emotionally freighted as the money exchanged on the tier above her.

"Hi, Kev, it's Gina," she said in her most adult voice. "How are you?"

"Hi, Gene—I'm wonderful!!!" he replied. "Good to hear from you! What's up?" Fatigued by the difficult reactions to her earlier assaults, Gina was beginning to think the happiness in our family was pathological. She had to keep knocking down exclamation points until Kevin, too, was reduced to flattened monosyllables.

"Shit . . ." he said. "Shit. I can't believe it." Despite the tens of thousands of dollars Kay and Jerry poured into higher education, the most intelligible replies Gina collected from the graduates were "Geez" and "Shit." Nowhere in her conversations with senior family members was there a glimmer of advice about what to do. Kevin's reaction was no help at all—incapacitated by grief, his immediate response was to get mad.

"I *told* her this could happen—I *warned* her last month," he said. "*God,* I'm gonna *kill* her for pulling a stunt like this." He had, in fact, expressed deep alarm when he learned of my diabetes last October. After some twenty years of freewheeling youth, he'd become a worrier of the first degree. Diabetes was the worst news to drop into Kevin's easily incited nervous system. Last year, his diabetic sister-in-law went into insulin shock during a visit and it scared the bejesus out of him.

"I *told* her to find another doctor after those jerks in Ann Arbor put in the tube—I'm gonna *kill* those bastards," he fumed. "When she comes out of this thing, we're gonna sue the *life* out of them." Kevin, the most ardent pacifist at Southern Illinois University in 1969, threatened to kill or sue somebody once a week. It was sheer ballast—it meant nothing. In truth, Kevin could no more kill someone than St. Francis of Assisi could do without birds.

By Thursday, Gina's journal was full of raw, undigested observations about the unusual methods family members employed to cope with their helplessness. Kevin expanded his hit list with every report—it now included anyone who presided over my illness in Ann Arbor and New York, as well as everyone who'd chanced a diagnosis anywhere in between. Kay and Jerry spent each morning at church, praying through Mass and kneeling in their pew long afterward, saying extra rounds on their rosaries. Paul sought comfort with his teacher, Dr. Ramesh Waghmare, a former professor of economics and longtime friend.

Paul found in Waghi, as he called him, the same uninhibited joy he loved in Jerry. A short, trim man with dark skin and brilliant eyes, Waghi's smile beamed with the same high intensity as our father's. Once, at a picnic Paul had hosted for the two families a few summers before in Ottawa, he had looked up from the barbecue grill and seen his two most influential "high beings" sitting together in animated conversation. Jerry was hard of hearing and, like me, occasionally had trouble understanding Waghi's musical Indian dialect. He caught only every other word, but the teacher's expressive face easily filled in the blanks. Wordlessly, Jerry nodded and grinned broad agreement, inspiring equally delighted nods and grins in return. As the hamburgers sizzled, unattended, Paul became entranced with the high-voltage light emanating from the lawn chairs across the patio. I quickly handed him my sunglasses. If he got knocked out, there went our dinner.

"The man is so *humble*," Paul said of his friend, wearing his KO'ed look. Humility in people dazzled Paul, one of the notable handicaps in my relationship with him. Kay and Jerry, who were at first concerned about Paul's deep interest in Hindu and Zen, were both relieved after they met this warm and compassionate man in person. However strange or mysterious Paul's spiritual path seemed from their devoutly Catholic point of view, it was obviously good for him. We all loved Waghi. I loved him because he was a dependably human high being, whose detachment was so complete he forgot to pack on moving day, before Paul and his wife, Debbie, arrived in their jeans and sweatshirts to help him load the truck. Waghi stood in his doorway, waving and smiling radiantly as Paul drove the rented U-Haul into the driveway.

"Ready?" Paul called, grinning back.

"Ready!" Waghi called. He meant spiritually, of course, because when they entered his living room Paul was stunned to find everything exactly where it had been for the last five years.

"Wagh . . . you haven't *packed* anything?" Dumbfounded, he looked in the kitchen. "You don't even have any *boxes*." They had to lease the truck an extra day—it sat empty in the driveway while Paul and Deb and Waghi and "Mama," as everyone called his wife Mangal, packed their household of cups and saucers, the hockey sticks and computers in the twins' room, and boxes upon boxes of books. A strong believer in the virtues of time management, Paul was sometimes rattled by the loose grip his friend had on the necessary details of everyday life. But the mental energy Waghi saved on daily tediums permitted him a larger view of life, and how it ought to be spent.

When the unexpected blow of my coma stirred fresh regrets about the strained affections between us the last few years, Paul brought his turbulent emotions to Waghi. His teacher's musical voice, together with the passages he shared from inspired yogis, gave Paul another way to think about comas. If he accepted the notion that all beings were advancing toward light, however ploddingly, a life-threatening coma might actually be useful. Being out of body, after all, was not an entirely dreadful experience. Waghi urged Paul to consider the possibility that a coma might be my peculiar route to a higher state of realization.

As Dr. Shunryu Suzuki explained in *Zen Mind, Beginner's Mind*: "Nothing outside yourself can cause any trouble. You yourself make waves in your mind. If you leave your mind as it is, it will become calm. This mind is called big mind . . . For us there is no fear of losing this mind. There is nowhere to come or go; there is no fear of death, no suffering from old age or sickness. Because we enjoy all aspects of life as an unfolding of big mind, we do not care for any excessive joy. So we have imperturbable composure."

Since Dr. Suzuki was dying of cancer when he delivered his lecture on "no fear of death," he persuaded his devotees to think of his imminent departure as a welcome transmission: "If when I die, the moment I'm dying, if I suffer that is all right, you know; that is suffering Buddha . . . that is not a problem. We should be very grateful to have a limited body . . . like mine, or like yours. If you had a limitless life it would be a real problem for you."

Since Paul considered the possibility that a coma could be a temporary, out-of-body journey into the mysterious waves of a higher state of being, Gina's report of unusual brain patterns did not upset this theory. Although Dr. McLarnon's neurological report did not use the exact words, "imperturbable composure," the results were essentially the same. Paul thought I could have no more comforting companion through a difficult spiritual passage than the high being he saw in his youngest sister, and expressed complete confidence in Gina's intuitive judgments. He recognized the thin membrane between us. Nevertheless, he volunteered to fly down from Canada if she needed his help.

She thanked him and asked him to stand by for another day or so. Since she was already having trouble communicating her unorthodox views to the hospital staff, Gina didn't think Paul's mystical views—and what sounded like incredible happiness over the phone—would aid her flailing credibility in ICU. The concept of coma as satori, for those who scrupulously believed in glucose factors and antibiotic drugs, would cause more eyes to roll back politely.

But Gina herself welcomed Paul's theory. When a person is drowning in despair, especially in army barracks or on hospital wards, the fragile contents of letters and phone calls becomes enormously important. Paul and Gina shared an immense gift of faith, and she had no difficulty accepting his spiritual diagnosis. Despair could accelerate the need to reach beyond reason even for rationalists like myself, who possessed no faith in anything we couldn't see and prove. I'd had enormous difficulty accepting the explanation of his madness Frank wrote two months before his suicide, but when I reread his letter on the train to Chicago, on my way to his funeral, I believed him.

For the three hours between Fort Wayne and Gary, I looked numbly out the window and wept, flooded with memories of the mountains of mashed potatoes he had consumed at my kitchen table that weekend, of the endless leaves he couldn't stop raking, of his last haircut—the best I'd ever given him—of his manic grin lighting up as I hollered, "*Yes*, goddamn it, I *love* you!" Why? Why eat, why rake, why have a haircut, why love if you know you're going to die? Why had he looked so wonderful to me, waving from the door of the Greyhound, when I knew as clearly as I'd ever known that he was not a well man? Already wrecked by grief and convinced I had nothing to lose, I took his letter out of my purse and reread it. Those six handwritten pages were responsible for the addled grin I was wearing when I greeted Jerry's "Hi, hon!!!" at Union Station thirty minutes later:

September 4, 1981

Dear Mary Kay,
    I feel like a man in the arctic who has just thrown his last log on the fire or like a man in the desert who has just swigged his last bit of

water. And he thinks, "If I thrash around awhile, I may find more wood or more water—there's a million to one chance, at least. But I'd rather enjoy my last moments of life and maybe hope and pray for a miracle."

I've made hundreds of applications in the last two months and been on dozens of interviews, all for jobs well within my ability. But the general feeling is that I'm overqualified or underqualified ... and there doesn't seem to be anything in between. This is the worst job market I've ever seen. Employers tell me that when they placed the same ad two years ago, they got only three or four responses. Now they get forty or fifty. The official rate of unemployment is seven percent (compared to six percent two years ago), but that doesn't take account of all the people who are driving empty cabs or selling the *Tribune* door to door.

I slept (or lay in bed at least) for almost 20 hours yesterday, from 1 P.M. to 9 A.M. It was absurd, but there was no reason to get up and I thought I might as well do what I most enjoy in my final weeks of life, before the money runs out and I have to commit suicide to keep from going back to Elgin ... and suicide seems the preferable alternative.

I feel half-dead now, since getting up this morning, which I wondered if I would ever do. It was like a resurrection when I found I had some voluntary will for a position other than flat on my back. I have a feeling of emptiness, nothingness, weakness, floating (toward the waterfall perhaps, the impending doom), drifting, quite different from "the feeling of absolute power," as you called it once. But it's not unpleasant, because I like to think the current bearing me along is ultimately benevolent, even if I have to go over the waterfall of death with it.

I read your latest essay this morning—sometimes I get the feeling about your writing that you are trying to weave a spell around what you say rather than saying it outright. Certainly I would have a hard time sketching in Roman numerals the outline of your thought, but then I might have a hard time diagramming my own sentences; I'm flying much too fast for that. But you are touching underground a current of meaning, or trying to, giving us the report on Alph, the sacred river, on limited instruments—or maybe my ability to interpret the message is limited. Anyway, I respect that you are in touch with something deep within you, the beat is flowing through you, and if I do not appreciate your dance and your incantation I can at least see that something is there, something is moving you, there is sense in what you write even though the completion of the network comes later to me; the lines of tension are drawing, redrawing, casting, recasting, like the little loops in your sewing that bit by bit draw the fabric into its destined shape.

I like to think that all things are true, but only partly true, in dialectical fashion, more true than what came before, less true than what comes after. Even Adolph Hitler was in at least one way better than the Weimar Republic, moving from the concept of a kingdom ruled by autocratic powers to the concept of the Deutsche Volk, the living organic unity, however monstrous and terrible was the war and the concentration camps. I have to believe that if I believe God is good. The reason we have suffering is that progress can only be achieved at a price, because goodness has to be made out of badness, and the raw material has to be refined by fire and mixed with alloys before it can become strong. This is what I like to believe, anyway. The alternative is to believe that we are subject to invasions of absurdity and chaos for no reason at all.

So I like to think, too, that something good will come from my madness, that something is being fashioned here by divine intelligence, monstrous and terrible as it may seem to those around me, and to me, too, in retrospect.

I'm talking out of my mind now, which scares me a little. I like to know at all times exactly what I'm doing. But Alph, alas (but Hooray! also) is wiser than we are, so we can only grope toward the music, play our all against his-her all and try again. I hope this all makes some sense to you, because I am writing now the way you do, by intuition rather than logic. Do you grope me?

I think I will go for another walk now, just drifting along as the current moves me, because in the current are all things, Victory and Achievement and Truth. But now is not the time for writing, or reading, or hunting for a job, or sleeping, but just for walking along.

"It is hard for you to kick against the good."

"Without Me you can do nothing."

"I lack the will to study."

Love,
Frank

10

THE CEDAR HOTEL

BY THURSDAY EVENING, Gina was in the same hyperalert, aggressively nurturant state I was in two and a half years earlier, when I had arrived in Chicago for Frank's funeral. As the train pulled into Union Station I had refolded his letter and put it back in the envelope, taken out my compact, and covered the bright pink patches of skin on my cheeks and forehead with a heavy layer of powder. I achieved, essentially, the pancaked aura of a tattooed lady trying to conceal her freakishness on her day off. It was ultimately a pointless disguise, since my skin heated up and broke out again the moment I joined my similarly inflamed relatives. Jerry saw me first among the disembarking passengers and launched his ebullient hello.

"We're over here!" he called, unnecessarily, for nobody in that corner of the massive waiting room could have dodged his luminescent grin. My mother and sister were standing beside him, smiling and waving only slightly more moderately, and together they formed the kind of visibly impassioned welcoming committee that might have given a more stoic arrival the bends. But my own emotions, already in high gear, easily matched theirs. Though my arms were pinned down by two suitcases and a shoulder bag, I flipped my elbows back and forth in a makeshift wave. I probably looked like an overweight turkey, flapping my wings for a futile takeoff, but I didn't care. This was my family; this was who we were.

Still a handsome and vigorous man in his late seventies, Jerry wove through the crowd to give me a hand with my luggage. The strangers around him opened a path and yielded the right of way, as if by some unspoken, unanimous vote he'd won the nomination for Best Greeter. Relieving me of my luggage, he immediately dropped it on the floor and encased me in a rib-crunching hug. Ever since the therapist at ISPI had questioned the inadequate affection relayed by formal handshakes, Jerry had returned, with immeasurable relief, to his bone-crushing habits.

Kay and Gina, only seconds behind him, joined us to form a tight, four-person huddle around my suitcases. Being unabashed public huggers, my family frequently blocked the roped intersections in train and airline lobbies, but this was an unusually prolonged and needy grip. A dark awareness of why we'd come together for this unplanned reunion hung heavily on the huddle. Smiling like four mad fools while tears streamed down from red-rimmed eyes, our unairbrushed faces looked beautifully human to me, so damp and sunny at once I imagined a small rainbow forming over us.

It was probably Kay who cleaned herself up first and reminded us that we had to keep moving. There were things to do. Jerry loaded my suitcases into the trunk of the car and then commenced a white-knuckle drive up the Kennedy Expressway to O'Hare Airport, where Paul was landing from Ottawa. We formed another rainbow in the international wing, before heading home to wait for Kevin's arrival by car from Southern Illinois. Once the troops were amassed, we began preparations for Frank's funeral.

We all cherished different parts of him, each of us becoming focused on the strange fragments of life he left behind. I found Kay in the basement late that night, sitting on the cot where Frank sometimes slept, staring at the pair of black shoes he left there. She was thinking about the calluses on his feet. I sat down on the cot next to her, watching her watch his shoes. She said it was hard to believe that just five days ago, he'd walked clear across the city from the room he rented in Uptown to have dinner at home, a trek that took him a little over three hours. He preferred walking to swifter modes of travel, especially when he had any serious thinking to do.

After dinner, he had taken off his shoes and socks to rub his feet before starting out again, and Kay had noticed the thick calluses covering his soles. She coaxed him to stay an extra hour so she could treat them. She remembered talking, sitting across the kitchen table from him, his pant legs rolled up to his knees while he soaked his feet in the warm sudsy solution she prepared. After he'd pickled for an hour or so, she put a towel in her lap, lifted one foot at a time, and went to work, filing down calluses and massaging skin cream into his overtraveled soles.

"He was so sweet that evening," she said, addressing his shoes. The soothing pedicure had apparently achieved what innumerable doses of Thorazine and lithium never could. "He was so relaxed afterwards," she said, "he let Dad drive him home."

"It's funny," she said, smiling ruefully at the creased black oxfords that had covered thousands of miles of city pavement. "Of all the ways to spend your last hours together—but I'm just so glad I *did* that."

I was glad, too, for the expression she wore that night relieved any worries about how Kay would come through Frank's death. If such a thing could be measured in the wildly fluctuating passions of my family, her grief would be largest—she knew him most intimately, fought hardest to save him, had the greatest investment in him. I knew those intelligent blue eyes could not look unflinchingly at suicide and remain unchanged. There were plenty of memories that could have left permanent traces of anger or guilt, had those chapters of their history dominated in the end. Instead, the innocence she lost during the long years of illness was replaced with solid compassion. Frank had an uncanny way of putting Kay in touch with her tenderness.

Frank's madness uncloaked secret selves in all of us—the outrageous acts and provocative taunts of manic-depression pushed Jerry to heights of rage he'd never experienced, before or since, and Gina was equally surprised to meet an angrier version of herself. But Kay was the most startling relative to meet in the altering environment of this disease. The change wasn't immediate—through the first decade of his illness she was the familiar, dependable leader, tracking down specialists, bolstering flagging hopes, listening and reading and examining herself at length. Once she understood, however, that neither medicine nor psychology were advanced enough to cure him, and that even her own herculean will and discipline couldn't help him, the perfectionism that drove her relationships with her children yielded to the vast store of mercy just below it.

I envied the love I saw the first time I observed it at ISPI, directed across the conference room to Frank. Wholly free of expectations, it wasn't the same unconditional love she wore in the movies of Gina's homecoming—the straightforward, untested affection that must have welcomed all of us as infants, before duty and responsibility complicated things. No, this was what unconditional love looked like on the other side of motherhood, after the expectations had all come and gone, after forgiveness triumphed over a turbulent history. Every time I saw her eyes expose that naked tenderness—the vulnerable part of herself my mother kept most private—I thought I should look away.

The jealousy I felt the first time I saw her undiluted love for Frank gradually subsided when I realized it would be mine, too, but only when Kay thought there was nothing more she could do. While her affection for me still carried a formidable load of expectations, I couldn't see or hear her criticism now without recognizing that it was all flourish, the ceremonial trumpets she had to sound before feeling entitled to play the most harmonious, most elevated strains of love. When Gina, unfamiliar with the transition notes, heard Kay sigh, "I suppose there's nothing we can do," she mistook it for defeat. Had she been privy to the earlier sighs, however, she would have recognized mercy being ushered in—those sighs announced a kind of general maternal amnesty for all previous crimes. Gina, bearing the prolonged dishonor of her multiple incompletes, might even have felt jealous if she knew what a tremendous quantity of forgiveness would be heading my way.

That was what the business with Frank's feet was all about— Kay was practicing the tenderness he evoked in her. It was a perfectly Zen gesture, caring for a callus when a suicide was right around the bend, a scene the poet Basho might have praised as a lesson in pure detachment. I was sure the religious implications of the ritual weren't lost on Frank, who tended to interpret all actions spiritually—most certainly, a spontaneous foot washing after dinner on an unusually Holy Thursday. Of all the mixed emotions Kay must have felt staring at his shoes in the basement that night, the one overwhelming all the others was unqualified affection. I knew she would emerge from Frank's death satisfied that she had done everything she could. She loved him right down to the calluses on his feet.

The physical symbols Frank left behind were indeed meager—
Kay got his creased black shoes, I inherited his stocking cap. But
the distribution, haphazard and unofficial as it seemed, was
ultimately appropriate. His stocking cap, the headgear he used to
muffle the voices, was probably the most useful bequest he could
have given me. The private emotion I managed to keep buried,
until Frank's sickness unleashed it, was a terrific fear of becoming
insane myself.

That I could *follow* the mad tracks of his mind, even on the
deviant paths he took through psychiatric wards, worried me
enormously. I, too, swung wildly between poles of joy and
despair—never as far as he did, but never fully insured against that
possibility either.

"You never seem angry with me," he said during one of my
visits at the Reed Mental Health Center. "Everyone else in the
family can get angry with me but you. What's wrong with you,
M.K.?" he teased, aware of my fears. "What do you think that
indicates?" he prompted, quoting Kay's famous question. He
loved to get a rise out of us—it made him feel potent, engaged, the
center of our universe. He laughed, taunting me with the suggestion that I just might qualify for a cell of my own, right next to his.

How could I be angry? How could I genuinely wish he'd "come
down" from his gleeful highs when I knew where it would
eventually take him? His manic antics even made some sense to
me, when I got past my embarrassment for him. One evening in a
Fort Wayne restaurant I had tried to have a rational discussion
with him, dutifully urging him to consider the consequences of
recent actions that, if continued, were certain to land him in a
hospital again. But he had been flying so high with joy he had no
tolerance for grim lectures.

Abruptly, he had gotten up from the table and broken into a
little dance, performing an Irish jig and singing: "My name is
MacNamara, I'm the leader of the band, I play at wakes and
weddings, I'm the finest in the land . . ." He had amused himself
for several minutes before he noticed the dumbfounded stares
from the other patrons and decided to bring them in on his joke.
He stopped dancing and spread out his arms, taking in the whole
of his audience with a contagious, resplendent grin. With a low,
gracious bow, he addressed me in a dignified British accent,

borrowed from one of his internal characters: "And that, darling, is the only point I wish to make this evening."

He then sat down again with complete beau geste, as if he had successfully concluded a little spat we were having, laughing with enjoyment at my embarrassment. So, of course, did everyone else in the dining room. Trust a crowd to side with a charismatic madman over a doomsaying rationalist every time.

Only the most controlled person could hear Frank's laugh, his manic speeches, and not be taken in by them. It was the laugh of a man who sees joy when all the stops have been pulled out from a mind. Daffily in love with life, in love with *you*, he did in fact make coming back to reality seem a ridiculous goal. How can you really wish reality on someone so consumed by happiness?

It was enormously difficult to come away from public incidents with Frank without losing track, however momentarily, of who was nuts and who was not. His actions, though bizarre, didn't necessarily classify him as a lunatic—Gina had danced in public, in *taxicab* shoes, and she wasn't crazy. And Frank's restaurant audience had laughed with, not at him. Did that make them psychotic by association? Even among the doctors who committed him and the police who arrested him for "creating a nuisance," there was a grudging admiration for his bold unrepentance, as if below their uniformed authority they suffered from a dearth of joy themselves. Through Frank I saw that even perfectly stable, presumably well-adjusted people were prone to envy his abandon, recognizing the purgative powers of madness. The question of insanity, from my own close perspective, was not a clear yes or no but a matter of degrees.

Frank had become craftier by his final breakdown, hiding the give-away symptoms that landed him in civil and mental jails. He tried to contain the compulsive pacing, the perpetual insomnia, the speaking in verse. I had watched him, grinning into his mashed potatoes the last night we had dinner together, when he had refused to share what, exactly, he thought was so funny.

"I can't tell you," he had said, when I begged him to tell me what was up. Something was certainly Up.

"I can't tell you," he had repeated resolutely, "because you'll try to talk me out of it." The words seem transparently obvious now, but they weren't at the time because there were any number of schemes I'd tried to talk Frank out of in the last ten years. I had discouraged him from legally changing his name to Jesus Christ; I advised him not to run for governor as a third party, planetary candidate; I vowed to call the police myself if he proceeded with his plan to extinguish the eternal flame on JFK's grave in Arlington Cemetery. He was convinced it was a bad idea to promise anything "eternal" on earth—he thought truth changed too rapidly to rely on permanent symbols. None of my threats ever stopped a plan-in-progress, any more than Kay's filing down his calluses relieved his itch to keep pacing. I had stifled my urge to interrogate him any further, while he tried unsuccessfully to suppress his grin through dinner. I saw his knees swaying wildly under the table, keeping time with the beat, the beat, the beat.

It took every ounce of his willpower to remain seated, to choose his words carefully, to keep his secret plan sealed behind his translucent hazel eyes. "It's one of those times when the irrational will become rational," he offered cryptically. "I'm in 'that magical moment when *is* becomes *if . . .*'" He caught himself and stopped quoting e. e. cummings, replacing the rest of the poem with his quiet, lunatic grin. That smile was my personal legacy from Frank. I did, eventually, come to believe his last outrageous act was rational.

Kay reacted to his death with tenderness, I with uncharacteristic faith, and Kevin had a likewise unusual response. Kevin, the most handsome and truly lighthearted member of the family, was seized with an immense, unprecedented fury. He was going to kill everyone. When he heard questions about whether Frank could be buried in a Catholic cemetery, since Canon Law viewed suicide as a mortal sin, Kevin was enraged at the unnecessary pain it added to our parents' ordeal.

"After all the contributions Mom and Dad have made to that church, I can't *believe* this. I'll *kill* those guys if they can't let go of one lousy cemetery plot. Canon Law—gimme a break," he fumed.

Like Frank, Kevin was an ex-seminarian, the most skeptical breed of Catholics. Having spent their formative years observing the adolescent behavior of future priests, they had a hard time bestowing the superhuman qualities their former classmates were supposed to gain upon taking final vows. Even after adding the heightened dignity of "Father" to their boyhood names, Frank still saw his roman-collared friends as the boys who once threw spitballs at Father Jerome and thoroughly enjoyed it. Kevin's reverence was similarly qualified—he could have been a priest himself if he hadn't left Quigley Seminary voluntarily in his second year, and he was excruciatingly aware of how fallible *he* still was. In private conversation, he ignored the convention of "Father" and referred to the officials presiding over Frank's burial as "those jerks."

"What's the point of punishing a guy after he's dead? What a religion," he said, shaking his head. "This funeral isn't for Frank anyway—it's for Mom and Dad. I'm gonna kill those jerks if they blow this call."

Mercy prevailed over Canon Law and Frank was granted a plot in St. Mary's Cemetery. The decision hardly soothed Kevin, however, for there were more jerks at every turn. He questioned the competence at the funeral home, where the mortician couldn't guarantee an open casket for the wake; at the newspaper office, where the obituary writer misread my hasty, handwritten copy and assigned "Frances Jude Blakely" the wrong gender; at the florist shop, where the clerk reported there weren't enough white gardenias on hand to make a whole wreath. These small disappointments and offenses kept Kevin moving. His legacy from Frank was an unquenchable thirst for justice. He was so parched after his first full day of funeral planning he had to take a break and have a few beers with his old college pals. Kevin would be all right—an energetic anger lifted him out of despair and a sufficient quantity of beer rescued his sense of humor.

It was Paul's reaction that worried me most that weekend. He was neither angry nor relieved; he had no last memorable visit, no letter, no black shoes or stocking cap to meditate upon. In the last few years of illness, Paul hadn't argued with Frank to come back to reality with the same ferocious zeal I had. With sublime maturity, he'd accepted Frank's madness as his inevitable destiny, as the unfortunate karma he must have collected during one lifetime or another. When one cure failed after another, Paul came to terms with the fact that Frank would have to struggle with bouts of madness for the duration of his life.

For a man dedicated to achieving spiritual detachment, Frank was a major trial. Frank's main avocation was prodding incessant "I love you!"'s out of embarrassed relatives. Paul's imperturbable composure in the face of high-spirited performances was irritating to Frank, who needed the involvement of an audience to keep his juices flowing. So perhaps there was an element of punishment when Frank left him empty-handed at the end. Or maybe he thought Paul, only fifteen months behind him, was so advanced on his own spiritual path he didn't need an explanation for death. Whatever the reason for not saying good-bye, it hurt. Boy, did it hurt.

Paul spent most of the night talking to Waghi before he left Ottawa, but his pale blue eyes still wore a look of unrelieved shock by the time he landed at O'Hare the next afternoon. He had a copy of something by Sri Krishna Prem, the former Ronald Nixon of Cambridge University, tucked under his arm, but it was hard to believe he'd gotten much reading done on the plane. His jaw muscles had deserted him completely, dropping his mouth in slack-jawed astonishment, while his eyebrows rode high on his forehead, exposing the full whites of his eyes. An uncontrolled tic vibrated noticeably on his right temple, and the keen, light blue brilliance of his eyes was buried below the rubble of a smoky confusion. Upon arrival, he bore all the composure of a man who'd just been asked to please stand up a little straighter for the firing squad. Staring down the multiple barrels of grief aimed at him, he couldn't decide whether he wanted a blindfold or not.

Something essential to his inner harmony had been shattered by, not just death, but deliberately chosen death. Despite Waghi's assurance that Frank's decision didn't have to mean he'd abandoned his path—in fact, suicide may have been directly *on* his destined route—Paul took little comfort from it. Even if he accepted suicide as ultimately no more grievous than natural death, it would relieve only part of his pain. There was still the unsaid good-bye, the meaningful conversation forever denied.

I ached for him. Though we didn't have much in common by then—I was a seasoned back-talker, in the midst of introducing not only feminism but the first divorce to three generations of unbroken marriages—I did know something about the torment of being stuck with leftover words. His malfunctioning detachment and my aggressive nurturance made us an unusually compatible pair that week, as necessary to each other, say, as an exceptionally rusted tin man and a homesick, bereft Dorothy who happens to have an oil can.

We talked, uneasily at first, but eventually fell into the intimate, familiar rhythms that bounced steadily across the Ping-Pong table almost two decades ago. As in the old days, we began conducting a kind of unofficial grief patrol, looking out for stray regrets and arresting conversations that might upset Kay and Jerry, Kevin and Gina. When the whole crew met to divide up our funereal duties, Paul and I, now the two eldest siblings, volunteered for the hardest job.

Jerry and Gina took responsibility for finding a photograph of Frank for the wake, since there was a question about whether the casket would have to remain closed. He was a difficult subject to capture on film. The framed portrait from his college graduation hanging in the dining room, where one member of the family or another would get stuck for long minutes, staring and remembering, didn't really satisfy. Age hadn't affected much change in his youthful features, but experience certainly had. The unknowing twenty-one-year-old who smiled below the tasseled mortarboard was a flat facsimile of the intricate character who finally evolved from him.

They decided to enlarge a recent snapshot Frank's friend Marlene had taken on their tour through Germany that year, during his last calm period. Hardly anyone besides Marlene would risk traveling with Frank because of his maddening habits on the road—he never looked at a map, ignored recommended routes, and neglected to specify when he would return. It must have been a chilly evening when the picture was taken, for the beaver collar of his overcoat was turned up against the wind. I knew the scent of that beaver collar intimately, having smelled the Frankness it emanated season after season. He'd hugged me from the deep interior of that coat a hundred times.

It was just before dusk on a Bavarian night, and a dim, opaque light blurred all images except the slender profile of his face. He seemed to be disappearing into the darkening edges of the photograph, as if he'd made the weighty decision to remain in Brigadoon, giving up his only chance to step back through the fleeting crack in time. Waves of dark black hair curled onto his forehead, yielding to the night breezes, as he stared abstractedly at some vision outside the range of the camera. Thought was weaving an unconscious beauty across his face, in the quiet resolution of his eyes, the sweet sadness in his wan smile. Simultaneously serious and mischievous, enigmatic and sharply lucid, the picture captured the paradox of Frank.

It took Jerry and Gina most of the afternoon to frame the enlarged print at the do-it-yourself shop. Selecting a color for the mat took the longest, as they debated about whether to match the unusual light of the sky or the warm dark fur of his collar. Periodically that week, all of us had become engrossed in small questions, about the lettering on a gravestone or the color of a mat, grateful for the distraction from the larger questions that defied ready answers. After prolonged deliberation, my father and sister selected a muted brown-gold color, an excellent choice from my point of view. It directed the viewer's attention to exactly the right place in the portrait, to the translucent hazel eyes in the center of the scene where certain, inescapable facts radiated from his face about how he lived and who he was. To the astute observer, there was further valuable information explaining the circumstances of his death.

"In a seer, what part of the human anatomy would necessarily be required to take the most abuse? The *eyes*, certainly," J. D. Salinger wrote in *Seymour—An Introduction*. "However contradictory the coroner's report—whether he pronounces Consumption or Loneliness or Suicide to be the cause of death—isn't it plain how the true artist-seer actually dies? . . . I say that the true artist-seer, the heavenly fool who can and does produce beauty, is mainly dazzled to death by his own scruples, the blinding shapes and colors of his own sacred human conscience."

The clear prisms of Frank's eyes confirmed that diagnosis, as well as his own hunch that madness, at least in his case, was "a spiritual fever." Anyone who looked directly into those intense eyes would have to know that his death was unavoidable. Frank could no more have stopped himself from that final act than he could have stopped seeing, searching, knowing. That Bavarian snapshot, taken only months before the death itself, relieved any lingering illusions I had about whether I could have saved him. There was no saving a man with the flimsy gravity of human love once he's in orbit with divine inspiration.

I saw more of Frank in Marlene's wonderful photograph than I saw in the body, three days departed, displayed at the wake. He'd been recolored all wrong. Funerals are not for the deceased, of course, but for the mourners, and Frank would not have begrudged us that one last, vicarious look at him.

When word came back late that afternoon that his corpse was sufficiently repaired for a half-opened casket, Kay took charge of the wardrobe details. She went through the clothes he kept at home, looking for an appropriately sober ensemble to deliver to the mortuary. He was a deeply casual, cardigan-sweater-and-corduroys guy, often prone to odd dashes of color with a pair of yellow socks or fuchsia tie, usually embellished with a gravy or mustard stain. I suggested a number of intriguing combinations, together with his stocking cap and beaver-collared overcoat, which seemed by then to be permanent extensions of him. Kay wasn't satisfied with the eccentric choices her search turned up and asked me to accompany her to a men's clothing store in Jefferson Park, where she'd been outfitting the family for twenty-five years.

For his final audience with friends and relatives, she selected a smartly tailored black sport coat and striped red silk tie. She nodded at my request to bury him in his own, lived-in pants, since they wouldn't be visible in the closed part of the casket anyway. They were the proverbial brown shoes he would have worn with the tuxedo. For reasons that weren't remotely rational, I thought we should try to make his corpse comfortable in the grave.

Her last sprucing up of him was as diligent, as dedicated, as the sugar water she applied to his cowlick before Mass on Sunday mornings in the fifties. For this woman who devoted years of her life to grooming her children, Frank wore a brand-new tie and spotless sport coat to the wake, with a small white carnation in his lapel. My last physical impression of him was as a pale-faced young man on his way to a prom. He would have loved it.

The weighty responsibility Paul and I volunteered for was the task of "collecting his personal effects," as the coroner's office routinely described it. We drove downtown and spent a full hour in City Hall, where we had to prove our immediate relationship to the deceased with birth certificates and notarized documents, then fill out an impressive number of government forms. An official paper was finally stamped and ceremoniously handed over,

giving us authority to break the coroner's seal on his door at the
Cedar Hotel. We were instructed to summon the police once we
arrived there. A squad car pulled up within minutes of our call.

Paul and I and two Chicago patrolmen entered the lobby, such
as it was. At one time the Cedar Hotel was a classy Rush Street
property, when jazz and blues quartets kept music lovers from all
over the city up and dancing until 4 A.M. Hard times had since
fallen on both the building and its tenants. The dilapidated,
unrenovated lobby, dimly lit, smelled of old wood and alcohol. As
our foursome passed through the entrance we collected silent,
wary stares from Frank's former neighbors, mostly transients—
musicians long between gigs, men with stains on their trousers,
women who wore too much lipstick.

"Frank has penetrated more subcultures of this city than anyone
else I know," Paul said, shaking his head in amazement. It was
true, it was true. He had lunch with prostitutes, made friends on
psychiatric wards, met criminals in jail, prayed with the suburban
families at the Unitarian Church in Norwood Park. Representa-
tives from most of these factions came to his funeral—how they
knew about it was a mystery to us, since the obituary never ran.
There was a small, ragged platoon sitting in a back pew whom no
one in the family recognized, but their handkerchiefs and, in one
case, sleeve, were as damp with grief as ours. Frank's charisma
was incredible. People loved him because he loved them—openly,
demonstratively, for free. In a sense, the unkempt group in the
back of the church were the legacy Frank left to all of his
survivors. To this day, I couldn't walk past the street people in
New York City without feeling I knew their lives, better than I
wished I did.

The police accompanying us approached the glass-enclosed cage
in a corner of the lobby, an unadorned, bullet-proof registration
desk where a clerk collected daily rents. He mumbled some
apology when he handed the police officer the key. I thought he
meant for Frank, the fact that he had died, but he meant for the
room, which had been broken into the same day the coroner had
sealed it. Bureau drawers were pulled out and dumped on the floor,
a wallet lay open on an ancient chiffonnier, the cabinet door above
the washstand swung open on its hinge. It was the work of one
goddamned disappointed thief. Frank had already given away the

last of his money—very possibly to some of the occupants of the back pew—and there were no drugs except a few remaining aspirin next to the empty bottles on the nightstand.

The police filled out another form, reporting the break-in. The checklist we answered was a straight "no" ticket—no TV, no stereo equipment, no typewriter, no radio, no jewelry, no valuables to speak of. Paul signed the complaint—or noncomplaint—and the officers left us to our private work. The "personal effects" we collected easily fit into the two large duffel bags Paul and I had brought along, with plenty of room to spare. Frank was the lightest traveler I knew.

Paul kept his eyes trained on the job, concentrating on the dumped contents of the drawers. He quickly packed a duffel bag of brightly colored socks, a light windbreaker, then immediately began slowing down. "Should I pack all his clothes?" he asked, looking up with wildly distressed eyes. Detachment was impossible when you were holding the underwear of someone you loved.

"What for?" I asked. "We'd only have to pack them again for the Salvation Army. Just his papers, I think. Maybe anything personal the folks might want to keep."

"Right," he said, relieved. Standing up, he walked over to the chiffonnier and cleared the few items on top, packing an old watch even the thief had rejected.

While Paul worked with singular determination, collecting Frank's physical effects, I wandered about the room in distraction, collecting the psychological ones. I did not believe in ghosts—perhaps the one blessed relief of agnosticism—but I *had* felt a peculiar sensation the moment I entered the room. It was normal, I assured myself, to feel an emotional surge in such a loaded environment. Visits to the Lincoln Memorial and the Vietnam Memorial had produced surges, too. It was perfectly natural, imminently explainable, to mourn tragic deaths.

Except that I wasn't mourning, at least not exclusively. I kept feeling, to my total astonishment, a pervasive excitement. It was not a rational excitement—it didn't even feel like my own. My first reaction to seeing the empty pill bottles on the nightstand, the plastic cleaner bag on the bed, was pure agony. Almost immediately however, as if my head had been yanked open and another brain dropped inside, I felt unbelievably *happy*. Looking at the aspirin, I thought, "No pain." When I saw the plastic bag, "Don't leave a mess."

Here I was, standing in the room where Frank last breathed, feeling not only happy but *grateful*. I didn't even suffer the doubts of poor Abraham, questioning voices from above regarding the sacrifice of his beloved Isaac. I knew Frank's time was up with hospitals and jails and halfway houses; he'd paid his purgatory dues in full before he left this planet. He said he didn't belong here anymore and, from the evidence around me, I was inclined to believe him. The view from the only window in the room looked directly at a brick wall across an empty air shaft. There wasn't anyplace I could look without feeling assured, knowing his method, pumping with the nervous excitement of his escape. Even the grimmest symbols of death didn't register terror in my exuberant, irrational condition.

I noticed a chair wedged tightly between the bed and the radiator, placed strategically under the window, and went over to inspect it. A rope was tied to one leg, coiled neatly in a circle, and looped in a noose at the other end. Only a very calm and steady hand could have achieved the perfect symmetry of those intricate knots: "Not afraid," I thought. The coiled rope was such a cliché of horror, like the hanging moss on the cover of a Gothic novel, I thought Frank had probably gone to the library to learn how to do this. After the hours of careful work, I was glad he'd decided against the rope.

"Paul, look at this," I said excitedly, intending to point out Frank's clear rejection of senseless pain, for himself and for his family. "This must have been the plan he abandoned." Paul looked over from the chiffonnier, but the bed between us blocked his view of the rope on the floor. He saw the chair positioned under the window, however, and didn't want to see the rest. Wearing the same shaken, firing-squad look he had at the airport, this time he chose the blindfold.

"Please," he said, becoming pale. "I don't want to re-create any scenes here." Looking stricken, as if he'd been delivered a terrible blow, he weakly returned to his packing. I was sorry the instant I took in his undetached grief.

More than anything, Paul didn't want to think about the act of the death itself. What he didn't know, and god only knows how I did, was that nobody alive could ever really see death anyway. It was invisible by nature. "You can't act death," Rosencrantz declared in *Rosencrantz and Guildenstern Are Dead.* "The *fact* of it has nothing to do with seeing it happen—it's not gasps and blood and falling about—that isn't what makes it death. It's just a man failing to reappear, that's all . . . here one minute and gone the next and never coming back—an exit, unobtrusive and unannounced, a disappearance gathering weight as it goes on, until, finally, it is heavy with death." I felt an enormous fear that Paul, blindfolded and struggling to collect the physical artifacts of the room, would be crushed by the tremendous, unforeseen, psychological void of death. He had so many backed-up words—to me, to Frank—pouring silently into the room it thoroughly drenched my excitement. I sobered up immediately.

"Okay," I said. "Let's pack up and get out of here."

It was Paul's face that I focused on the next day, when I stepped up to the pulpit at the funeral. In the division of labor the family worked out, it was my job to deliver the eulogy. Still in the peculiar, almost euphoric mood that had enveloped me at the Cedar Hotel, it was the easiest writing I'd ever done. I simply sat down and recorded the flood of memories rushing through me. The hard part was reading it in church to my family, sitting together in the front pew, their eyes loaded with grief and aimed at close range. I knew if I saw anyone cry—and the possibility was very nearly guaranteed—the inevitable lumping of my own throat would render me mute. Only Paul had remained dry-eyed, thus far, so I entered those deep blue, penetrating tunnels to carry me through.

It was the eulogy Gina chose for her monologue when she returned Thursday evening, after thinking about brain damage all afternoon. Before she left Chicago she took Kay's manila folder, labeled simply M.K., from the family files and packed it for the trip. It was a bulging collection of news clips, essays, letters, and contained a typewritten copy of the eulogy Kay and Jerry requested after I'd returned home. Rereading it that afternoon, she concluded that my aberrant brain waves could possibly be the result of a lingering distress over Frank's death. In fact, I was feeling no pain whatsoever—even the irritating tube in my throat didn't upset me that evening, after the guards started the pleasant, absorbing dream again that afternoon. The despair she perceived was actually a product of her own mind, but after seven days of trying to fathom mine she was losing track of whose was whose. It was easy to do in this family.

Preaching, which came easily to me, was quite a different experience from listening to my own sermons. Had I not been in a state of imperturbable composure, prepared to dream, it would have been deeply embarrassing to hear the unveiled passion I'd hurled from the pulpit that morning two years ago. Still, I had to own the thing, having written it myself. Gina's voice had regained its full dramatic power. What's more, she didn't stumble over the God-talk included, since it was far more compatible with her own views than mine. I'd been surprised to find it in there, wondering where it had come from, but I had the distinct impression that eulogies, once written, ought not be revised. While Gina read the eulogy, hoping to open my eyes, I remembered reading to Paul, succeeding in watering his:

I asked my parents if I could give the eulogy this morning—there are some things that Frank told me last weekend, and through these last few years when we learned better and better how to talk to each other, that helped me accept the finality of today. He brought me his papers and writing last weekend, asking me if I would be his "translator." Maybe if I understood them, he said, I could make him understandable to other people. That's what I think Frank wanted me to do: to take this great grief he must have known we would be feeling today, and translate it into a meaning that will lessen the pain of it and leave the love he felt for us intact.

Frank's life looks lonely and sad to us because he didn't live the way most of us live. Two things separated him, set him apart, two things that caused his entire adult life to be spent in constant, painful conflict: the great brilliance of his mind, giving him knowledge and insights beyond what most of us are able to imagine; and his illness, the devastating fever of his mind that took this brilliance and twisted it, reshaped it, sent him down dark and fearful paths. Until the last day of his life he tried to balance these two elements of his being. "I feel like a missionary inside my own mind," he said once, "separating the angels from the demons."

Much of his life is incomprehensible because we share neither his brilliance nor his madness. But it's important to remember, especially today, that Frank didn't think his life was wasted. He always felt that his madness was given to him for a reason. In one of his letters, he wrote: "I like to think we're like the bacteria in a banana, each of us doing our own little thing, but in the process, the fruit is ripened for God's digestion."

I think—no, I know—that Frank understood his madness better than anybody. Better than the doctors who treated him, better than the advisers who counseled him, better than all of those who loved him and tried to help him did. "My madness," he said once, "is a form of prayer." Frank thought his whole life was a prayer.

We called it madness when we talked—we didn't use the clinical term "manic-depressive" or the scientific language his doctors used. Frank described it as "loving God so mightily sometimes my circuits blow." The madness, he said, was the "faulty wiring in the equipment." But he never despaired, the way I did; he never doubted that God loved him.

In this grief today we're tempted to look at Frank as an unhappy man. He wasn't though. Yesterday, on the train ride to Chicago, I remembered so many examples of his wit. He had a great capacity for joke-telling. I thought, wryly, that if I asked him what he would like me to say at his funeral he might have smiled and said, "Why don't you ask why Mayor Jane Byrne isn't here?"

During a visit at Reed once, I said that I had him to thank for introducing me to the inside of psychiatric wards all over Chicago. "True. But aren't you glad, though, to have met a few Martians?" he asked. "Doesn't every serious writer need a few Martians in her life?" He was in his highly excited state that day—the Excelsior phase, I called it: "Whenever you're wearing your Excelsior eyes, I know we're in trouble again."

"As you should," he agreed. He had a fine concept of the absurd. The last time I visited him at Elgin, I asked if we could go for a walk on the grounds instead of sitting on the ward. He took some chips out of his pocket—the white tokens patients earned and traded in for privileges—and handed them to the caseworker he called the Warden. As the caseworker opened the door Frank smiled at me, sideways, and said, "I hope you're grateful. We can go for a walk today because I combed my hair this morning." He was not lost to the irony of his circumstances.

We talked that day about everything. He seemed marvelously sane to me, although it was clear he wouldn't be able to manage his life well outside the hospital. He asked me that day, as always, if I loved him.

"Yes," I said, I loved him very much.

"Why?" he asked, as he always did.

"Because you're a fool," I said, "and I love fools."

"But Jesus said, 'There are no fools,' " he challenged, quoting St. Mark.

"I know. But I think what Jesus really *meant* was that we are *all* fools," I replied, quoting Seymour Glass. "I think you are the King of Fools." And then I asked him if he loved me.

"Yes," he smiled, and I asked why.

"Because I think you might be the Queen."

We talked about love again last weekend, and Frank said he felt inept at showing the family how much he loved us. When he wrote to Kay and Jerry this week, thanking them for being his parents and standing by him all through these long and difficult years, it was a love letter written in much the same spirit Jesus might have thanked Mary and Joseph for being his parents, loving him on this earth, knowing that we might learn what love really is only when we are with God, when we are no longer trapped by the limitations of our human bodies and our human minds. That is the kind of love Frank reached for his whole life.

I often felt, as most of us who loved him did, that I never did enough for him, that I failed to save him from the ravages of his illness. I told him I felt guilty, sometimes, when I thought about him.

"It's arrogant for you to feel guilty, Mary Kay," he admonished. "You don't understand my madness. *I* don't understand my madness. Only God understands this madness, and why it's been given to me. It's arrogant for you to presume to know what only God knows. You shouldn't feel guilty." That is the kind of crazy he was.

I know if there's one thing Frank would want me to translate this morning, it is the guilt hovering over us today. He would want us to translate it into a prayer, for that's what his madness was—a divine, inscrutable prayer. Pray to the God he loved, or to Frank himself, because I know he will hear it.

And I believe he is with the God he loved. When he knew that his time was up, when he was certain that he had learned everything there was for him to learn here and decided to be, now, with God, he must have felt all that a human being can feel before death. But I know there was a certainty about it for him. I know his suicide was *not* an act of despair. It was an act of faith. It was a death from exhaustion, from thinking and striving and loving. And it was his strong desire to be with God.

This grief, this engulfing sadness we feel today is our strong missing of him, the great loneliness for his presence among us. I will miss him terribly. But there should be no guilt, and no despair over his death. He would have none of it. He would call that human, and ask that we go beyond it—directly to God. Frank loves us still, I am sure.

11

THE ENERGY CIRCLE

3/30/84

I read M.K.'s notebook this morning. It was just sitting out there, and I couldn't stop myself. In truth, I don't think M.K. is the type of person who needs to be embarrassed by her notebook. It is so clear an indication that her sincerity is not something she abandons in the privacy of her notebook. There's so little difference between the Mary Kay I know and the Mary Kary that writes those entries . . .

The only thing she does there that she wouldn't do in public—at least not until she has chosen the words that would not alarm—is to catalog some of her exhaustions, to talk on paper pretty honestly about the damages to herself that her aggravations over the past few years have caused. I thank god for the relief from her own discipline and courage that must give her.

So while I feel from my own activities on the pages of notebooks like I've fairly committed a crime by reading hers, I can't feel like I wish I hadn't done it: I wish there were more clues to how she's really braving it, toughing it out, and maybe a hint as to how I might help her with some of it.

God, I do love her. I haven't loved her well—it was just last month that I didn't get to Fort Wayne to see her performance with Joan—but I do love her. If she wakes up I want to be closer to her, I want to take the trouble with her, accept her invites, feel more like an important sister to her.

I wish I could stop, for a few hours while I'm with her, being so goddamn self-conscious. There is a constant monitor in my mind: Now I'm writing a suffering letter to Barbara, now I'm out with the amazing Phyllis Wender, now I'm trying to talk with nurses and doctors and be the mature family relative who can handle it. Nowhere in there am I actually feeling this situation, wanting Mary Kay out of it with all my soul and energy. Today when I hold her hand I'll talk to her with every bit of affection I feel for her, even if it makes me weepy and scared.

"She's looking better, don't you think?" Larry asked when he joined Gina at the hospital Friday evening. Gina looked at my blank face, the passive pumping of my chest, the multiple needles in my purpled arms. Compared to *what*, she wondered. What was he seeing that she didn't see? Because she knew him as a strictly rational man—a lover of facts, the cautious player of the long shot—she was surprised when he leaped from reality with blind faith. He was actually *smiling* as he looked at me, as if brain damage hadn't made any dent at all in his munificent opinion.

He'd just returned from Connecticut, where he kept our appointment with the realtor and signed a two-year lease on the house we found there last month. Since we'd planned to cosign, the realtor was puzzled when Larry arrived alone and asked if I were still in the picture, as it were. Yes, Larry assured, but halted before he explained my absence, considering the number of questions he'd have to clean up if he let "coma" drop from his lips. He described my condition briefly as "a severe case of the flu," and promised I would stop by the office as soon as I was feeling myself again.

The trip to the pleasant coastal town we'd chosen for our future home seemed to revive him. Before he returned to the city he took a walk along the shore on Todd's Point, remembering the glowing February sunset we'd watched there last month, after finally locating a place that met our complicated space and school and commuting requirements. Sitting in the car, holding each other in a loose embrace under the overcoat he draped over us, we were happy not to talk for a change, not to think about all the financial, health, and stepparenting issues. For the first time in two years, we sensed the luxury of time ahead of us. It was nice to rest my head on his shoulder and not be consumed by the usual frantic hunger to soak up enough of him to last through another month of phone calls. Imagine. We were going to have time to waste.

He, too, was eager to live in the common environment of daily routine, even looking forward to the burnt dinners and smoky kitchens that inevitably came with my companionship. He wanted to open the shower curtain and find my stockings drying on a hanger; to come in the back door and trip over the kids' ice skates; to know what it was like to be aggravated with me, how long it would last, why it didn't matter. Two years of fantasies rushed in on him as he signed the lease, causing a kind of emotional gridlock that prohibited the entry of depressing facts. He even entertained the flu excuse himself, since the drama of brain damage didn't fit the future he wanted to imagine that afternoon. While the waves crashed over the jagged rocks on Todd's Point, imperceptibly wearing them down into unimposing granules of sand, Larry believed we were just as surely gaining on this thing—maybe by tonight, maybe by tomorrow morning.

Signing a lease is a kind of vow for a serious man, and Larry drove back to Manhattan fervently committed. It was undoubtedly love, not reason, that prompted the remark about how much better I looked. Gina watched Larry with simultaneous disbelief and gratitude, just as I watched Howe stand by Darren's incubator eight years ago, loving him beyond reason.

"Maybe she looks better because I combed her hair," she said, unable to share his optimism but unwilling to shatter it, either. Her own current, mild panic had been incited by Dr. Greenbaum's comment, just a few moments before Larry arrived. The chief stood at the foot of my bed for several minutes, frowning as he read my chart. Usually those frowns preceded vigorous action, orders for more tests, stronger medications, another suctioning. By Friday afternoon, however, most of the physical symptoms had been diagnosed and resolved. Pulmonary functions, blood tests, and electrocardiograms were all within normal ranges. Except for peculiar brain waves, there was no longer a medical indication for the coma.

"She should be coming out now." He frowned. "Sometimes it takes another day or two after glucose tests return to normal, but . . ."

But hers have been normal for at least *three*, Gina knew, from her own unauthorized readings at the foot of my bed. She waited nervously for the order that would follow such an extended frown. Judging from the gravity of his jaw, she expected a whopper— possibly some test or treatment from "nuclear medicine." Being unfamiliar with hospital defense departments, she wasn't sure exactly what the troops in nuclear medicine did, but when she overheard the phrase that day she suspected they were in charge of last resorts. Instead of an order, however, Dr. Greenbaum issued an uncharacteristic sigh.

"She should be coming out." He sighed again. "Let's give her another day."

Then what, Gina thought. Without conscious permission, her eyes moved to the respirator plug in the wall socket, the fragile connection between me and my life. She didn't want to contemplate the questions concerning that plug, any more than she wanted to consider the dilemma discussed at Julia's dinner last night.

True to her belief that minds work better when bodies are not wanting, Julia roasted the leg of lamb she'd promised earlier that week. The most serious questions in New York City required the most involved culinary attention, and Julia recognized a seven-course crisis when she saw one. Long after dessert, after all shoes and ties and remaining self-consciousness had been abandoned, the dinner guests were slumped comfortably on the couch cushions in Julia's living room. In that hair-down, heart-exposed last hour, they took up the pressing question Kay raised before hanging up that afternoon. She asked Gina to make arrangements with the hospital chaplain for the Sacrament of Extreme Unction.

The question of last rites troubled Gina on a couple of fronts. There was the time factor: Yesterday marked the seventh day of the coma—was that *only* seven, compared to Elaine Esposito's record 37 years and 111 days, or was that oh my god, *seven*, compared to almost everyone else alive? Since the main point of last rites was to prepare the recipient for death, Gina had to turn her whole mind around before arranging such a ceremony. After twenty-four hours of churning thought, she hadn't progressed more than a few degrees in her acceptance of death.

The other problems resolved around how I would feel about having my senses anointed by a priest, especially one I'd never met. She knew I was not automatically inclined to think fondly of priests. I wasn't a "fallen away Catholic," the term applied to cases of lapsed or lazy faith. As her godmother, I had been rigorous in my religious instruction, warning Gina to watch out, to examine every man-made rule for signs of clerical ignorance or arrogance. Did she have any right to invite a priest into the final moments of my life when I'd dedicated the last ten years to keeping as many as possible out?

My decision to leave the Church was anything but frivolous. As a youth, I was not only a pious Catholic but one who worshiped St. Maria Goretti. The tragic death of the young virgin, as depicted in the *Lives of the Saints*, made an indelible impression on my prepubescent mind, providing exactly the kind of role model a martyr-prone adolescent would adore. Choosing sure death over the possibility of sin, Maria became the victim of a violent sexual assault. It was a death scene perhaps only Ingmar Bergman could have been trusted to handle symbolically on film: While all the farmers who might have rescued her knelt down on the fields outside, praying the Angelus, she was stabbed seventeen times with a pitchfork in the hay shed.

I still remembered a day-long retreat in 1962, when the girls in my eighth-grade class were separated for a gender-specific lesson in sexuality. A handsome young priest described our future bodies as "vessels of sin"—the breasts and curves we were growing into at that very moment, nipples tingling even as he spoke—and offered us the beautiful Maria as a kind of patron saint of purity, who prized virginity above life itself. In our aroused, thirteen-year-old minds, her death represented the triumph of chastity rather than a tragedy involving murder and rape. The latter, in fact, was never mentioned in the *Lives of the Saints*, nor was an autopsy conducted to determine whether Maria might have been violated anyway, against her will. Rape was never the sin under investigation.

While Frank's eighth-grade retreat left him with enormous self-loathing whenever he felt the normal sexual arousals of adolescence, causing him to sing Tantum Ergo at the top of his lungs every time he entered the bathroom, mine left me equating my budding sexuality with violent death. When I studied the life of St. Maria Goretti in 1962, I wanted to be just like her. It never occurred to me, then, to be enraged that the wrong sin was on trial.

After spending ten years imprisoned by the attitude that women were "vessels of sin," my belated release from that damning sentence was followed by a period of pure hostility. I was outraged that an all-male, celibate hierarchy made decisions about birth control and abortion and motherhood without being remotely interested—being, in fact, aggressively *dis*interested—in what women themselves had learned from living those experiences. Did they think they knew what sexuality, reproduction, or raising a child was all about by meditating on it?

My fury at the misogyny of the clergy was the hardest part of my feminism to bring home, the most painful affront to my devoutly Catholic parents. It was as if we belonged to two different religions: Theirs was one of hope and dignity, the Church that welcomed the sons and daughters of Irish immigrants through its doors fifty years ago, offering material help through a Great Depression and the Second World War. For my parents, Catholicism was a joyful celebration of family, bonding us together through the sacred rituals of baptism, communion, penance, confirmation, and marriage. My family's affections were so intertwined with religion, it was almost impossible to separate them. Misunderstandings abounded: When Frank left the Church in 1969, my parents felt they had failed their responsibility to him; when they remained loyal to the Church after he left in such pain, he thought they didn't love him. This tragic mixup led him to commit the most loveless act of his madness.

All of us were furious with him that day—especially me, since he expected my support for an act specifically designed to upset our parents. He'd interrupted a Sunday service in their parish in front of five hundred friends and neighbors, causing them deep humiliation. The police arrested him and returned him to Reed, where he'd escaped the night before. When I visited him that afternoon his mind was still in a state of high mania, despite the large injections of Thorazine that slowed his speech and dragged his pace to a shuffle.

Unrepentant, he defended himself against my charges of heartlessness, claiming it was his duty as mystic and seer to expose the hypocrisy of the Church—whatever the cost, even the love of his earthly parents. Would Jesus have waffled on his duty to clear the moneychangers out of the temple just because the subsequent newspaper reports might cause momentary embarrassment for Mary and Joseph? Frank didn't think so. Even though the action hadn't produced its desired effect—he imagined the faces in the pews filling up with light and the congregants vowing to lead purer, unhypocritical lives forever after—he thought it was worth the risk. Showing no signs of slowing down as he shuffled in a circle around the dayroom at Reed, he justified his action with a long list of grievances against the Catholic church.

"Okay, you have grievances," I hotly conceded, pacing along beside him. "But keep your battles on your own goddamn turf.

You were cruel to innocent people—you went out of your way to make your point in Kay and Jerry's parish instead of your own."

"That *was* the point," he shouted back, looking at me with pure incredulity. "And how can you call them innocent people? They went through the *scruples* with me, fifteen years ago! How can you and Paul defend them when they're still supporting a church that permanently *damaged* us?" He railed on, defending the superior virtue of truth over love, quoting St. Paul, quoting Jesus Christ: " 'I am The Way, The *Truth* and The Light.' Do you hear Love—do you hear *Obedience*—anywhere in there?" He was shifting into high gear, revving his engines for takeoff when I hit the brakes.

"No!" I shouted, with such intemperate volume it stunned both of us. "You're dead wrong and you know it!" I yelled. There was a big difference between telling the truth and smearing his ego around, I said. "You don't want Kay and Jerry to 'know the truth'—you want them to 'Follow Me!' " He stopped pacing and stared at me.

Slowly, through the opaque overlay of Thorazine, his face brightened in a peculiar, radiantly lucid smile, an expression that had appeared once or twice before when his mad incantations were halted, almost humbled, by the unexpected arrival of common sense. Standing very still, he waited for me to catch my breath and continue.

"You do," I said, regaining some of my lost composure as he quieted down. "That's exactly why you criticized me, last Thanksgiving, when you accused me of coming home with a homicidal glint in my eye, prepared to slay anyone who didn't agree with me. You said agreement had nothing to do with truth: 'You have to tell your truths, you have to live them yourself, but it's really *none of your business* what anyone else does with your truth.' You said detachment doesn't abandon love, but goes beyond it. God, you made me *repeat* it a million times." I remembered everything he'd said that Thanksgiving, suddenly gifted with total recall. Our conversation stuck in my mind because, in part, I was distressed that the only family member who seemed to understand me that year was the one confined to a psychiatric ward.

Crazy or not, his theory made sense to me: Truth should be held self-evidently, without expectation, without the burden of anyone else's agreement. It put truth in perspective for me, sharply focused above the confusions of love and ego, canceling out both the need to please and the need to accuse. I found the theory useful as a daughter, a writer, a mother—not least, as a sister talking to the madman who divined it, urging him to practice it himself.

Frank was in such firm possession of his ego by the time he was composing his farewell letter to Kay and Jerry in the Cedar Hotel, he was able to release his most difficult truth with complete detachment, no regrets, and sincere thanks. At peace with himself, with his family, I doubt he would have objected to a Catholic funeral—the provocatively un-Catholic death was his own, but he left all decisions about the burial to the mourners.

Gina wasn't sure I would feel the same way about last rites. Was I willing to lend my body for a Catholic ritual that would comfort not me but my family? Coming fresh from the God-talk I had written in the eulogy and her own emotional conversations with the family, Gina was inclined to think yes.

Larry voted a qualified no. From his completely secular point of view, last rites were useful only for the shock therapy they might provide: "If anything could make her sit bolt upright, it would be a priest sprinkling holy water on her head," he said.

They finally settled on the compromise suggested by Joan, whose opinion about both mothers and priests most closely reflected my own. Joan spoke to Gina and Larry at least once a day, since she was the manager of several telephone trees emanating in the Midwest. When Gina consulted her about whether to grant Kay's request and call a priest, Joan's answer was yes and no. Yes, honor your mother and promise last rites for Mary Kay; no, forget about calling in the priest. It wouldn't be a lie because there were several religious services, more or less, being held for me in various parts of the country that Friday night. One or another—or all of them together—were sure to satisfy the ceremonial intention of Extreme Unction.

In Fort Wayne, the program for the Sisterspace Coffeehouse had been canceled and replaced with a ceremony the organizers billed as an "energy circle." It was a kind of meditation service performed by members of the Fort Wayne Feminists, a group I had joined ten years before when I left the Church. If I still felt anything that could be classified as a spiritual impulse by 1984, it generally occurred in the company of that eclectic congregation.

Joining the Feminists was a move I like to think my patron saint, Maria Goretti, would have made, had she heard the inspired speeches at the Take Back the Night march in 1974. Joan was one of the most gifted speakers I'd ever heard—brilliant, witty, compassionate, angry. She brought politics right to your front door, where you lived, where you loved. Fluent in Catholic, an Irish mother of five, she seemed like someone I'd loved my whole life.

Joan was one of the Feminists' founders, referred to informally as the Grandmothers—an honorable title conferred on the women who attended "the first meeting." Nobody knew exactly when it was or how many women were there, but it must have been some spectacular meeting, possibly as astonishing as the one the apostles once had, when little tongues of fire appeared above everyone's head.

The Feminists distrusted hierarchies of any sort and operated more like a large, political family, moving quickly to influence public decisions while working slowly on personal change. At every meeting, patience had to be extended to the new arrivals, or "baby feminists" as the veterans sometimes called them. A baby feminist, just dipping her big toe in the shallow end of women's rights, had so far learned to say phrases like, "I believe in equal pay for equal work, but I don't believe in all that other crazy stuff." The "crazy stuff" usually meant abortion rights or lesbian rights or other words that were hard to say out loud in Indiana.

It took a long time to become a feminist—those who'd been at it awhile were suspicious of "overnight conversions." As Cathryn, a psychology professor and founder of both the Feminists and the women's studies program at Indiana University once said, "You cannot wear a skin you didn't grow yourself." In Fort Wayne, if you were going to march around shouting "Sisterhood is powerful!" you were expected to show some evidence of it in your life. You couldn't, say, stand up at a rally of sympathetic women and declare, "Equal pay for equal work!" and then neglect to mention it to the personnel director at work. Becoming a "troublemaker," whether you had nothing or everything to lose by speaking up, was everyone's responsibility.

As feminism was practiced in Fort Wayne, beliefs discussed at collective meetings turned into political action. We organized a rape crisis center, lobbied for a battered women's shelter, raised funds for a displaced homemaker program, and began two family businesses—a bookstore and coffeehouse. Spontaneous task forces were invented as needed. The Unity Coalition campaigned for the ERA, the Justice Coalition for the impeachment of a sexist judge, and when the Women's Health Organization was being harassed by antiabortion groups, the local newspapers received letters signed by the Catholic Grandmothers for Abortion.

The volume of activity by the mid-seventies gave the city council the impression there were several hundred of us, but in fact most of the work was done by fifty or so women (fewer during the softball season) on very little money. The poverty and fatigue made us testy at times, unwilling to entertain new proposals. One of our younger and more impulsive members proposed a march on a local formal-wear store that rented tuxedos to men but didn't make prom dresses available to women. It would have been an illegal march since she hadn't bothered to get the appropriate permits, but she dared us to show some courage. There were a lot of rights the women in my political family were willing to risk a jail sentence for, but prom dresses didn't turn out to be one of them.

The prom-dress campaigner was what the Fort Wayne Feminists called a Growing Girl—a sister so absorbed in her own issue, she failed to see its relationship to others. We thought the case was closed but it opened again, to our deep chagrin, when we invited a famous activist to Fort Wayne for a lecture at our university. As a Midwestern branch of the revolution, we were touchy about the stereotype that Indiana was a backwater state and took pains to correct that impression. After a rousing speech Flo Kennedy opened the mike for questions, and the first one came from our Growing Girl: "What should you do when the women in your city are too apathetic to participate in a march, even when there's a clear case of discrimination?" There was an audible groan from about fifty women in the audience, and the speaker read the situation instantly: "Then I guess you'd better plan something that doesn't take so many people," she said.

While the Growing Girls sometimes embarrassed us in public, they also provided a lot of the fun and just plain goofiness every political movement needs now and then. One time, a local TV station manager refused to cancel an outrageously sexist game show called *Three's a Crowd*. (Points were earned when the women in the boss/secretary/wife team correctly guessed the boss's answer to such questions as, "Which TV dog most resembles your secretary's bra: Snoopy, Lassie, or Old Yeller?") The station manager dismissed the complaints as "form letters" from organized fanatics. The Growing Girls were incensed, having carefully penned several personal notes themselves. They proposed a Zap Action, a last resort when more legitimate means of getting the point across failed.

On this particular occasion, a pickup truck was secured, a half dozen women donned overalls, rubber boots, and stocking caps, drove to a farm a half hour outside the city, and shoveled what remained in the pen after a small herd of well-fed pigs quit the sty. Just after dusk, six barrels of the still steaming stuff were deposited on the lawn in front of the TV station, with a poster declaring this carefully worded explanation:

DEAR MR. METCALF,

HERE'S SOME FEEDBACK, SO TO SPEAK, ON *THREE'S A CROWD*. WE HOPE YOU DON'T MISTAKE THIS FOR A FORM LETTER.

The two other local networks received anonymous tips about the incident, just in time for the evening news. The show was subsequently canceled. The next spring, a bright green patch of grass marked the fertilized spot, a lush tribute to the spunk and spirit of the Growing Girls.

When Joan decided to run for county auditor in 1974, she organized a campaign team of inexperienced but dedicated friends that Democratic Headquarters amusingly labeled "the Green Ladies." The Green Ladies won, free of any debts to the party bosses. When Joan brought her staff together the first day in office, she presented the options: We could play it safe and go for reelection, or we could go for broke and blow whistles for four years. We chose the whistles.

With forty patronage jobs secured for four years, the auditor's office became a temporary haven for women in transition: Women between careers, between marriages, emptying their nests, filling them up, burning out, and just beginning. A poet and songwriter worked in the Deeds Department, and I became her deputy auditor, with my background in literature. It was grim work, hunting for symbolism in columns of figures. But if the work was sometimes boring, the company never was.

During Joan's term, the auditor's office was a lively stop for the corps of reporters who covered the City-County Building every day. She used the daily interviews to speak publicly to the state legislature, the county commissioners, Republicans and Democrats, the superintendent of public education, and, most vehemently, to the bishop, when anti-ERA groups were allowed to leaflet and collect funds in local churches. She revealed to the press the total amount of tax exemptions he was risking.

No institution was exempt from Joan's critical scrutiny, even the media itself. When the *Journal Gazette* sent a questionnaire asking her to evaluate the accuracy of a recent feature about her, she filled in the space under "any general comments" with a few questions of her own: "Is 'feisty' a word ever used to describe tall men? Only short men, animals, women, and children are 'feisty.' Was General MacArthur, Abraham Lincoln, or Mayor Robert Armstrong ever called 'feisty'?" She filled in the last question, "Any overall feelings or comments?" with her straightforward request: "Please have 52% women editors, 14% blacks, and 34% white males from now on."

Though we poured enormous effort into the ERA campaign in Indiana, it still seemed a miracle when the state legislature finally ratified the amendment. Talk about a joyful confirmation ceremony—we partied and danced all night. If the Unity Coalition could persuade that reluctant assembly into the twentieth century, we were sure Oklahoma and Arkansas couldn't be far behind. Instead, we watched in despair as the whole country succumbed to the backlash against civil rights that began with the eighties. The year before I left Fort Wayne for Ann Arbor, I stood on a curb next to Roz, a black woman who'd just moved to town, watching the Ku Klux Klan march through the streets in white hoods.

"Lord, girl, what are we doin' here?" she asked with a low whistle, shaking her head. "Why don't we just give this place back to the folks who had it first and get out of here?" There was no place else to go, of course. The same battles were being fought everywhere—the only difference between Fort Wayne and Chicago was that the enemy here wore white hoods and bright orange hunting caps. You could see them clearly. There was no danger of lapsing into apathy in Indiana—you see a klansman in the street, you know where you stand.

Maybe that's why my friendships there were so important. The dangers were obvious, the work was never done. When the Reagan administration took office in 1980, the already limited funds for women's programs virtually disappeared. After Medicaid funds for abortion were cut, a Friday afternoon ritual called the Women in Need Happy Hour was instituted. In any crisis, the Fort Wayne Feminists' first response was to throw a party. The weekly happy hours were much like the Irish wakes that brought my own extended family together again and again, where we laughed and mourned and collected donations for the survivors.

Nevertheless, it was depressing to watch all the changes we'd made rapidly reverse. After Joan's term expired, daycare, flexible hours and job sharing disappeared from the auditor's office. She gave each of her staff a plaque at the end of our tenure, with twenty-one pennies in the shape of the woman symbol representing the few cents more we gained during her term. The earnings gap in the county budget opened wide up again, without any protests from the new auditor. The distinguished Senator Birch Bayh lost his reelection in the Republican sweep through Indiana, and an inexperienced conservative named Danny Quayle took his place. Joan was profoundly depressed by the losses: "If you want to see what difference we've made, put your elbow in a bucket of water, take it out, and study the impression you've left." Joan looked back over her four years of public service and wished she'd gone to medical school. "At least I'd be a doctor now," she said. "And it would've been easier."

I couldn't hear her despair that year without feeling somehow dismissed by it. Maybe she hadn't permanently altered the culture of the City-County Building, but she had certainly influenced and inspired forty individual women. I, for one, would never be the same. Didn't I count? While she mourned the losses, I delivered rhapsodic monologues about how her staff, wiser and more courageous for the time we spent together, would carry on the knowledge we acquired. No election could take that away from us. In my secular view, we had a chance to realize the only kind of immortality guaranteed to human beings: One life can stamp and influence another, which in turn stamps and influences another, on and on, until the soul of human experience breathes on in generations we'll never even meet. While I was waxing romantic about our past, Joan concentrated on the depressing realities ahead.

The year we left the auditor's office brought the first strains in a long, affectionate friendship. The twenty-year age difference that never mattered to us suddenly did to potential employers. When it was time to find new careers after a bold experiment in politics, I was in my early thirties and she was in her fifties. Her high visibility as the "feisty" auditor gave potential employers pause— speaking out carried a price, and Joan was charged in full. Maybe she'd opened doors and inspired confidence in other women, but the personal benefits she reaped for her efforts were nil.

After ten years of working side by side, our mentor/protégé relationship underwent its first split, requiring an operation as traumatic and delicate as a heart transplant. Especially since it had been an extremely successful partnership, since valuable gifts had been exchanged with exuberant affection, the distant period that followed was hard on both of us. Achieving peerage without pain was no more possible than giving birth without labor. If the protégé was to use the acquired gifts she had to make them her own—even if she appeared to be squandering them; if the mentor was to nurture independence she first had to secure her own— even if it seemed she was withdrawing her love. When Joan isolated herself in an impenetrable cocoon of privacy in the winter of 1980 to tend to her family and her own future, I knew that process had begun.

We strung the eventual separation out for another year. Still addicted to working together, we let a friend talk us into forming a consulting business with her. It was the worst idea we ever had. While the three of us had plenty of experience in political organizing, we had no genius at all for marketing a business. The name and motto we selected was a prime example: "Natural Changes, Inc. A consulting firm on the changing roles of women and men." One of our clients threw away the introductory package we sent because he thought "Natural Changes, Inc." was some kind of New Age granola company. Joan was the first to see our major problem: We were essentially asking companies to pay us for inciting a revolution among its women. We might as well have asked the Pentagon for contributions to the nuclear freeze movement.

Joan and I argued more that year than the previous six. She kept wanting to quit. I kept urging her to stay. I described our work as "helping women." She saw it as "selling out." Instead of clarifying issues, the arguments provoked my insatiable need to be understood, my worst application of "Follow Me!" Joan tried to convince me her rejection of Natural Changes wasn't personal—she still loved me, she assured me. She left our failing enterprise to work for the Census Bureau and teach labor studies at the university. I received dozens of memos signed "Love, Joan" that year, but her ferocious affection kept getting buried under the debris of my self-doubt.

I received an award from Women in Communications at the Headliner Dinner that spring, and I was upset when Joan not only didn't join the small throng congratulating me at the podium afterward, but walked out of the banquet hall. She left because she knew she would see me later, but I misunderstood when I saw her and Cathryn slip quietly out the door. I thought I had somehow disgraced myself. To be honored by the local media could mean that I'd established myself as an "acceptable feminist"—which according to my own definition was a contradiction in terms, like "military intelligence." Had I sold out?

Guaranteed prime space on the Sunday op-ed page each week, I wrote often about women's issues—and collected a respectable volume of irate mail whenever I did. But I stepped back from the front lines every now and then, writing a holiday reflection or family reminiscence, sometimes a humorous essay with no point at all except sheer amusement. Joan was not opposed to fun—she masterminded brilliant comedy at Sisterspace coffeehouses and unforgettable "closing ceremonies" at hen conventions—but she had no time for pointlessness. I interpreted her silence at the awards dinner as disappointment that I wasn't advancing issues as forcefully and directly as she had done when the microphone was hers as the county auditor.

"You don't use the power you have," she said that winter, when I finally penetrated her silence. What power? What power did she think I had?

Witnessing the enthusiasm of the small mob at the podium, Joan and Cathryn thought I now preferred the company of my media friends. I blamed the misunderstanding on the old problem of charisma—"I'm not the one trying to be's with them, they're the ones trying to be's with me!"—but nobody bought it. I'd chosen that night to sit at the table with the editor-in-chief instead of my women friends. I seemed to be courting fame deliberately.

Fame in a small city brought more problems than pleasures. Money would have been nice, if I could have selected the trauma celebrity would bring. Instead, I was poor but famous, a condition that drained me. I felt like an impostor when exaggerated rumors preceded me with new acquaintances, when anyone stared at me with an appreciation larger than life. One does not "talk" under such a stare; one "holds forth." I found it exhausting to dismantle the distance celebrity created. Surrounded by friends who thought I'd become too important to bother with the little matters of their everyday lives, I felt alone in the crowd the last year I lived in Fort Wayne. I'd lost my place as one of the gang.

After moving to Ann Arbor, I suffered a long bout of what psychiatrist Oliver Sacks called "incontinent nostalgia." I remembered my experiences as a baby feminist, a Growing Girl, the honor of becoming a Grandmother before I left, even though I hadn't attended "the first meeting." My mind went blank in the absence of friends—I was a translator who'd lost contact with the original material. Flooded with memories and longing, I made no attempt to make new friends. For one thing, I was exhausted all the time. For another, I felt like a freak with a "big head." Despite a lifetime of warnings from Kay, I'd gone ahead and gotten one. As a national columnist and contributing editor to *Ms.*, I attracted large crowds when I spoke to women's groups but almost no invitations to dinner. Fame, however cardboard, made people nervous when it sat down right across the table from them. I wore my loneliness in Ann Arbor like a hair shirt and ashes—a woman doesn't spend ten whole years worshiping St. Maria Goretti and then let go of martyrdom one, two, three, just like that.

My social life existed on a few weekends when I traveled back to Fort Wayne. The welcome was always warm, but I was no longer included in the intimacies bred through daily life. Loneliness made me hungry, so perhaps I overreacted when I tasted a small slice of my former life. In February 1984 I had driven to Fort Wayne, tube and all, to perform with Joan in a fund-raiser called "Together Again." A huge crowd came to the reunion; we brought the house down, and put a record deposit in the Women in Need fund. I was ecstatic. I thought we had discovered a way to keep working with each other—I imagined taking our show on the road, maybe even to New York City. Joan received my enthusiasm with polite indifference. She didn't know how to make it any clearer that she didn't want to be mushed around anymore with consulting firms or other pointless schemes. She had a serious revolution to conduct. When she found my winter coat hanging in her guest closet after I left, it occurred to her I might be losing it altogether.

One month later, Joan called Ann Arbor and learned I was in a coma in New York City. She spread the news among friends in Fort Wayne, who did what they always did in a crisis: They organized a fund-raiser. They wanted enough money in the Women in Need fund to insure a long recovery. Joan collected intelligence every day from the staff at St. Vincent's and circulated reports through the telephone trees, extending as far as Maine in the East and California in the West. When I still hadn't awakened by the eighth evening, my friends in Fort Wayne gave up on a medical solution and took matters into their own hands.

Some fifty women gathered together on Friday night for the energy circle—a ritual we sometimes performed on Halloween, at the annual Witches and Amazons Coffeehouse. We did it mostly for fun, casting spells and chanting incantations over truculent legislators, but this time the family was completely serious.

Holding hands, they sang songs and meditated about Grandmothers, who had committed themselves for the long haul, however depressing or hopeless the war began to look. They took turns telling stories, remembering the sublime and ridiculous moments we'd spent together, laughing of course, crying and hugging each other. A Friday evening service at Sisterspace could match, plea for fervent plea, the passion rising from the pews at a Baptist service in the heart of the Bible Belt. Joining hands and singing in harmony, they sent a mighty wish for my recovery across seven hundred miles to my hospital bed.

12

THE WOMAN WITH
THE WHITE LIGHTS

EIGHT EX-PATRIOTS FROM FORT WAYNE heard about the energy circle planned for Friday night and, unable to attend the Sister-space service, held one of their own in California. Smaller huddles formed in other parts of the country: Carolen and Ann hugged each other to fend off grief in Kansas City; Paul and Debbie spent the evening with Waghi and Mama in Ottawa; Phyllis called long distance and talked courage to Kay and Jerry now back in Chicago; and Kevin got on the phone that evening to Gina. "This is it," he declared, at the end of his patience. "We've got to do something about this."

Gina never found out what Kevin did—she didn't know of any all-night law firms that accepted suits on Friday evenings. She herself bought a bottle of red Chianti and joined Larry, Susan, Carrie, and T.C., Carrie's husband, all similarly equipped, for a New York version of the energy circle.

They met at St. Vincent's before heading over to the Italian restaurant in Greenwich Village where Carrie made reservations. Susan wanted to say good-bye that night—she was leaving the next day to return to Juneau.

"Should I cancel my tickets?" she'd asked Carrie Friday afternoon. She was depressed that after traveling more than five thousand miles she'd never once looked in my eyes.

"Susan . . . we don't know how long this thing could go on," Carrie said. "I'll be right here—I'll check on her every day. You can call me every night." Susan accepted the sound advice but it didn't make saying good-bye any easier. Looking at my comatose form, it was hard to believe all the partying we'd done six months ago in Juneau. Last September, when I was sent to her coast for an assignment in San Francisco, I promised Susan I'd "stop by" on my way back—geography was never my strong suit. It turned out to be one of the happiest miscalculations I ever made.

I landed the day before the celebrated all-day pig roast at her friend Pete's cabin, out on The Road. Street names and directions were never a problem in Juneau, Alaska, since there was only one road out of town. About thirty of us played volleyball, drank beer, danced, drank wine, played music, passed a joint, laughed, sang, and committed ridiculousness of the highest order. By the time Pete announced that the pig was finally ready, shortly before midnight, half of his guests could no longer handle a knife and fork.

I had the time of my life and Susan, who often chided me for working too hard, was delighted to witness my flair for decadence. "M.K., ten people told me they've fallen in love with you tonight—men *and* women," she teased. "How about you, M.K.? Did you let yourself fall in love with anybody tonight?" I was in love with everyone, I said. Introduced as Susan's friend, the feelings the assembled company had for her were instantly extended to me. Workaholic that I was, I took on "Susan's Friend" as my job description, and wanted to make it my lifetime occupation. Six months later, that career and several others had come to a dead standstill.

Susan was as wrecked by the coma as Carrie had anticipated. All week she patted my arm and attempted to cheer herself up with private little jokes: "M.K., I've got two *pounds* of smoked Alaskan salmon with me . . . and a little something from Pete that's even better than whatever you're on. You know what I'm saying?" But she was out of jokes by Friday night. She said good-bye with a long, heavy sigh.

"God, even in a coma, she's beautiful," she said, by way of farewell. "She's still beautiful isn't she, Carrie?"

My friend since adolescence, Carrie rarely thought about how I looked, any more than it would occur to stop reading in the middle of a gripping novel, close the cover, and see if the author's name was still on the spine. She knew the jacket art was there, but it wasn't what usually mattered to her. Carrie was more interested in the stuff inside my head, particularly what I had to say about motherhood, since I was ten years down that road and Carrie had just started. Three months earlier, she had begun an extended maternity leave from a successful career with Time Inc. It was almost unimaginable good luck that my work put me in the same city with this friend of twenty years, at this particular juncture in our lives.

I relied heavily on her insider's view of Manhattan mores and the magazine business, calling her whenever I needed to right my course: "Listen to what just happened. . . . Is that *normal?*" I provided the same kind of sanity check for her whenever she returned from the pediatrician: "He told me to put ice cubes on her feet to keep her awake while she's nursing! Isn't that *cruel?*" We took turns pointing out the hazards through the sharp turns required by editors or children, or both. When Carrie looked at me she was searching for something intelligent, funny, confident, droll, exasperated, angry, inspiring. Beautiful was way down on the list.

"Yes," Carrie admitted. "She's beautiful."

Carrie and Susan stepped aside and someone else moved in, picking up my hand and squeezing it hard. I recognized Gina. She'd been squeezing my hand all day, sending little pulses of electricity through my arm.

"Goodbye, M.K.," she said, kissing me on the forehead. "We have to go to dinner. See you tomorrow, Sis."

I felt Larry's warm, full lips kiss my cheek. Someone patted my arm and then someone else kissed me. Feet shuffled in the background as many arms began sliding into sleeves. Zippers closed.

"Good-bye . . . Good-bye . . . Good-bye." They were gone.

Seated around the large table Carrie reserved in a corner of the restaurant, the group watched silently as T.C. opened the first bottle of wine and poured out five glasses. The meditations from this particular energy circle were not a single, unified surge designed to travel seven hundred miles—they were five separate, short-range sparks, going in different directions and occasionally colliding with each other.

Larry talked about the house in Connecticut, excited about the view from Todd's Point and how it would look in the spring.

Speaking as though the move scheduled for next month were still on, he kept saying "we"—"we have to reserve a moving van," and "we'll have to paint the third floor for the kids." He talked as if "we" were not remotely affected by brain damage, and Carrie had to wonder if there wasn't something seriously wrong with him.

She felt almost angry when he didn't acknowledge the possibility that my life was being permanently altered by this coma. She certainly had to think about it. Having spent nine of the previous eleven months being pregnant, she was freshly trained in worrying about brain damage. It was a healthy pregnancy from beginning to end, but going through amniocentesis meant waiting for results, and waiting for the assurance of "normal" always caused anxiety. Once questions about brain damage were raised, the answers weren't the kind you could go either way on. A yes or a no affected your whole life.

Carrie worried while Gina, true to her promise in her notebook, was feeling this situation with her whole soul. At least once during dinner, everyone at the table had stopped to stare, fork in midair or match burning low, arrested by her uncanny physical resemblance to me. Her inflections, her gestures, the slight nasal sound of her cold—she acted and sounded exactly like me, too. She even told the same stories and joked the same way. "It's almost spooky," Joan told Larry that afternoon after talking to Gina on the phone. "I had to keep reminding myself it wasn't her."

Sitting next to Gina, Susan remembered all over again why she didn't want to leave. She needed something to take back with her, some eye contact, some vital sign that I wasn't washed up in my career as Susan's Friend. On Friday night, there was no chance of having the heart-to-hearter Susan always saved for the last day of a visit, when we looked unblinkingly at our lives, untangled knotty problems, shrugged at the lunacy, and recognized how much we loved each other in spite of—or because of—these private revelations. That talk always came at the end of the week, I suppose, because exchanging intimacies all night left us speechless the next day, capable only of sinking into a window seat on a plane and daydreaming at high altitudes.

She reconsidered canceling her reservations back to Juneau. She didn't care about the money she'd lose, but how long would she stay? The outside chance of a thirty-seven-year coma was a long leave of absence from work. Everything that could be done medically had been done, according to today's report; the tests results all indicated that I was "normal." She had to suppose my condition tonight was the one I could be in the rest of my life. There was no promising evidence to merit postponing her flight.

It fell to T.C., my friend of the shortest duration, to keep the conversation moving through these four different preoccupations, all focused on the same person. It was like trying to conduct a symphony when the musicians were all reading different scores— a lighthearted oboe played out of time with a melancholy violin, cymbals clanged while a trumpet moaned. Here was where the red Chianti came in handy. T.C. poured. Everyone talked. It was a three-hour prayer, as New York services in the chapels of Italian restaurants often go.

"Good-bye . . . Good-bye . . . Good-bye." It keeps ringing and ringing in my ears. Like a needle stuck between grooves in a record, it's driving me crazy. I'm so agitated . . . upset with my friends. I can't believe they just put on their coats and left me! They were going out to dinner, and not including me!

Okay, I can't walk, but there has to be a wheelchair around somewhere. I've been pushed around all day on some kind of stretcher—couldn't they have taken me to dinner on a stretcher? If they really loved me, they would have found a way to include me.

The more I thought about it, the more upset I became. I felt so lonely. People I loved kept walking out on me. I'd alienated significant members of both families, political and biological; and still to come, a year of separation from the kids. Madness, divorce, fame, distance—the facts of my life conspired against me. Joan walked out of the Headliner Dinner, and now five of my closest friends just went off to dinner without me. Goddamn!

I was so hungry—it seemed like I hadn't eaten in days. And I hurt. My throat hurt, my arms hurt, I hurt everywhere. I had a pounding headache. My eyelashes were stuck together, glued with a heavy accumulation of sleepers. A chemical heat filled my chest, heaving it up and down. I was miserable—pain roared through every zone in my body.

And I was *mad*. I was sick of the goddam tube and all the needles—I wanted out of this crazy place, with its mind-bending dreams. Through with being the good prisoner, I heaved my legs over the side of the bed.

They worked! I kicked, then excitedly kicked again. I didn't know where this kicking would get me, except in a rage, but it felt wonderful to move. I banged my wrists against the iron bars, trying to free myself from the loose cotton handcuffs. The tube lines shook, and I heard glass clinking against steel overhead. I made *noise*!

"Mary Kay! Are you in pain?" a woman's voice called, as footsteps hurried into the room.

What does she think? Of course I'm in pain! How would she feel if somebody rammed a fat tube down her throat? I hear a sound roaring up from my lungs, a tremendous yell of rage. The scream moves up my throat, gaining volume until it hits the tube. The gigantic roar sputters out weakly in a faint, muffled cry.

"Oh, Mary *Kay*!" the woman said, excited and alarmed by my feeble wail. "I'll get something for the pain. But this is good. Hang on! This is good!"

This is good? What kind of sadists are running this place? Oh, the pain. Everywhere, unstoppable pain pumping through me.

The woman, true to her word, returns almost immediately. She massages the tense muscles in my right leg and then pokes a needle into my thigh. A warm, pleasurable sensation ripples up my leg as she continues to pat me softly. The twitching muscles relax. She keeps rubbing, patting, calming tensions until the pain vanishes under her fingers. A soft white light beams through my closed lids. My rage melts in the warm affection of the light.

Maybe she isn't so bad, this woman.

I wonder if she'd like to go to the cafeteria with me. Surely there's a cafeteria somewhere in this place. I've been rolled down a lot of halls here. Buildings with long hallways always have cafeterias. We could get a sandwich—god, am I hungry. Maybe a cup of tea. I'd love a cup of tea. I wonder what she looks like.

Cracking my eyes, I peer through my stuck lashes. Shadows. Shades of light and dark. A woman in a white dress standing near me, long dark hair and olive skin. She wavers in the light, as if she were not quite solid. My own body is floating in air, filling with light and pleasure through her magic fingers. Oh, sweet friend.

"Okay? Are you okay now?" the woman asked as she patted my thigh. My legs felt like two feathery pillows lying limp on the bed. "You're okay," she assures me, answering her own question. "I'll be right back. I think we'll let Dr. Greenbaum know about this little incident."

She was turning me in? I couldn't believe it. Another friend leaving—and no dinner again! Angry, betrayed, I protested, trying to swing my legs into action once more. I kicked limply with pillow legs.

"Still in pain?" she asked, alarmed. She picked up my arm and pressed two fingers against my wrist. I tried to pull it back, but my arms were as limp as my legs. She must have deadened my arm with an Oriental acupressure technique on my pulse.

"I'll be right back," she assured me, and hurried from the room.

I didn't care if she ever came back. I didn't want to care whether anybody came back. It was foolish to care, expensive beyond measure to love people who kept slipping through my life. There was no point in pursuing love, so terribly fragile, so mortally human. It must have been in defense against being left, being the last one still wanting, still needing, that drove Dostoyevsky to his private hell and "the suffering of being unable to love." Floating in my cell, hungry and lonely, I felt myself sinking into that dark layer of mind.

The loneliness of being unable to love could not be worse than the perpetual pain of wanting to be loved. I thought if I let go of all desire, if I abandoned all yearnings—as daughter, sister, wife, mother, mate, friend—there would be no more disappointment, no more desperate need to be understood. If the loneliness became unbearable, at least there would be no more torture from the agonizing dilemma of truth versus love. Truth would no longer be thrown off course if the need to be loved did not exist.

"Mary Kay," a woman calls softly from a great distance. "Are you in pain? I have something for you."

Yes, yes, so much pain.

Tenderly, she anoints a patch of skin with a cool liquid. It feels good. Everything she does feels good, even the little pinch she gives me next.

I like her.

I love her . . . No, don't. Don't be seduced into caring. She will leave you. Everyone leaves, sooner or later.

The woman approaches my bed with a thick sheaf of papers, yellow pages torn from a legal pad and covered with a tiny handwriting. She might have found them in my briefcase—or perhaps at the Cedar Hotel. It looks more like Frank's handwriting than mine. Without sound, she informs me through some kind of telepathy that an important message is buried in the manuscript. She wants me to "translate" the pages. Jesus Christ. Here we go again.

I roll my head slowly side to side to tell her I can't. I don't want to translate anything. I'm through with reading other people's minds. She nods, understandingly.

Suddenly a bare wood frame springs up around my bed, like the skeleton of the uncanvased circus tents in the kids' rooms. She begins to fasten the pages inside so that I can see them clearly. She keeps papering until I'm under a canopy of lined yellow pages. Then she smiles and waves her arm generously, inviting me to read. I look into rows and rows of indecipherable symbols and letters. The words make no sense to me. I'd have to learn a whole new language to translate the message. I raise my eyebrows to show her I don't understand.

But she already knows, for she has visual aids. She starts attaching images to the pages, photographs about the size and shape of the holy cards I collected in my youth. Although I don't recognize the faces I'm sure I know them. The instant I look at them, the pictures light up and start moving. Unlike the holy cards, the light doesn't radiate in spiked halos around their heads or from open wounds of martyrdom, as though sainthood were too subtle for the ordinary viewer to take in. The light just lets these faces be. Nevertheless, I have a strong impression of holiness. Despite my reluctance to learn the language, I want to know who they are, how we ended up under this canopy of yellow pages together.

"*Use the power you have*," the woman thinks to me. What power? What power does she think I have?

She turns up the lights in the room and I love these people more and more. The brilliant white light soaks my head, my whole body, and I feel a burst of ecstasy. I still cannot grasp the words, but I read their faces, coming closer to their truths in this penetrating brilliance. A peculiar knowledge seeps into my head through the strange capillary action of light. This is the first time I've ever translated without depending on words, without any speech.

A worry surfaces: Are they dead? What if I take the trouble to learn who they are only to discover they're gone?

It doesn't matter, the woman thinks to me. *We can never be separated. If I absorb the lights, if I translate the messages and pass it on, even death cannot part us*. The light is so inviting, I feel my mind expanding into hers, into the people in the pictures— everyone's at once. Amazing power in this collective head—and amazing relief! No boundaries between who I am and who they are. My loneliness evaporates in this collective consciousness. I am a group.

I feel drenched with love from all directions. An enormous affection sinks into me and waves exuberantly through me, like the electric energy I used to feel holding hands and singing songs at Sisterspace. I would join the circle of friends for the closing song at the coffeehouses, swaying and singing with friends, and come as close to religious inspiration as I ever expected to feel. That same gorgeous ache of passion now wells up in my throat as I remember the lyrics to the song by Madeleine Pabis: "*Don't push the river, she flows by herself . . . Her cool waters soothe me, why go somewhere else? Why go-ooooooooh somewhere else?*"

The ache in my throat swells as my friends sing to me, I sing to them, our voices harmonizing. The woman with the bright lights smiles, the faces in the pictures beam. They love me. It's so ironic that after letting go of all claims for affection, I am loved beyond my wildest expectation. I thought choosing truth meant giving up love, but without trying at all to please I have suddenly become pleasing. In the spectacular peace of the white lights, truth and love no longer exist on opposite sides of an equation. I realize that truth, unashamed and unencumbered, is so powerful it magnet-

ically attracts love. When truth stands up radiantly, love can't help itself. It bows and follows.

I felt a tight squeeze on my hand and recognized the signal at the end of the song. I squeezed back, acknowledging affection. It was the little charge of electricity we always gave each other before we unclasped hands at Sisterspace—not unlike the secret handshake lodge members in the Fraternal Order of Elks used to seal their loyalty oaths. It meant: "I'm here for you."

"I think she's smiling!" the woman squeezing my hand said excitedly. I recognized Gina's voice. Had Gina finally made it to Sisterspace? I'd invited her dozens of times—I knew she would love it—but she was always busy.

"Doesn't it look like she's trying to smile?" she asked, sounding as happy as I'd ever heard her. I knew she would love the company at Sisterspace. A pair of warm hands gently held my cheeks.

"Mary Kay?" a male voice asked. It was Larry. Larry? Was Gina doing an imitation of Larry? Had *Larry* joined the Fort Wayne Feminists?

"Are you awake?" he asked urgently. Awake? Had I been dreaming? I cracked my eyes and saw him wavering in the light. Our faces were so close our noses almost touched. Where was I? Was the woman with the bright lights a dream? Then why were the music and light still filtering through my head? My limbs were still pillows, my body still floating. I could barely keep my eyes cracked, the pull of sleep was so heavy on my lids.

"Mary Kay," he called softly, holding my face in his hands. He moved his thumbs back and forth across my cheeks, as though to verify I was actually here. He smiled with huge affection, larger and hungrier than anything I'd ever greeted in the past two years of coming and going. Even though I remembered kissing him late last night, when he came home from work and crouched next to the futon, he kissed me now as if a single night's sleep were an unbearable separation. Gripped by the enormous wanting in his eyes, I tried hard to shake my sleep. I wanted to assure him, "I'm here."

I couldn't speak—I was still wearing the gag, which Larry saw clearly but for some reason chose not to remove—so I had to communicate with my eyes. I fluttered my lids a few times to beacon the telegram: "Am right here. Stop. Not to worry." He seemed to understand completely, for every time I blinked he grinned even harder.

"You just don't know how happy I am to see you!" he said, reluctant to let go. When he stepped back instead of crawling into bed with me, I saw Gina standing immediately behind him. I wondered what Gina was doing in our bedroom, how she had become so familiar with Larry. She was rubbing his back affectionately, intimately, as if some large secret had passed between them in the night. Phyllis was there, too, wearing the happiest expression I'd ever seen on her face. Since these three people didn't go together, I couldn't figure out whether I was in Washington or Chicago or New York.

The geography question was further complicated by my friend Alice, from Fort Wayne, smiling quietly on the other side of the bed while tears streamed down her face. Carrie and Susan were standing together at the foot of the bed, looking happy but enormously fatigued—maybe we were all in Juneau, Alaska, reaching the end of an all-night pig roast. Everyone looked slightly intoxicated, smiling with nonsensical joy but showing visible signs of wear. It must have been some wild party—I wasn't feeling all that hot myself.

Phyllis was wearing a neck collar and I was immobilized, flat on my back. We must have been in a terrible accident on the way home—I recognized now that we were all in a hospital room. Each nursing some private wound, the faces showed traces of receding pain, but as I opened my eyes everyone was enjoying the punch line of an enormously funny joke. The accident had apparently turned out all right since the mood surrounding me was pure celebration. My friends kept laughing to themselves and shaking their heads side to side, speechless, as if it were just too much. I assumed I'd been the source of the joke, since everyone was staring at me with expansive appreciation. I had no idea what I'd done—I knew it wasn't something I'd said because I couldn't talk. Whatever it was, I'd never faced a more appreciative audience. All I had to do was blink my eyes and they were ready to applaud.

They smiled, my eyes smiled back, they smiled more. We were like a family of chimpanzees, mimicking expressions without thought. I felt the goofiest pleasure in this shower of affection. I didn't have to speak, think, work—I didn't even have to breathe, for a machine had been provided to do that for me. All I had to do for immediate approval was look at them. The love flowing back and forth between us was absolutely effortless.

"You've been in a coma," Larry said. He kept repeating "coma," wanting me to understand. It seemed to mean a lot to him, requiring some kind of acknowledgment. I nodded, to show I'd heard him. His response to this simple gesture was nothing short of glorious. He picked up my hand and kissed it passionately, as if putting "coma" behind us represented some kind of vow. The kiss seemed to promise we would live happily ever after, surrounded by wonderful friends, in an atmosphere of love and affection.

A pleasant drowsiness fell over me and I closed my eyes again. In the confusion between sleeping and waking, between the messages of the dream and the baffling appearance of my friends, one fact seemed clear: All I had to do to ensure this happiness forever was to remain faithful to the truth. It seemed so simple.

13

WAKING UP

"MARY KAY!" a man's voice called excitedly. "Open your eyes!"

"Mary Kay!" two more voices joined in, then three: "Mary Kay!"

Through the slits of my eyes I saw the fuzzy outline of three men leaning over me, their silhouettes wavering unsteadily in the bright background lights. The glare intensified the sharp pain already stabbing my temples. I'd awakened that morning with the worst hangover I've ever had in my life.

The place had been a madhouse all morning. Phones kept ringing incessantly, drilling my ears every five seconds. I heard the guards talking excitedly in the hall, trading rumors of a break-in late last night—except they identified it oddly as a "break-through." They were so preoccupied with the robbery they ignored the phones. The only way to restore peace was to answer them myself—and leave the receivers off the hook.

I knew I couldn't walk but thought I could crawl down the hall, and I attempted to slide out of bed by throwing my legs over the side. My right thigh crashed into a metal bar. I was recovering from the surge of pain that sent through my spine when one of the guards discovered me, swung my calves back into the center of the mattress, then issued a sudden cry of surprise.

She called excitedly for reinforcements. Footsteps pounded down the hall as voices shouted urgently to one another: "She opened her *eyes*? Are you *sure*?"

"Call Greenbaum!"

"It's Saturday."

"So what?"

"Right—he'll be ecstatic!"

My cell soon filled up with a crowd shouting my name. The din amplified my pounding headache. Irritated, I squinted against the glaring lights. Where was I? I remembered arriving in New York, having the flu. Saying goodnight to Larry—was he here, in my cell? Someone was fastening my ankles to opposite sides of the bed, forcing my legs into a spreadeagled, forty-five degree angle. Three lunatics were leaning over me, yelling my name. Dream deprived, irritated, pinned down in a vulnerable position, I was not remotely interested in answering their stupid questions.

"Mary Kay, can you see my hand?" the leader asked, holding his hand just inches above my face. "How many fingers am I holding up?" he asked, extending three.

Who *is* this asshole? Ignore him. Close your eyes.

"Mary Kay—don't . . ." I recognized Gina's voice.

Gina? Was Gina here, in New York? Did she know these guys? Did she really want me to participate in this stupid questioning? I struggled to open my eyes. I saw Gina standing next to Larry, both looking anxious and pale, apparently suffering hangovers of their own.

"This is important, hon," she said. "Can you count the fingers? Can you tell us how many?" Jesus. I couldn't believe Gina was asking me if I could count to three. Rolling my eyes back to show my annoyance, I nevertheless tried to hold up three fingers. I could barely move them.

"One . . . two . . . three!" the leader yelled. "She responded!" There were hoots and cheers. Gina and Larry smiled—I'd passed some critical test. The examiners left the room, talking feverishly and planning more tests. Gina and Larry followed, asking whether I now qualified for the "respirator" test. When the room finally quieted I was too agitated to rest. From my own point of view, the test had been a disaster.

Just lifting three fingers had sent a roaring pain up my arm. I barely recognized the two thin, bony spindles extending before me as my legs. Staring in disbelief at the metacarpal bones protruding sharply from my wrists, I had no trouble counting to five, then ten. The skin on my arms was purpled and yellowed, and I couldn't lift my head from the pillow. I could remember "metacarpal," but couldn't get a grip on "coma," the word Larry kept repeating in my dream. Everywhere, I ached. What had happened to me?

*   *   *

"We're going to take you off the respirator, Mary Kay," a sober man in a plaid sport shirt said, walking into my room with Larry and Gina and a team of technicians in hospital scrubs. I recognized the green creatures. They looked thoroughly human in the broad light of day—their faces were wracked with worry.

"I want you to take a deep breath as soon as I remove this tube," the leader instructed. Chimpanzeelike, I absorbed the doubts on the faces around me. What if I couldn't breath? Would I die? Suddenly I was afraid I didn't know how. Breathing, like sweating, was something I'd never thought about—it just happened. What muscles or reflexes were required? My fingers hadn't moved without monumental effort—would my lungs? Before I could check the answers, the tube was out.

Gina, Larry, the green creatures all shouted loudly: "Breathe, breathe, *breathe!*"

Swallowing hard, I felt a tremendous ache well up in my throat. My tongue was thick and swollen. A heavy deposit of plastic stuck to the insides of my teeth and my jaw ached from clenching the tube. My lips were parched and cracked. The raw skin under the adhesive tapes on my mouth and cheeks stung sharply in the exposed air, and my chest was burning with chemicals. While these strange, alarming sensations bombarded me I was suddenly elevated, seemingly deus ex machina, by a cool rush of air filling my lungs. Again, I heaved in; again, the rush. I was breathing.

Larry and Gina beamed. The green creatures applauded, and even the sober man in the plaid shirt broke into a wide grin. As a reward for passing the breathing test, my wrists and legs were untied. Oh, joy! I was being released!

Without my gag, I tried to thank my liberators, but I still had no voice. A small, weak, grunt was all I could produce.

"What is it, M. K.?" Gina asked, smiling indulgently. "Do you need something?" I nodded. I needed a wheelchair to get out of this place.

"What, hon—what is it?" I tried to lift my arm to draw the outline of a wheel, but it fell limply on my stomach. I moved it in a circular motion, indicating the method of transportation I needed to go home.

"You're hungry!" Gina declared, misinterpreting my sign. "Is that what you want—some dinner?"

Once she mentioned it, dinner sounded like a wonderful idea. I was starving. I nodded, willing to postpone my departure long enough for a bite to eat.

"Could we get her some food?" Gina asked. An efficient woman in a white uniform glanced at her watch.

"The food cart won't be here for another hour—I'll go down to the kitchen and get something. What does she like?"

"French, Italian, Japanese," Gina joked, mocking hospital cuisine. "She likes everything." I'd never seen her in such high spirits.

Larry grimaced as he lowered my dinner onto the tray table. I looked down on a platter of gray-green peas, something brown and lumpy floating in a pool of thick gravy, mashed potatoes, a square of red Jell-O, a carton of milk, and a plastic container of ice water. After the insulting numbers test and the scary breathing test, I approached the eating test enthusiastically. I loved mashed potatoes. Slowly, with enormous concentration, I secured the fork in my hand. Almost immediately, it dropped in my lap. I looked up, afraid I'd flunked the test and jeopardized my release.

"Do you need help?" Larry asked. I shook my head, pouting, determined to prove myself. This amused Larry and Gina, but they suppressed themselves and indulged another solo attempt.

I picked up the fork again, slid it through the peas and gravy, aiming for the mashed potatoes. The fork jammed into the stiff white mass and stuck there. The impact dropped my wrist into the pool of gravy. Larry and Gina found this hysterical. They were like two kids with an incurable case of the giggles—everything I did amused the hell out of them.

Hunger eventually won out over pride. Larry fed me. I had trouble swallowing and Larry, intuiting my difficulty, put a straw in the ice water and held the container while I took a long, slow drink. The cold water soothed my throat. He spooned a cube into my mouth. I sucked it until it melted, then asked for another with my eyes. Spooning cube after cube, he smiled, as if some ache in his own throat were being relieved with mine. After a satisfying dinner of ice cubes and Jell-O, I was ready to go home.

Several problems quickly presented themselves: I couldn't walk, there were four IV tubes stuck in my arms, and all I had on was a flimsy hospital gown. My mind worked feverishly to solve these last obstacles. Surely there had to be a wheelchair around somewhere—maybe one with extended poles where we could hang the IV bottles. I could wrap myself up in one of these blankets on the bed. So far so good. In my mind, I had rolled out the door under a canopy of clinking glass and I was sitting on the curb, swaddled in a blanket, while Larry hailed a cab. From there I saw my one remaining problem: there would be two or three steps of icy slush to navigate between the wheelchair and the cab. Those three steps represented a chasm between me and my freedom. I had to have some protection for my bare feet.

Trying to remember what I'd done with my shoes—or whether I even had any on when I came to this place—I must have looked disturbed.

"What's wrong, hon?" Gina asked, becoming alarmed. "Are you in pain?" I shook my head no. I was in pain, but that wasn't my immediate problem. I wiggled my bare feet but they didn't understand.

"Do you have an itch?" Larry asked. *No*, I shook my head sadly, my eyes filling with tears of frustration. I was back in familiar territory, possessed once more with the need to be understood.

"Oh, Sis—don't cry," Gina moaned. "What can we do?"

"Can you write?" Larry asked.

Yes, I nodded, brightening. Certainly I could write. He found a pen and small pad of paper and placed it on the hospital tray. With extreme care, I applied my knowledge of the Palmer method while Larry and Gina waited, tension mounting. My talent with a pen, however, proved no better than my skill with a fork. The message I wrote was a kind of intricately knotted line graph leading absolutely nowhere. I suppose they might have been alarmed about brain damage had I looked pleased with myself, but I turned in my writing exam with pure gloom. An alarming failure, even to me.

Unable to speak, incapable of writing, competent only in nodding yes or no—despite these challenging handicaps, my tolerant companions were undaunted. There was an important thought stuck in my mind, and they wanted desperately to get it out. Larry had another brilliant idea: He made a chart of the alphabet and pointed to the letters one by one, while Gina kept a record of each yes or no. With tight economy of words and no misspellings, I delivered my first written thought. The only problem was that the chart contained no space bar, so the two words of my message had to be jammed into one:

NOSHOES

The grins that had been building as they acquired the seven letters faded as Larry and Gina tried to decipher the foreign word.

"Nosh . . . Nosh-ohs?" Gina attempted a pronunciation. She wondered if I wanted a Mexican dish, something with cheese and jalapeño peppers. I shook my head no. Without sound, I mouthed the words slowly, taking a long break where the space was supposed to be. They watched intensely, mouthing silently with me. A light went on in Gina's eyes.

"No *shoes!*" Gina yelled, like someone who'd won the jackpot on *Wheel of Fortune*. I nodded ecstatically. "No shoes!" she repeated, grinning broadly, happy to communicate word for word, soul to soul. Her joy was no less resplendent for the fact that my message made no sense whatsoever.

"What does it mean?" Larry asked her.

"I don't know," she said, her laugh subsiding, shrugging her shoulders as if we'd both been caught committing high foolishness together. "What *does* it mean, Sis?"

Delighted to elucidate further, I wiggled my bare toes. I nodded at my feet and then looked up and out the door, trying to indicate that with any kind of footwear, "I'm outta here." Larry was the first to catch my meaning.

"You want to go *home?*" he asked. I nodded happily. I wanted to go home more than anything.

"Oh, hon." Gina moaned, hating to disappoint me. "You can't go home. Dr. Greenbaum said if everything goes well you might be released in three weeks."

Three weeks! I started to cry, which made Gina immediately begin to cry. Even Larry, the Vulcan, became perceptibly moist. Three more weeks of unceasing dreams . . . I knew I would go mad.

For the next two days my moods swung wildly from anger to joy, depending largely on the company and dosage of painkilling drugs. Gina and Larry swung with me—feeling happy when I smiled, blue when I cried. Even the staff and the green creatures caught my contagious passions. Only the man in the plaid shirt, who appeared the next day in a crumpled white lab coat, approached me with detachment. Frowning slightly during one of my manic moments Sunday afternoon, he stood next to Larry at the foot of the bed.

"How do you think she's doing, Dr. Greenbaum?" Larry asked, smiling at me with undiluted approval. I fluttered my eyelids—I felt silly waving my eyes, but I remembered how happy it made him the other day. Dr. Greenbaum hadn't attended that particular scene.

"To be honest, she seems a bit juvenile to me . . . but then I don't know what she's usually like," he replied, willing to be open-minded about bimbo behavior. "Does she appear normal to you?" he asked Gina.

For two days, since I'd first opened my eyes, Gina had been delighted to play bimbo with me. But the party was over for her. She was leaving tomorrow—Kay was on her way—and she had sobered up considerably. The question of brain damage was still open: I still hadn't spoken, became upset without apparent provocation, smiled at odd times, and seemed to be losing my appetite. Greenbaum's blunt question about whether my behavior looked "normal" rattled Gina.

"I might have thought so," she recorded in her notebook before packing it several hours later, "if she had not appeared suddenly juvenile and un–Mary Kay–like to me. I said I didn't think she was exactly juvenile or normal, and felt obligated to tell him she was a writer and a 'pretty intelligent woman.' "

Had Gina left a day earlier, during the height of postcoma glee, she might have left a free woman. As it happened, she had to drag the weight of possible brain damage home with her. When she came to say good-bye Sunday evening, she had to face the truth that I did not bear any resemblance to a "pretty intelligent woman." I was a thirty-six-year-old, ninety-pound, sloppily sentimental baby. I cried when she left. With Gina, I knew I was losing my music, my reading, my joy.

Larry was similarly afflicted by her departure. Gina was his first, week-long experience with the pleasures of family. In the nine days they spent together, he had someone to take the trouble with him, someone to care and love and worry as passionately as he did. Going solo after such heart-to-heart companionship was wrenching. Forty-one years of only child independence collapsed into a strong craving to live in a family. He felt stabbing withdrawal pains as Gina stepped aboard the airport shuttle at Grand Central Station. Everyone in the family had trouble letting go of Gina.

Most of the calls jangling the phones the morning I woke up were from Fort Wayne. The fifty friends who attended the energy circle the night before were calling to find out if it had worked. When I opened my eyes Saturday morning, the participants believed it was their spiritual wish that had reached me, although my medical experts were inclined to think it was the sensory stimulation of the telephones. I myself thought there might have been an element of vanity involved, since one more day in the coma meant my rebirth would have coincided with April Fool's Day.

When my friends in Fort Wayne couldn't get through on the phone, mail began pouring into my room. By the third week more than four hundred letters had arrived, something of a crisis for a woman who feels obligated to answer all her personal mail. My friends urged me to "take care of yourself," and sent a large check from the Women in Need fund to ensure a long recovery. It was much easier to come out of a coma when a wealth of affection was waiting for you. Joan described what those nine days were like on the other side:

April 2, 1984

My Dearest Mary Kay:
The wonderful news from Larry yesterday was that you were awake! Wide awake! Probably as the pain and the discomfort and the realization of what has happened to you seeps back into your veins, you will be wishing you could sleep through some of the healing. But for those of us who stood vigil while you were in that coma, we thrill at each report of your progress—and believe me, little sister, where you are now is progress.
On Sunday morning, March 25th, I opened the hall closet and there was your winter coat which Jim had told me he would mail back to you—only, of course, he mailed Laurie's coat instead. I called to make arrangements to exchange the coats and Howe answered and told me you were in a coma . . .
There began a telephone tree that circled this country . . . I talked to Cathryn in Maine . . . Carolen in Kansas City . . . Ann . . . Jeannette

... Marge ... Claudia and Norma ... Harriet and then, of course, the word spread. Some of your students called students who had moved to California and they told Marge and Carol who called me before I had a chance to call them ... the Auditor's Office gang was in constant touch. Sue and Ro did the calling there ... I had to stop Colette and Sarah from getting a group together to storm the hospital the first few days you were in the coma ... Mary has been after me every day. She has a group she calls. Mary gets mad at me every time she calls because I never ask Gina or Larry all the questions she wants answers to. She is so mad because you are ill. ...

The reality of "coma" sank in as I became aware of the extensive physical damages. As I discovered my wounds, my staggering ineptitude, the recovery time that seemed interminable suddenly seemed too brief. It had taken me ten years to grow from a baby feminist to a grandmother in Fort Wayne, Indiana, and now I had only three weeks to shape up the juvenile, incompetent youth who woke up in New York. It was depressing to find myself at ground zero at age thirty-six. Being "born again," despite euphoric reports from fundamentalists, was a very mixed blessing.

There were glorious aspects of rebirth, certainly. It was an extraordinary experience to be loved unconditionally, as an adult. Unlike the absolute love that welcomes an infant into the world, this passion was more powerful and electrifying for the forgiveness it contained. Human love, hurdled willfully over serious breaches and heart-stopping words, was divine enough for me. Kay, who'd loved me longest and had the most to forgive, came to New York with amazing quantities of the stuff. There is perhaps no stronger joy on earth than being greeted with unqualified affection by the woman you've aimed to please your whole life.

When Kay arrived in ICU I had recovered my voice, but not a significant portion of my mind. Still woozy with painkillers, I told her about the fantastic discovery I'd made the night before, when I looked through my window and witnessed a clandestine drug operation in the building next door. The curtains of my room had been accidentally left open and I'd observed the most bizarre speakeasy scene. Women in small white hats made rounds with cigarette trays while two pianists played a duet on a ten-foot long, pink piano. I suspected a drug operation because everyone in the place whispered to each other, and two men exchanged secret papers. Kay looked through the only outside window in my room and saw a brick wall.

"Maybe you just imagined it," she suggested gently, without much hope of persuasion. She released a tremendous sigh, a vintage issue from her deepest private stock. It wasn't the first time she'd heard a wild delusion from one of her offspring—my ten-foot pink piano was a harmless schmoo compared to the stories she'd heard in ISPI. I invited her to come back at midnight to see for herself.

That night I looked at the brick wall and saw the vision again. It disappeared when a nurse came into my room and drew the drapes across the inside window, shutting out the bright lights reflected from the nursing station across the hall. Just before the drapes closed, I saw two women working behind the long pink counter while another, in a white nurse's cap, walked by with a medication tray. Kay and I laughed the next day when I revealed the mystery behind the clandestine drug ring. It was wonderful to laugh with her that afternoon, to see her relief that I wasn't crazy after all. That laugh was even more gratifying for the passion I had seen in her eyes the day before, when it was clear she loved me even if I was.

It was in the benevolent atmosphere of ICU that Kay met Larry, with whom I would soon be "living in sin." I hadn't yet explained to my parents I was moving in with Larry, but the coma resolved that little piece of unfinished business. The actions she observed during her week in New York made words unnecessary. She watched him feed me, comfort me, anticipate my needs. Midweek, they took a trip to Connecticut to see the house and visit the schools we'd chosen for the kids. She heartily approved of my choices, and the subtle suggestion of marriage came only as an afterthought, almost out of obligation. She was clearly uninterested in taking up the habits of criticism again—praying for me through a nine-day coma had purged all grievances. While she couldn't approve my "living in sin," compared to death, it was a manageable offense.

The first week of recovery brought other good news: I was lucky, Dr. Greenbaum said, to come through without heart or brain damage. My lungs had actually improved. The shadows were shrinking steadily. The five intravenous antibiotics that had to drip through my veins for three weeks had already closed in on the various encampments of germs, including the ferocious empyema infection. The trauma of the coma ultimately liberated me from the loathsome tube.

Unlike that of the born-again fundamentalists, however, mine was a qualified joy. Maybe their happiness was uninterrupted because they went straight from being born to being born again, without any messy little deaths wedged unpleasantly in between. Resuming life, after the devastation of a coma, was a fearful and risky business. Incompetent in the simplest tasks, I had to learn how to live all over again—beginning with the basic principle of remaining conscious.

How had it happened that nine days of my life disappeared one night—and could it happen again without warning? Was the coma the result of being a diabetic, or a diabetic with a pulmonary tube, or a diabetic with a tube and a serious case of influenza, or a diabetic with a tube and the flu and one beloved, irretrievably gone madman? Was the coma caused by the outrageous chemical accident in my body or a psychological explosion of grief in my mind? By the time my voice returned, I had a long list of questions for Dr. Greenbaum.

Having met me in a coma, he was pleasantly surprised to find a functioning mind behind the juvenile exterior; I was relieved to discover a warm, witty friend, a doctor who regarded his patients as people instead of humble subjects.

"So, what's on your list today?" he said each morning, taking a seat and anticipating a barrage. Since I was fluent in chart terminology, we had extensive conversations about "sarcoid" and "necrotizing nodules" and "rheumatoid factors." He hypothesized that the chemistry of my body was so unbalanced that a common case of the flu might, indeed, have tipped me over the edge. There were things I could learn about managing diabetes, he assured me, that would prevent another disaster. He cleared up worries about my continuing mood swings and recurring dreams: "You've had enough drugs to keep a junkie happy for a year."

He accepted my departures from standard routines—sort of: "If you want Larry to bring in Chinese food tonight, go ahead. Why do I know you would anyway, whatever I said?" He was clearly a fan of "feisty," amused when I refused to wear a hospital gown and donned my sweats for my self-prescribed exercises the last week. I shuffled through the ward pushing my IV bottles on a pole, like an arthritic jogger with a cane bearing the slogan WILD WOMEN DON'T GET THE BLUES.

In truth, I had to wrestle with the blues every day. I felt a deep sense of failure and regarded the coma as a sign of weakness and ignorance. I was ashamed that when the going got tough, I keeled over.

"I suppose you could think of yourself as weak and vulnerable," Greenbaum admitted, familiar with the tomes of my medical history and the author of at least five hundred pages himself. "Or you could think of yourself as strong and resilient. You've recovered from some exceptional disasters. What you've come through would have flattened a fullback on the Giants." He said he was inclined to think of me as strong and resilient—but that I was entitled to my own opinion.

Dr. Greenbaum stopped by to cheer me up or slow me down several times a day, and when he couldn't answer my questions he arranged meetings with specialists who could. One afternoon, the chief of staff paid a call. He congratulated me on a dramatic recovery and asked if I would mind answering a few questions about the bizarre data on the emergency-room report. As he delicately put it, he wanted to document that "we inherited these problems." The data on the emergency-room report were the kind that could easily inspire a lawsuit. He didn't have to worry. People who feel shame for keeling over don't sue—they take their comas home and brood over them.

Since catching the flu had become synonymous with death for me, I developed an irrational fear of germs. And although I'd never experienced insomnia before, I now wrestled with an overwhelming fear of sleep. The last time I'd willfully closed my eyes, I lost nine days of my life. Not just ordinary work days—I'd checked out of the most ambitious week I'd ever planned. I'd slept through eight lunches and dinners with editors and prospective publishers, four meetings with writers, a week-long reunion with Susan and Carrie, a prehoneymoon week with Larry, two job interviews, and I'd left an audience of three hundred people staring at an empty stage.

I was embarrassed that all of the significant people in my life had to be told: "She's in a coma." I felt my credibility was forever damaged—there was no use acting dignified anymore, pretending composure. Who would believe my perpetual claim—"I'm fine!"—after I'd dropped off into a coma? No one. The great pretenders had been publicly exposed.

Contemplating my release, I wondered how I would ever fit myself neatly, unobtrusively, into the real world again. I sympathized with Frank's feelings of "otherness" when he returned from a high, having to apologize to the people he loved for acting out damaging delusions. In the hospital it was easy to talk to nurses and doctors who saw comas every day, but the world outside would have to receive me with either polite skepticism or outright shock—the demeanor they might adopt, say, when a new acquaintance at a cocktail party drops the fact that two millenia earlier she was the queen of Egypt. Few people in possession of an exotic experience can keep it to themselves. I knew I couldn't. For one thing, I'd been afflicted with a strong impulse to confess ever since my youth. Invariably when anyone offered a compliment on an outfit I'd sewn myself, I felt obliged to mention the mistakes.

"Honey, you don't *have* to tell everyone about the hidden safety pin," Kay advised. "Just say, 'Thank you.' "

I always said, "Thank you, but . . ." I thought opinions would be revised if admirers knew a safety pin was holding everything together—that it was dishonest, somehow, to withhold the information. The fact of "coma" was attached to my life like a red zipper in a white dress, a detail so arresting and deviant it demanded notice. It was something I felt any prospective audience/reader/colleague/editor had a right to know, an item that, if I were a completely honest woman, would be listed on my résumé under "personal experiences." I thought anyone entering a contract with me had a right to know that I'd spent nine days in outer space.

Even if I suppressed the impulse to confess, however, it was impossible to disguise the way the coma altered me. I still felt the coma lights glowing through me like a neon sign, blinking on and off with every subject, every task I picked up. Completely rewired by nine days of hallucination, my mind reeled with flashbacks when certain faces or conversations triggered them. While one part of me worked hard to pick up the pieces of my life, another part of me sat back, arms folded across her chest, asking why, what for, was I sure, did I really need to reclaim every shard of broken pottery? This new presence was not someone willing to remain in the closet, as it were, appearing only when convenient. She was all over the place, presenting her opinions about my life every ten minutes. I had become, if not a group, a pair of inseparable twins.

After I was transferred to a general-medicine floor for my last week of recovery, Larry had the luxury of his first Saturday morning without a crisis. Instead of bolting a quick breakfast at Poppy's Deli on the way to the hospital, he bought a *Times* and cooked an elaborate omelet at home. He opened the paper to a story about a couple in Brooklyn whose baby started choking at the dinner table. Suddenly, between gulps of coffee, he felt himself fall completely inside their minds. He knew their panic watching the baby turn blue, frantically calling 911, trying to answer the operator's urgent questions: "Is she breathing at all?"

For three solid weeks he'd managed to bury that panic himself, but reading the story of a couple he didn't even know in Brooklyn, tears began streaming down his cheeks. He cried again when he sat on the edge of my bed, repeating the story to me. Was I a sadist, to love him most when he was pained?

Suffering wasn't the only avenue to compassion, but certainly one of the most direct and, in my case, most heavily traveled. When I saw Larry's pain I knew there would be less explaining to do whenever he saw me weeping over the newspaper. Was it necessary to suffer to learn a deeper capacity to feel, and therefore love? Wasn't empathy enough—did passion have to be experienced? The difference between empathy and compassion was essentially the same as watching a high diver and being one. It might be a thrill to see the spectacular leaps from the cliffs, but no one in the audience has the woozy, pit-of-the-stomach sensation the diver has. That wooziness, I think, has to be what brings the divers to the cliff's edge, over and over. If Larry were serious about wanting to spend the rest of his life with me, some direct experience in going over the brink was appropriate preparation.

*   *   *

"I'm gonna *kill* you if you ever pull a stunt like this again!" Kevin called with a promise to kill me; Paul called every day wanting to talk. I called Jerry and collected a select bouquet of exclamation points, and Gina called me to relieve lingering worries about brain damage. With every call to friends and relatives, I had to relieve concerns. I explained the flu theory, the various infections, the five antibiotics that had to drip through my veins. After three weeks of continuous bombardment, the multiple infections were completely wiped out: "My god!" my friend George exclaimed. "You've been nuked!"

Lists of things to do crept gradually back into my life. I asked Larry to bring my briefcase and set up a temporary office in my room. While I was working one afternoon, a florist arrived bearing a tree flowering with exotic lavender blooms. Pale satin ribbons, pink and green, streamed down from a gold card attached to the trunk. A small parade of nurses and aides followed the florist into my room for a closer examination.

"Good grief," I said, "Cardinal O'Connor must know I'm here. Maybe the pope!" The tree was a gift from Nancy and Dona, my editors at the *Times*. It towered above the floral arrangements now overcrowding the windowsill, the dresser, the bed stand, with several more lined up against the wall. My hospital room/office had the quiet, sweetly scented aura of a funeral home. Most of the bouquets were from editors, a reminder that one of the reasons I'd been hauled back to life was that I left without finishing all my deadlines. "I've been in a coma" was the best excuse I'd offered so far for being late. Every morning, between glucose tests and consultations with specialists, I added a few lines to the riddle of responsibility for the Cosmo girls. But I was far from committed to my former career. I ultimately turned down Miss X's offer for "The Politics of Pretty." The next deadline I gave myself was to satisfy a long-standing incomplete: I wanted to translate the papers in Frank's blue suitcase.

Vogue sent a second bouquet when the three essays they submitted for the National Magazine Awards put them in the finalists' circle. I was invited to join the editor's table at the banquet in April.

"What're the National Magazine Awards?" I asked Julia, calling her at work.

"They're like the Oscars of the magazine business," she explained. "There's a huge banquet each year at the Waldorf-Astoria." I remembered the Headliner Dinner. Here we go again.

"It's next week. Do you think you can come?" Julia asked, excited for me.

"Maybe," I said. "But all I have to wear is my purple vest." The Waldorf-Astoria seemed like exactly the right place to trot out that old relic of the sixties. Maybe with a few lavender blossoms from the *Times* in my hair.

Though I had no intention of reproducing in this lifetime, I got my period before I left the hospital. I asked Kay to bring the tampons I kept in my suitcase. She arrived that afternoon carrying a vast disapproval behind her blue eyes, which she hadn't decided quite how to release. It took several hours before she found the right words to vent her unhappiness: While searching through my suitcase to collect my list of personal items she found a small leather case containing two joints—a Valentine's Day gift from one of my friends.

It was clear we were in for a long discussion. I couldn't believe Gina hadn't cleared the decks for me, so to speak, before Kay arrived. Gina went through my journal, my briefcase, my purse, but had never opened my suitcase. The coma laid bare my whole life—like the victim of an authorized robbery, I felt personally exposed. Of all the sins that could be turned up in my absence, Kay found only the venial offense of two joints. I suggested that might be reason for celebration.

But two joints looked like major criminal activity to Kay. They meant I wasn't perfect, and she was unhappy about having to resume the role of perfecter. The brief period of unconditional love had been rudely and abruptly terminated by her discovery in my suitcase. I explained that two joints were about equal to a double martini, which hardly relieved the woman who never proceeded beyond one whiskey sour. In the interest of reestablishing peace, I offered her one of the chocolates Carrie had brought that morning. ("Oh god, I can't believe I forgot you were diabetic," Carrie had moaned.)

Kay eyed the chocolate but refused. "I can't," she said, "I'm allergic."

"I know," I said, smiling. "But this seems like the perfect time to bring on a case of laryngitis." We were back in the familiar territory of conditional love. Still, having experienced the more divine stuff of intensive care, I knew the peaks of unqualified affection were there. Without much difficulty, I could look past the criticism in her eyes and remember that she loved me.

After a month in the hospital, where meals were delivered to my room, my sheets were changed daily, and uniformed personnel inquired about my welfare almost hourly, I experienced separation anxiety the night before my release. My two main tasks that month were to remain conscious and keep breathing; tomorrow, I had to face hundreds of personal responsibilities that would become my own again.

I became hyperalert to what was ahead of me. Why *had* I been hauled back—what was I supposed to do with my life? Newborns are not expected to have a reason to be upon birth—they're slated to spend the next two decades in childhood, adolescence, young adulthood. For reborns, however, life was an entirely different matter. Being born at thirty-six, I was looking at middle age, old age, and death. There wasn't a lot of time to fool around if the last item in that succession were to bring peace. It seemed I had to figure out almost immediately who I was and what I was doing here.

A reborn had to consider not only the spiritual questions that arise in midlife, but myriad physical issues as well. My roommate in general medicine gave me a brief glimpse of what the rental equipment we lived in would look like after another four or five decades of hard use. Mrs. C.—a remarkable eighty-six-year-old woman recovering from her third case of pneumonia—and I were in about the same shape when my wheelchair was rolled into her room a week earlier. We each started out at ninety-five pounds, both required to reach a hundred before we got out.

Mrs. C. was a spirited competitor. "I gained half a pound today and that girl didn't," she told her son proudly one afternoon, nodding toward me. Larry overheard her and smiled. He suggested placing large scoreboards at the foot of our beds, labeled MRS. C. and THAT GIRL. Mrs. C. rose slowly and steadily but my body, more than forty years younger, soon overtook hers. After three weeks of being weak and helpless, walking stiffly in pain, my flexibility and strength finally began to return. Such gains were forever denied my roommate. No law could be written to relieve the last, cruel discrimination of age.

In addition to the indignities of her physical limitation, she had to bear the subtle differences in our care. I was perpetually greeted with the belief that I would get better; Mrs. C. often faced the less enthusiastic attitude that she was more or less through. When I complained of pain, my doctors were concerned. When she did, her doctor chided her for "whining."

He was careless with her orders. I heard him agree twice to change the diet prohibiting dairy products, allowing her to have a carton of milk with her cereal at breakfast. Two mornings in a row, she had to ring the nurse's station when it didn't arrive with her tray. She explained that the orders had been changed, but no one believed her. I watched her cry as she poked a spoon into her second bowl of dry cornflakes. It was so heartbreaking, my rage at her doctor inspired my first solo walk down the hallway, rolling my IV bottles on a pole. I refused to go back to bed until they gave me a carton of milk.

"How did you do it?" she asked when I returned. "I told them I heard your doctor order it," I said.

"I did, too," she said. "But they think I'm crazy."

Spending a week with Mrs. C. was one of the last gifts of my coma. I understood that the pain I was shedding would return again, if I lived long enough; that I would no doubt be considered crazy some day, unable to convince anyone I could handle a carton of milk. But I saw, too, that it was possible to live through these humiliations with dignity. Mrs. C. courageously got on the scales every day, determined to heal, fully anticipating another spirited round of life outside the hospital. I found her a worthy competitor. The last morning we spent together she gave me a brief look at why it might be worth it to keep breathing, to keep welcoming life, mortal though we are.

A young nurses' aide came in on her day off to give my roommate a home permanent. She was a sweet girl of about nineteen who understood exactly how an eighty-six-year-old woman might feel about entertaining visitors "when my hair's such a mess." After the shampoo Mrs. C. was in high spirits, propped up with pillows in a chair the aide and I pulled in from the lobby. I was sitting on my suitcase, waiting for Larry, making myself useful by handing the curling papers to the aide. Mrs. C. was in rare form, telling stories of her glory days. The three of us, ages spanning almost seven decades, were giggling like girls. More than any painkillers Mrs. C. had that week, the home permanent made her feel terrific.

The stench was dreadful and the room was a mess, but I couldn't think of any place I'd rather be than in that hospital/beauty parlor, participating in that strictly female ritual. Watching an old woman inspire compassion in this girl, seeing this girl inspire joy in an old woman, I could see my theory of immortality clearly: one life stamps and influences another, which in turn stamps and influences another, on and on, until the soul of human experience breathes on in generations we'll never even meet.

"All we ever do is walk from one little piece of holy ground to the next," Salinger once wrote. Anyone viewing life from the general-medicine floor in St. Vincent's that morning had to know it was true.

14

ANOTHER I

RETURNING TO REALITY, even as a tourist, was never a purely amusing journey. I remember standing on weak legs, elbows propped up against the windowsill, watching a hard rain fall on Manhattan the night before I left St. Vincent's. Rush-hour pedestrians fought their way down Seventh Avenue, leaning into strong winds that turned their umbrellas inside out. Life outside the hospital was hard on people. I knew I would be whipped about by the elements once I entered the streets again, consumed by overwhelming passions and ambitions. Put me in the company of seven million bananafish and—I can't help myself—I swim with their school.

Despite my propensity to join the madding crowd, I had the unshakable feeling that however much I reapplied myself to life it would never be quite the same. I thought I wasn't really supposed to be here. I had been scheduled for death but—like other important deadlines I'd missed—I didn't make it. The years ahead of me seemed like pure gifts, unearned bonuses to spend however I liked. I felt radically altered by my nine-day sleep, a passionate psychological journey that uncovered old, unextinguished yearnings. After awakening on March 31, I gradually discovered that the life planned by the woman I had been no longer fit the woman I'd become.

I'm embarrassed that when the going got tough I keeled over into a coma, but it did not turn out to be a tragedy for me. While I slept, my family and friends conducted the equivalent of a nine-day wake, remembering all the reasons they loved me, feelings they wished they'd expressed but hadn't because we thought there was plenty of time. These words, stuck in private minds, poured out when I awakened. It was an amazing experience to wake up into an atmosphere of unconditional love, as an *adult*, knowing that my family and friends had forgiven me. The understanding I worked so hard for through hundreds of pages and thousands of words had arrived, ironically, during my extended silence.

The coma was far harder on the people who loved me, who spent nine days wishing me back into existence, than it was for me, captured by fantastic hallucinations and visions. It forced everyone to stop and think, to abandon the mindless path of the starving processionaries and find food. There were undoubtedly more dignified ways to reach the emotional truces we subsequently established, but dignity had never been part of my karma anyway.

Although I never plan to repeat the coma experience, I've had to suppress a kind of giddiness, an unstoppable happiness, about having survived it. I have more sympathy for the maddening behavior of "born-again" Christians—although I still don't share their particular visions, I have some empathy now for their embarrassing urge to "witness." Though agnostics have difficulty identifying with spiritual feelings, the moments of blinding illumination during the coma left me light-headed with happiness and love. My friends have told me that's exactly what sanctifying grace feels like, when believers receive the gift of faith. I suspect it's also exactly what morphine feels like, when a person in pain receives an injection. Either way, whether divinity or drugs was responsible for the euphoria, the peacefulness I felt during the coma occurred again and again in the months that followed. I cannot recommend a coma as the cure for depression, but it did provide the peace of mind that had always eluded me.

Invariably, physical pain brought important changes, providing "the protective psychological hardiness that comes from being hurt," as biographer Ted Morgan described F.D.R.'s struggle with polio. "It was this spiritual battle, this passage from despair to hope, this refusal to accept defeat, this ability to learn from adversity that transformed him from a shallow, untested, selfishly ambitious and sometimes unscrupulous young man into the mature figure we know as F.D.R."

I recognized versions of this spiritual battle among the people I

loved—Ryan, lowering his blue beak on the curb in front of
Marie's; Howe, saying good-bye to me at the airport; Larry,
reliving his loss through the strangers in Brooklyn; Kay, staring at
Frank's shoes in the basement; and Frank himself, who avoided no
pain at all. Everyone I admired had to battle with something
terrible, coming through with a perceptible limp but nevertheless
stronger than before. Even after all the madness he endured, Frank
thought something valuable was being crafted through his struggle. And here I was, freshly released from the most dramatic
physical collapse of my life, grateful for another round.

I spent the next month in New York with Larry, regaining
strength before returning to full-time motherhood in the Midwest.
If Larry worried at my slow progress, he kept it to himself, sharing
with me only his confidence in my full recovery. I remembered
only one evening he let it slip, when I was standing in front of the
refrigerator with the door open, stuck in one of those everyday,
what-am-I-looking-for? stares. He was standing in the doorway,
waiting with his empty wineglass, his eyebrows rising steadily
toward his hairline. I knew the thought crossing his mind.
"Brain damage?" I said. He smiled, caught red-minded.
The same intense scrutiny and repressed suspicions would greet
me during each reunion with friends. I didn't mind. I was still
dazzled by the otherworldly experience of the coma myself. There
was something different about me—I saw it clearly, whenever I
looked in the bathroom mirror. There was a subtle but stunning
difference in the face staring back each morning, hardly recogniz-
able as my own.
I'd forgotten what I looked like without physical pain. But now,
in private to the bathroom mirror, when no conversation or
thought was employing my face, I saw a woman whose composure
was imperturbable. After running around the bases of fatigue and
fear and poverty, collecting the wear and tear, scars at my left
temple and right collarbone, peace had become home base. It was
either the coma or the long unplanned rest or the extraordinary
affection of the last two months, but something had taken the
trouble from my eyes.
"You love peace," the fortune cookie message taped into my
journal declared. I did. I loved the woman who looked into my

eyes in the bathroom every morning, despite the daily trials or griefs I'd put our face through the day before. She was the presence who awakened with me in the hospital, the inseparable twin who wouldn't leave me alone. Looking at my existence through her calm, optimistic eyes, the requirements of my unwieldy life seemed actually do-able. While I became obsessed with deadlines and pressures once more, she would shrug our shoulders in the mirror each morning and think: "If nobody dies, it's not an emergency."

As my strength returned so did old habits of mind. A familiar sense of loss hung over our handshake when I stopped by Dennis Greenbaum's office to say good-bye. I think he was feeling it too, because the wry and witty chief of Critical Care couldn't come up with a single joke.

"Say hello to Larry and Gina for me," he remarked wistfully. For three weeks he was an important part of my hospital family, a committed partner with Larry and Gina in healing me. Caring for the critically ill was risky because patients kept dying, but it was just as important to maintain emotional detachment from the survivors. Just as we became ourselves again, just as we could hold up our end of a conversation and entertain visitors, we moved out. With luck, forever. In most cases we preferred to forget the days spent in ICU and the people we met there altogether. After resolving serious griefs with his patients, the chief didn't get to participate in the subsequent joy. Succeeding in his job—and in my case, he'd succeeded spectacularly—his patients couldn't wait to leave him. I promised to stay in touch, but we both knew it wouldn't be the same. Like a parent launching a grown child into independence, he shook my hand with mixed congratulations and regrets. It was a scene I would be enacting again, in the opposite role, when I left my sons in Ann Arbor at the end of the summer.

The coma became the deciding factor about where the kids would live for the next year. It would be a whole year before I regained my strength. I needed rest, and Howe craved responsibility. "Don't worry about anything," he said at the end of our first long, emotional conversation after the coma. "Take care of yourself," he said, then added the words lost in the wind outside the New York Air terminal last month: "I love you." He never wanted to be stuck with that phrase ringing inside his head again.

Those nine days in March were as revealing from his side of the coma as mine. He mourned the loss of "friend" as passionately as he would have mourned the loss of "wife." The bitter pain of divorce paled next to the possibility of my leaving the planet altogether. Previously invisible responsibilities became excruciatingly obvious in my three-month absence from Ann Arbor: He took the calls from the coaches for soccer fees, wrote the checks at Kroger, wrestled with nightmares about how he would manage it all without me. How had I managed it, he wondered. The desperate pleas I'd spoken or written unsuccessfully for almost three years were instantly understood in that one brief period without words.

The relationship looked different to me, too. Somewhere between the studio, the ambulance, the emergency room, ICU, and Coronary Care, I lost my emerald engagement ring. When it wasn't among the personal items returned to me after I awoke, a hospital security officer visited my room to fill out a report. Though he initiated an investigation of possible theft, I suspected I'd lost the ring without anyone else's help. It didn't fit my finger anymore. It kept slipping off in the shower, in the kitchen sink, even in bed once during a fitful dream. I reported the loss to the hospital detective, but in truth I'd been losing my engagement ring for years.

Though I'd taken off the wedding band almost three years before, ending the marriage, I had tried to keep the love we once shared. I thought that our history and the strong attachments to our parents, in-laws and the two sons we both loved bound us together indefinitely. From my altered perspective, I knew now that the effort to "keep" love was misdirected. It was impossible to possess love—it had to be continually attracted by revealing, over and over, who we were. History was important for its lessons, but held no legitimate claim on current passions.

While losing the engagement ring depressed me, my inseparable twin took it in stride. The grief and guilt woven into my relationship with Howe were threads of my existence the born-again woman wasn't interested in picking up. Owing no debts to my past, she loved or didn't, based on the particulars of present realities. Loving Howe with detachment was the most difficult passion I had to learn. In the thought-laden weeks following the coma I began to shed the pain of divorce. Guilt was an imperfect form of love; I wanted to know what we looked like outside of that awful bond. It meant I had to stop feeling responsible for pain belonging exclusively to him; to stop expecting recognition for favors I had no business doing. If we were to love each other now, it couldn't be based on The Way We Were. It had to spring from The Way We Are.

Joan had prescribed "listening to your body" while it healed, but in my case there was no chance of ignoring it. One morning in June, shortly after I'd returned to Ann Arbor, I was in the shower rinsing the shampoo out of my hair and suddenly felt a soft mass moving down my back with the stream of water. I looked down at the drain and saw a large clump of silver strands, like a soft, stretched-out Brillo pad. I lifted the ball to examine it and gasped when I discovered my hair.

I called Dr. Greenbaum to report the disaster, asking if it was normal to lose hair after a coma. He'd never heard of it, but promised to look it up. Dr. Whiteside hadn't heard of it either. My friend Carolen in Kansas City finally supplied a name for it: delayed hair-loss syndrome. Dr. Watsky later identified it as telogen effluvium. Generally, it occurred two to three months after a traumatic experience. The beautician in Ann Arbor told me it was common among hospital patients. She had learned in beauty school that intravenous solutions don't provide the nutrients and proteins hair needs to grow. When she combed a lock of my hair and held it up, we saw a thin, transparent line about an inch above my scalp, marking the week I spent in the coma like a bizarre halo all around my head.

I had a few inches cut off to stimulate the growth but my hair kept falling out. Brushing it each morning, cleaning handfuls from the hairbrush, became a horrifying daily event. After two weeks of heavy loss, I could see my scalp clearly under the thinning silver strands. In despair, I returned to the beautician to cut a few more inches off, trying to salvage the source of my vanity. But my hair was so limp and thin, I eventually had to cut it all off. I came out of the beauty parlor the third time with a kind of spiky, asymmetrical crewcut. ("Good grief, you've gone *punk!*" Phyllis said, the first time I walked into her office looking like a clown. "No, this haircut is an accident," I explained. "Like everything else, I got into punk backasswards too.")

Being long trained in analyzing physical symptoms for signs of psychological stress I had to wonder why I lost my hair, which Larry thought my most attractive feature, the same month I was moving in with him. I was in no position to disregard the messages my body sent out. Was it conducting some kind of unconscious test? I knew Larry had loved me with a tube sticking out of my ribs, he'd love me through a coma, he'd even loved me through the possibility of brain damage. But would he love me bald?

Losing my hair put me back on square one with the vanity issue. The indignity of my see-through crewcut was worse than the bent curls in my second-grade picture. I turned on the bathroom lights each morning and looked in despair. The woman looking back shrugged our shoulders and thought: "Nobody died."

Kay and Jerry arrived in June to help me pack up in Ann Arbor. Four women friends came from Fort Wayne to load the truck. "They're so *strong*," Kay remarked in admiration as Sheryl and Sue easily hoisted my three-cushion couch. I wanted to tell her these four friends were the organizers of the Burly Woman Coffeehouse, an annual event at Sisterspace to celebrate the Lesbian Caucus, but managed for a change to keep this interesting fact to myself and let her draw her own conclusions. "You don't know how lucky you are," she observed, shaking her head at the end of the weekend. "You have such wonderful friends."

George arrived on Saturday to drive the truck. Kay, Jerry, and the kids followed us for two days on Interstate 80. When our small caravan pulled up in front of the three-story Victorian we'd rented in Connecticut, Larry suddenly found himself in the thick of family. After knocking around by himself for three months, six of us moved in on him. I arrived bald and plural, as it were: Loving me meant loving the whole damn group.

The kids spent the summer with us before moving back in September to attend school in Ann Arbor. They were cautious with Larry at first. To live harmoniously with this excruciatingly neat, organized, efficient man, they had a lot of new rules to learn. Ryan was most keenly observant that summer, amazed by the careful procedure Larry used to dish up a bowl of ice cream. After scooping three servings, he placed a fresh layer of plastic wrap over the remainder to prevent freezer burn, then rinsed the sticky lid before putting it back on. Ryan, never having seen anyone clean a cardboard carton before, asked for clarification of the rules: "Are we supposed to wash *all* the garbage?"

One afternoon in late August I watched Darren from my office window on the second floor, riding his bike down the street as if forty devils were after him. I loved to watch his recklessness. He was wearing his red racing shorts and a white cotton shirt, looking so splendid I started to cry. My tear ducts operated on an independent reflex network, watering my eyes at kitchen tables, in darkened auditoriums, at the sight of certain jerseys on the soccer field. Whenever one of my children was on stage, I was certainly Jerry's daughter. Two years ago Darren, dressed in a rabbit costume and playing Thumper in a second-grade production of *Bambi*, prompted a flood that required two full tissue packs to mop up. I loved to see him riding fast in those flimsy nylon shorts. That summer, I recognized we'd spent half the years mothers and sons generally had to live together, and that the remaining half would be equally divided between Howe and me. The sense of diminishing time caused me to take nothing for granted.

Though truth rarely arrived without a price, there were two events that delivered invaluable information about motherhood to me. The first was during the therapy session at ISPI, when I lost my innocence about expert opinions. Twenty-some years after the fact, Kay was blamed for following the pediatrician's rules about not "coddling" her firstborn son. A vow formed in my mind that night which, through the years, has evolved into this theory: Don't ever accept an expert's opinion if it violates your own, because the experts can change their minds. Ultimately, you stand alone, and your own instincts are the only safe ground to stand upon. Only your own opinions will be defensible in court some-day. That theory, though it cost Kay dearly for me to learn it, has given me innumerable guilt-free days with my children, as we've broken one rule and then another.

The second event was the wrenching good-bye at the end of the summer of '84, when my nest emptied abruptly eight years before I expected it. After enjoying the pleasure of their company for a solid decade, I had to watch Ryan and Darren move seven hundred miles away. They loved their father as much as they loved me, and I knew the best interests of my sons meant maintaining a close affection for their dad. It became my job to be happy for them, to conduct the back-and-forthing between us without friction or jealousy. The separations I had to withstand made me a better mother than I actually was. When they returned the next year, I expected to meet two different, more independent people. The possessiveness that gripped me periodically was finally spent on that August departure, when I recognized that my sons were increasingly "guests in the home."

The passages in motherhood were hardly subtle in my case—at a distance of seven hundred miles for nine full months, I couldn't miss the truth that my sons were no longer to be had, to be kept at close range. Their happiness now depended on their independence. My role was to stamp and influence and release them into the current. That, I supposed, was what these departures became for me—lessons on how to let go, to trust the influences.

There were pleasant little surprises. I discovered children's love was dependable, even long distance. They weren't letter writers by any means, but I got a collect call at noon one Wednesday from Darren.

"Hi, Mom," he said calmly in his flat, telephone monosyllables.

"What's wrong, Darren?" I asked. "Aren't you at school?"

"Nothing's wrong," he said. "I just got out of gym." A light bulb went off in his head when he passed the phone outside the cafeteria, and he thought he'd give me a buzz. "I only have a minute," he explained. "I'm on my lunch hour." It knocked my socks off. His lunch hour. It gave me a buzz for the rest of the day.

Gina remained true to her notebook vow to be a "more important sister" to me. In between visits she sent long, emotional, not to say outright radioactive letters from Chicago to Connecticut. The vigil in St. Vincent's was the most emotional experience we'd shared so far, and we came back with dramatically different reactions. Perhaps because Gina's nine days were spent thinking about me (my private wars, my deep exhaustion), while mine were spent dreaming about what in the world was worth coming back *for* (maybe Gina's dances, certainly the laughs), this particularly rocky journey reversed our usual roles. She wanted to analyze, while I wanted to play.

In an eleven-page, single-spaced monologue that arrived the month after my recovery, she called my illness the "most radicalizing experience" of her life. ("God, I'm even starting to talk like you.") Churning with passion, it took her two full months to compose it.

April 20, 1984

My Dear Old Tyger That Sleeps (through my visits),

You were awfully sick by the time I got to New York . . . I watched you struggle with the respirator and felt absolutely exhausted for you. I had to wonder how much one gal—even a willful, determined one like you—could take. I never had to feel like you'd give up (and I want to thank you, right here and now, for that). But I'm embarrassed about how much it took for me to realize I still had things to say to you.

I mean, I *love* you—that much I suppose you know. And I know you love me, so that's not the problem. What I'd like to put an end to is our excruciating *patience* with each other. We are so goddamn *cautious*, M.K., not to intrude on one another's privacy with this great cumbersome affection. We're so polite to each other, there must be something we're not telling.

I read your journal one morning before going to the hospital. Please don't feel strange—you're not the kind of person who has to worry about her journal being read while she's still alive. All I read there that seemed new was your candidness about how tired you really were. I know you'd mentioned it, but somehow I missed the point.

I want to tell you it drove me *crazy* that I couldn't figure out what the tragedy was the night of January 15th. What news came over the phone that night? How come I didn't know? How come I never realized how lonely you were in Ann Arbor? How come it was OK if I missed your programs in Fort Wayne? How come I told everybody else I read your journal one morning before going to the hospital, but I haven't told you?

I talked to you all afternoon about your journal . . . it was a wonderful conversation—I'm so sorry you were comatose. Honestly, as I told Susan (she was appalled that I could do that to you, read your journal while you slept defenselessly), you don't have any hideous alter-ego hiding in the privacy of the pages. I read it as if you were talking to me . . . and then I remembered I was eavesdropping on a conversation you were having with yourself. What I felt awful and just nauseous and weepy about was that you might never really talk that way to me in person . . . that you might never feel like you could take a rest cure inside my bear hug for a change.

God, what a treatise! Since I began this "new sister" routine in
April and am now just finishing the same letter in June, the bare facts
seem to stand in testimony against me. Still, I *do* feel differently about
some things: I'm determined that you should know me, finally, in all
my sophomoric splendor. I don't know why that should feel so
difficult, but it does. I think part of it comes from knowing that with
this new adulthood of mine there is a strong possibility that we'll
come to see some things differently.

I dread the first time we end up on opposite sides of an argument,
M.K.—and it's not because I feel like I won't be up to the debate. It's
just that I know when it's over I'll feel so god-awful *lonely*. Do you
remember a time feeling frightened by the growing importance of your
opinions? I've spent so many of my formative years feeling boldly
different from other people because of the ideas I got from members of
my family. I'd feel absolutely dulled and witless and alone if I should
ever be disconnected from that familial freakishness. I know Salinger
has already written all about this, but unlike Buddy Glass, I *like* the
idea of the membrane being so thin between us.

Anyway, it's getting late and I seem to be digressing further. The
one message all of this scribbling is meant to contain: I love you. So
while I struggle with my inability to mail letters, make phone calls,
organize plans to get together, and even have whole two- or
three-year-long seizures of growing up—know that much; that I love
you. Know I always will.

Gina's letter described the lessons of nine "radicalizing" days,
ending with a long list of changes she wanted in our relationship.
"I'd like to arrive on your doorstep, just once, without feeling like
I'm asking you to help *me*," she wrote, resigning from the position
of "little" sister. Berating herself for not paying closer attention to
my infrequent comments about fatigue, she was also sure there
were important facts I'd completely neglected to say: "I'd like you
to learn to talk helplessly, M.K., because I need to feel like I can
help."

I felt overwhelmed by the size of her yearnings, intimidated and
ecstatic by her needs. In my reply, I told her that I hadn't been at
all disappointed in the way she loved me. It worried me that she
seemed to be in a terrific hurry to pay back all the love she felt she
owed. I asked her to make her peace with her charisma:

It's possible you will never "love back" to the degree and quantity
that people love you. You may have to relax about settling up your

emotional accounts. I can't see how you'll ever catch up, even in the family. It makes no sense for you to feel guilty or apologetic for not loving us well enough. Shaping and molding and thinking about you has probably done more to bring out what's good, what's worthwhile in the rest of us than anything else.

Am I really protecting you from my helplessness? I could hardly be more dazzlingly transparent: I drop off into comas, my hair falls out. My body's collapsibility is a constant embarrassment to me. I go to grotesque lengths with my neediness—softball-sized growths out from my rib cage! Isn't it just *incredible*, what my body does for attention? I live with this vulnerability as if it were an indispensable part of being human. I imagine it shows up all over me like Day-Glo paint.

I don't think love requires us to be in agreement. Maybe you'll need, in fact, to disagree with me, to define your mind from mine—this thin membrane between us can be a damned nuisance. So much shaping and molding you have to throw off! I think you have no choice but to disagree with us.

It wasn't going to be easy for Gina, the most lovable member of the family, to become disagreeable. Until now, she'd been content to be a silent partner during disputes, leaving it up to me or her brothers to advance difficult or unwelcome ideas. Here she goes, I thought when I read her letters, full of urgent pleas to be understood. God knows, I didn't envy her. The first rift truth inevitably brings to love is the hardest. The loneliness she dreaded was only a temporary passage, however—if she stuck with her truth, love would return more solidly and dependably than before. She might even find that by revealing who she really was, she would discover an affinity with people she'd never imagined.

I was amazed to become a member of the group I'd actively avoided joining before the coma, when it was important to establish my credibility among the sane and rational. Before I left New York at the end of May, I walked down Sixth Avenue to have one last pastrami sandwich at Poppy's Deli. I was delighted to see the old woman had returned to her usual place, wearing her navy-blue stocking cap despite the warm spring afternoon.

She had a new poster board but it bore the same message warning pedestrians: THE END IS NEAR. I dropped a few quarters into her cup.

"What happened to you?" she asked, observing my slow, stiff shuffle and skinny limbs.

"I was nuked," I answered, borrowing George's description.

"I'm okay now, though," I assured her. She narrowed her eyes to stare at me—through me, actually, as if scanning my soul with her X-ray vision. Whatever she saw convinced her I was telling the truth. The old woman accepted me as one of her group, inducting me into the small army of obsessed placard carriers who bared their souls on Manhattan sidewalks. It was pointless to deny my qualifications.

My lottery number had finally come up in the draw for sanity or lunacy, I guessed. She relaxed her intense scrutiny and took me into her confidence.

"Better warn the others," she said.

"Okay," I promised. I held out my hand and accepted the pencil she gave to believers.